Lectures on the Principles of Political Obligation

Lectures on the Principles of Political Obligation

Thomas Hill Green

Edited and Introduced by
Dario Bagnoli

Cambridge Scholars Press Ltd.
London and Adelaide

Lectures on the Principles of Political Obligation, by Thomas Hill
Green

Edited and Introduced by Dario Bagnoli

The main body of this book first published in 1895 by Longmans,
London
The introduction and some of the annotations first published 2002 by

Cambridge Scholars Press
79a Manor Waye,
Uxbridge UB8 2BG

British Library Cataloguing in Publication Data
A catalogue record for this book is available from the British Library

National Library of Australia Cataloguing in Publication Data
Green, Thomas Hill (1836-1882). Lectures on the Principles of
Political Obligation. Bibliography. Includes Index.
1. Liberty 2. Political Obligation 3. Political Science 4. Natural Law
I. Title

ISBN 1-904303-02-1

Editions Consulted

The present volume has been prepared by reference to three editions: The 1895 edition published by Longmans, Green & Co., the 1941 edition (a reprint from Green's Philosophical Works, vol. II), Kitchener's 1999 e-book edition (hereafter abbreviated "KE"), and the Cambridge University Press 1986 edition. The latter may be regarded, in some ways, as complimentary to the present edition in that it treats the manuscripts rather than early editions as sacred. No reference to it has been made in the present text.

Contents

Introduction

If the issue of the importance of one's life for the proper appreciation or even understanding of one's work has never completely been resolved, it may be because of inconsistencies between the two spheres such as the one visible in the case of Thomas Hill Green. Green, it has often been noted, did not leave the world a magnum opus which summarised his political beliefs, nor did he leave any clearly written and less than obscure document which unequivocally clarifies his position in the matters he discussed (Williams 1987, 400). And the two works he left us—though they enjoyed a wide readership and influenced thinking about the issues under consideration for decades to come—might well have acted against him rather than in support of his views, as their style is more likely to put the reader off, than to invite further or careful reading. Green's thought is clearly both remarkable and influential, yet this, it might be argued has as much to do with his activities as it has with the writings in which this thought is expounded. But maybe, as William points out, this is the source for the limitations of the reach of Green's thought among political theorists today.

Green played an active role in local political life for many years while at Oxford, serving as an assistant commissioner to the Schools Inquiry Commission, getting involved with the English temperance movement, becoming elected to the Oxford School Board, and then getting elected to the Oxford Town Council representing the North Ward in 1876. And it has often been observed that Green preferred to implement his views on the role of politics in life rather than express them in the form of writing. But despite his predilection of writing, and despite the general view that his perspectives and philosophy spread through word of mouth rather than through his writings, Green was a poor speaker on stage, and this meant that he was not well-endowed for a full career in politics (Cacoullos 1974, 31).

If Green was a poor speaker, as Cacoullos claims, and he was a poor writer, as Williams points out, then how did his thought reach such a wide audience, at least in the late nineteenth and early twentieth centuries (the above noted limitations among political theorists notwithstanding)? One may fruitfully look to the circumstances of his times for an explanation.

The nineteenth century is often characterised as a time when industrialisation and modernisation had led not to the betterment of life for all, but to the hitherto unprecedented gap which had developed between those who had taken advantage of technology, and the majority of the people who could not. The century had given rise to a growing awareness of inequality and exploitation, a consequence of which was a pressing need to solve problems of the below, and a growing repugnance to the perspectives of the above.

And with this in mind, let us turn to Green's most central concept in *Lectures on the Principles of Political Obligation*—the common good. One could argue that Green's Christianity and his sensitivity towards the socioeconomic divide between man and man were chiefly responsible for his insistence on a concept of goodness, but we need not venture into such territory since it involves a good deal of speculation and is not immediately relevant for a fruitful reading of the work. What is important to realise is that Green felt that the issue of goodness was in need of a proper argument if it was not to suffocate under the objections mounted against it. Above all, Green wanted to show that there was goodness that could stand on its own quite apart from other ends in whose service it could be used, as the utilitarians, for example claimed.

What I mean is this. The arguments against an absolute or non-arbitrary good were essentially as follows: Something can be good or bad only in relation to some end. If it helps attain that end, we call it good (for that end), if not, we call it bad (for that end). Unless this end is defined or understood, there can be no good or bad (which is non-arbitrary), since we would have no way of establishing the criteria which determine it.

The utilitarians used the concept good or bad in service of ends which, they considered, everyone agreed upon—maximum pleasure and minimum pain. But Green objected to this, considering it to be inaccurate. Perhaps the problem was that the utilitarians used the terms too broadly and almost invited objections from those who were devoted to absolute goods and bads. At any rate, Green thought that there was rather such a thing as the common good to which the above argument could not be applied since it conformed to it. There are absolute goods and bads, and are determined by whether they serve the purposes of the common good or not. Whether, that is they are good for all. Yet this doesn't seem to ward off the problem of what is "good for all."

Some idea of what is meant by this in the present book is given by Green in point 7 of his opening chapter:

"The value. . . of the institutions of civil life lies in their operation as giving reality to [the] capacities of will and reason, and enabling them to be really exercised. In their general effect, apart from particular aberrations, they render it possible for a man to be freely determined by the idea of a possible satisfaction of himself, instead of being driven this way and that by external forces, and thus they give reality to the capacity called will: and they enable him to realise his reason, i.e. his idea of self-perfection, by acting as a member of a social organisation in which each contributes to the better-being of all the rest."

The reader of this paragraph will be interested to get a better idea of what is entailed by the satisfaction of will and reason. And also whether what is entailed will give sufficient cause for Green's contempt for utilitarianism. But we are best advised to leave these matters for the reader of Green's works to look for them while reading the primary sources, rather than entering into these discussions here.

The common good then ought to be the aim of the law. How law achieves this is quite an intricate matter to which Green gives deep consideration. In so doing, he uses the idea of a natural law which is quite distinct from the law as determined by political institutions. He does not claim that such a natural law ever existed or could exist, but he does assert that it is the end of political institutions to bring about the state in which we can all live in a society ruled by such natural laws, since this is the only way to bring about the common good.

In the present work, Green assesses the application of his theory in diverse areas from the state's treatment of family relations to land law. I think the way in which this assessment is carried out is as relevant to us today as Green's thought to historians of British idealism.

Selected Bibliography

Anderson, Olive. 1991, "The Feminism of T. H. Green: A Late Victorian Success Story?" *History of Political Thought*, 12 (4): 671-93

Bellamy, Richard. 1990, T. H. Green and the Morality of Victorian Liberalism," in *Victorian Liberalism, Nineteenth Century Political Thought and Practice* (R. Bellamy, ed.)

Cacoullos, Anne R., 1974, *Thomas Hill Green: Philosopher of Rights*, New York: Twayne Publishers

Chapman, Richard A. 1965, "Thomas Hill Green (1836-1882)," *Review of Politics*, 27: 516-31

Chin, Yueh Liu 1920, *The Political Theory of Thomas Hill Green*, New York: W. D. Gray

Dewey, John. 1969, "The Philosophy of Thomas Hill Green" in *John Dewey: The Early Works, 1882-1898*, vol. 3

——. 1969, "Green's Theory of the Moral Motive," in *John Dewey: The Early Works, 1882-1898*, vol. 3

Diggs, B. J. 1998, *The State, Justice and the Common Good: An Introduction to Social and Political Philosophy*, Troy: Educator's International Press

Dimova-Cookson, Maria. 2000, "T. H. Green and Justifying Human Rights," *Collingwood and British Idealist Studies* 7: 98-115

Fairbrother, W. H. 1900, *The Philosophy of Thomas Hill Green*, London: Methuen & Co.

Green, Thomas Hill. 1890, *Philosophical Works*, London: Longmans

———. 1941, *Lectures on the Principles of Political Obligation*, London: Longmans, Green and Co.

———. 1986, *Lectures on the Principles of Political Obligation,* (Paul Harris and John Morrow, eds.)

———. 1999, *Lectures on the Principles of Political Obligation*, Toronto: Kitchener

Greengarten, I. M., 1981, *T. H. Green and the Development of Liberal-Democratic Thought*, Toronto: University of Toronto Press

Hansen, Philip, 1977, "T. H. Green and the moralization of the market," *Canadian Journal of Social and Political Theory* 1:91-117

Harrison, Ross. 2000, "Government is Good for You" *Proceedings of the Aristotelian Society*, 100: 159-73

Hoover, Kenneth R. 1973, "Liberalism and the idealist philosophy of Thomas Hill Green," *Western Political Quarterly* 26: 550-65

Jenks, Craig. 1977, "T. H. Green, the Oxford Philosophy of Duty and the English Middle Class," *British Journal of Sociology* 28: 481-97

Knapp, V. J. 1969, "T. H. Green and the exorability of property," *Agora* 1: 57-65

Lamont, William Dawson. 1934, *Introduction to Green's Moral Philosophy*, London: Allen and Unwin

Lindsay, A. D. 1933, "T. H. Green and the Idealists," in *The Social and Political Ideas of Some Representative Thinkers of the Victorian Age* (F. J. C. Hearnshaw, ed.),

Mehta, V. R. 1973, "T. H. Green and the Problem of Political Obligation," *Indian Political Science Review* 7:115-24

———. 1974, "T. H. Green and the Revision of English Liberal Theory," *Indian Journal of Political Science* 35: 37-49

———. 1975, "The Origins of English Idealism in Relation to Oxford," *Journal of the History of Philosophy* 13: 177-87

Milne, A. J. M. 1967, "The Idealist Critique of Utilitarian Social Philosophy," *Archives Europeennes de Sociologie* VIII: 318-31

Monson, Charles H. 1954, "Prichard, Green and Moral Obligation," *Philosophical Review* 63: 74-87

Morrow, John. 1982, "British Idealism, 'German Philosophy' and the First World War," *Australian Journal of Politics and History* 28: 380-90

———. 1983, "Property and Personal Development: An Interpretation of T. H. Green's Political Philosophy," *Politics* 18: 84-92

Muirhead, J. H. 1908, *The Service of the State. Four Lectures on the Political Teaching of T. H. Green*, London: John Murray

Mukhopadhyay, Amal Kumar. 1967, *The Ethics of Obedience: A Study of the Philosophy of T. H. Green*, Calcutta: World Press

Nicholson, Peter. 1990, *The Political Philosophy of the British Idealists*, New York: Cambridge University Press

Randall, J. H. Jr. 1966, "T. H. Green: The Development of English Thought from J. S. Mill to F. H. Bradley," *Journal of the History of Ideas* 27: 217-44

Richter, Melvin. 1956, "T. H. Green and His Audience: Liberalism as a Surrogate Faith," *Review of Politics* 18: 444-72

——. 1964, The Politics of Conscience: T. H. Green and His Age, London: Weidenfeld and Nicholson

Ritchie, D. G. 1887, "The Political Philosophy of the Late Thomas Hill Green," *The Contemporary Review* 51: 841-51

Rodman, John. 1973, "What is Living and What is Dead in the Political Philosophy of T. H. Green," *Western Political Quarterly* 26: 566-86

Sankhdher, M. M. 1969, "T. H. Green: The Forerunner of the Welfare State," *Indian Journal of Political Science* 30: 149-64

——. 1970, "T. H. Green's Concept of the Welfare State," *Journal of Political Studies* 3: 1-21

Sidgwick, Henry. 1902, *Lectures on the Ethics of T. H. Green, Mr. Herbert Spencer, and J. Martineau*, London: Macmillan

Simhony, Avital. 1993, "T. H. Green: The Common Good Society," *History of Political Thought*, 14 (2): 225-47

Smith, Craig A. 1981, "The Individual and Society in T. H. Green's Theory of Virtue," *History of Political Thought* 2: 187-201

Thomas, Geoffrey. 1987, *The Moral Philosophy of T. H. Green*, Oxford: Clarendon Press

Vincent, Andrew (ed.). 1986, *The Philosophy of T. H. Green*, Brookfield, Vt: Gower

Chapter 1
The Grounds of Political Obligation

1. The subject of this course of lectures is the principles of political obligation; and that term is intended to include the obligation of the subject towards the sovereign, the obligation of the citizen towards the state, and the obligations of individuals to each other as enforced by a political superior. My purpose is to consider the moral function or object served by law, or by the system of rights and obligations which the state enforces, and in so doing to discover the true ground or justification for obedience to law. My plan will be (1) to state in outline what I consider the true function of law to be, this being at the same time the true ground of our moral duty to obey the law; and throughout I distinguish moral duty from legal obligation; (2) to examine the chief doctrines of political obligation that have been current in modern Europe, and by criticising them to bring out more clearly the main points of a truer doctrine; (3) to consider in detail the chief rights and obligations enforced in civilised states, inquiring what is their justification, and what is the ground for respecting them, on the principle stated.

2. In previous lectures I have explained what I understand moral goodness to be, and how it is possible that there should be such a thing; in other words, what are the conditions on the part of reason and will which are implied in our being able to conceive moral goodness as an object to be aimed at, and to give some partial reality to the conception. Our results on this question may be briefly stated as follows.

The highest moral goodness we found was an attribute of character and so far as it issued in acts done for the sake of their goodness, not for the sake of any pleasure or any satisfaction of desire which they bring to the agent. But it is impossible that an action should be done for the sake of its goodness, unless it has been previously contemplated as good for some other reason than that which consists in its being done for the sake of its goodness. It must have been done, or conceived as possible to be done, and have been accounted good, irrespectively of its being done from this which we ultimately come to regard as the highest motive. In other words, a prior morality, founded upon interests which are other than the pure interest in being good, and governed by rules of conduct

1

relative to a standard of goodness other than that which makes it depend on this interest, is the condition of there coming to be a character governed by interest in an ideal of goodness. Otherwise this ideal would be an empty one; it would be impossible to say what the good actions were, that were to be done for the sake of their goodness; and the interest in this ideal would be impossible, since it would be an interest without an object.

3. When, however, morality of the latter kind has come to be recognised as the highest or the only true, morality, the prior morality needs to be criticised from the point of view thus gained. Those interests, other than the interest in being good, which form the motives on the part of the individual on which it rests, will not indeed be rejected as of no moral value; for no one can suppose that without them, or except as regulating them, the pure interest in being good could determine conduct at all. But they will be estimated according to their value as leading up to, or as capable of becoming elements in, a character in which this interest is the governing principle. Again, those rules of conduct, according to which the terms right and wrong, good and bad, are commonly applied, and which, as was just now said, are relative to a standard certainly not founded on the conception of good as consisting in the character described, are not indeed to be rejected; for without them there would be nothing to define the duties which the highest character is prepared to do for their own sake. But they have to be revised according to a method which inquires into their rationale or justification, as conditions of approximation to the highest character.

4. Such a criticism of moral interests—of the general motives which determine moral conduct and regulate such moral approbation and disapprobation as is not based on a strict theory of moral good may be called by the term a "theory of the moral sentiments." The criticism of recognised rules of conduct will fall under two heads according as these rules are embodied in "positive law" (law of which the observance is enforced on the individual by a political superior) or only form part of the "law of opinion" (part of what the individual feels to be expected of him by some person or persons to whose expectations he ought to conform).

5. Moral interests are so greatly dependent on generally recognised rules of conduct that the criticism of the latter should come first. The law of opinion, again, in so many ways presupposes a social fabric supported by "positive" law, that we can only fairly take account of it when we

have considered the moral value and justifiability of the fabric so supported. I propose therefore to begin our inquiry into the detail of goodness into the particular kinds of conduct which the man wishing to do good for the sake of its goodness is entitled to count good—by considering what is of permanent moral value in the institutions of civil life, as established in Europe; in what way they have contributed and contribute to the possibility of morality in the higher sense of the term, and are justified, or have a moral claim upon our loyal conformity, in consequence.

6. The condition of a moral life is the possession of will and reason. Will is the capacity in a man of being determined to action by the idea of a possible satisfaction of himself. An act of will is an action so determined. A state of will is the capacity as determined by the particular objects in which the man seeks self-satisfaction; and it becomes a character in so far as the self-satisfaction is habitually sought in objects of a particular kind. Practical reason is the capacity in a man of conceiving the perfection of his nature as an object to be attained by action. All moral ideas have their origin in reason, i.e., in the idea of a possible self-perfection to be attained by the moral agent. This does not mean that the moral agent in every stage of his progress could state this idea to himself in an abstract form, any more than in every stage in the acquisition of knowledge about nature a man can state to himself in an abstract form the conception of the unity of nature which yet throughout conditions the acquisition of his knowledge. Ideas do not first come into existence, or begin to operate, upon the formation of an abstract expression for them. This expression is only arrived at upon analysis of a concrete experience which they have rendered possible. Thus we only learn to express the idea of self-perfection in that abstract form upon an analysis of an experience of self-improvement which we have gone through ourselves, and which must have been gone through by those with whom the possession of language and an organisation of life (however elementary); but the same analysis shows that the same idea must have been at work to make such experience possible. In this idea all particular moral ideas all ideas of particular forms of conduct as estimable originate, though an abstract expression for the latter is arrived at much sooner than such an expression for the idea in which they originate. They arise as the individual's conception of the society on the well-being of which his own depends, and of the constituents of that well-being, becomes wider and fuller; and they are embodied in the laws, institutions, and social expectation, which

make conventional morality. This embodiment, again, constitutes the moral progress of mankind.[1] This progress, however, is only a *moral* progress insofar as it tends to bring about the harmony of will and reason, in the only form in which it can really exist, viz. in the characters of persons. And this result is actually achieved, in so far as upon habits disciplined by conformity to conventional morality there supervenes an intelligent interest in some of the objects contributory to human perfection, which that conventional morality subserves and in so far as that interest becomes the dominant interest of the character.[2]

7. The value then of the institutions of civil life lies in their operation as giving reality to these capacities of will and reason, and enabling them to be really exercised. In their general effect, apart from particular aberrations, they render it possible for a man to be freely determined by the idea of a possible satisfaction of himself instead of being driven this way and that by external forces, and thus they give reality to the capacity called will; and they enable him to realise his reason, i.e., his idea of self-perfection, by acting as a member of a social organisation in which each contributes to the better-being of all the rest. So far as they do in fact thus operate they are morally justified, and may be said to correspond to the "law of nature" the *jus naturae*, according to the only sense in which that phrase can be intelligibly used.

8. There has been much controversy as to what the *jus naturae* (Naturrecht) really is, or whether there is such a thing at all. And the controversy, when it comes to be dealt with in English, is further embarrassed by the fact that we have no one term to represent the full meaning of "jus" or "Recht," as a system of correlative rights and obligations, actually enforced or that should be enforced by law. The essential questions are: (1) whether we are entitled to distinguish the rights and obligations which are anywhere actually enforced by law from rights and obligations which really exist though not enforced; and (2), if we are entitled to do so, what is to be our criterion of rights and obligations which are really valid, in distinction from those that are actually enforced.

9. No one would seriously maintain that the system of rights and obligations, as it is anywhere enforced by law—the "jus" or "Recht" of any nation—is all that it ought to be. Even Hobbes holds that a law, though it cannot be unjust, may be pernicious. But there has been much objection to the admission of *natural* rights and obligations. At any rate the phrase is liable to misinterpretation. It may be taken to imply that rights and obligations can exist in a "state of nature"—a state in which every indi-

vidual is free to do as he likes—that legal rights and obligations derive their authority from a voluntary act by which individuals contracted themselves out of this state; and that the individual retains from the state of nature certain rights with which no legal obligations ought to conflict. Such a doctrine is generally admitted to be untenable; but it does not follow from this that there is not a true and important sense in which natural rights and obligations exist—the same sense as that in which duties may be said to exist, though unfulfilled. There is a system of rights and obligations which *should be* maintained by law, whether it is so or not, and which may properly be called "natural," not in the sense in which the term "natural" would imply that such a system ever did exist or could exist independently of force exercised by society over individuals, but "natural" because necessary to the end which it is the vocation of human society to realise.

10. The "jus naturae," thus understood, is at once distinguished from the sphere of moral duty, and relative to it. It is distinguished from it because admitting of enforcement by law. Moral duties do not admit of being so enforced. The question sometimes put, whether moral duties should be enforced by law, is really an unmeaning one; for they simply cannot be enforced. They are duties to act, it is true, and an act can be enforced; but duties to act from certain dispositions and with certain motives, and these cannot be enforced. Nay, the enforcement of the outward act, of which the moral character depends on a certain motive and disposition, may often contribute to render that motive and disposition impossible; and from this fact arises a limitation to the proper province of law in enforcing acts, which will have to be further considered below. When obligations then are spoken of in this connection, as part of the "jus naturae" correlative to rights, they must always be understood not as moral duties, not as relative to states of will, but as relative to outward acts, of which the performance or omission can and should be enforced. There is a moral duty to discharge such obligations, and to do so in a certain spirit, but the obligation as such, as that with which law has to do or may properly have to do, is relative to an outward act merely, and does not amount to a moral duty. There is a moral duty in regard to obligations, but there can be no obligation in regard to moral duties. Thus the "jus naturae"—the system of rights and obligations, as it should become no less than as it actually is maintained—is distinct from morality in the proper sense. But it is relative to it. This is implied in saying that there is a moral duty in regard to actual obligations, as well as in

speaking of the system of rights and obligations as it should become. If such language is justifiable, there must be a moral ground both for conforming to, and for seeking to develope and[3] improve, established "Recht;" a moral ground which can only lie in the moral end served by that established system.

11. Thus we begin the ethical criticism of law with two principles:— (1) that nothing but external acts can be matter of "obligation" (in the restricted sense); and (2) that, in regard to that which can be made matter of obligation, the question what should be made matter of obligation— the question how far rights and obligations, actually established by law, correspond to the true "jus naturae"—must be considered with reference to the moral end, as serving which alone law and the obligations imposed by law have their value.[4]

12. Before proceeding, some remarks have to be made as to what is implied in these principles. (a) Does the law, or is it possible that it should, confine its view to external acts? What exactly is meant by an external act? In the case of obligations which I am legally punishable for disregarding, the law, in deciding whether punishment is or is not due, takes account of much beside the external act; and this implies that much beside external action is involved in legal obligation. In the case where the person or property of another is damaged by me, the law does not inquire merely whether the act of damage was done, and done by means of my bodily members, but whether it was done intentionally; and if not done with the direct intention of inflicting the damage, whether the damage arose in a manner that might have been foreseen out of something which I did intend to do; whether, again, if it was done quite accidentally the accident was due to culpable negligence. This however does not show that the law can enforce or prevent anything but external action, but only that it is *action* which it seeks to enforce or prevent, for without intention there is no action. We talk indeed of a man acting against his will, but if this means acting against intention it is what it is impossible to do. What I call an act done against my will is either (1) an act done by someone else using my body through superior force, as a means, in which case there is an act, but it is not mine (e.g. if another uses my hand to pull the trigger of a gun by which someone is shot); or (2) a natural event in which my limbs are affected in a certain way which causes certain results to another person, (e.g., if the rolling of a ship throws me against another person who is thus thrown into the water);[5] or (3) an act which I do under the influence of some strong inducement, (e.g. fear of death, but which is

contrary to some strong wish). In this case the act is mine, but mine because I intend it; because it is not against my will as = intention. In saying then that the proper, because the only possible, function of law is to enforce performance of or abstinence from external actions, it is implied that its function is to produce or prevent certain intentions, for without intention on the part of someone there is no act.

13. But if an act necessarily includes intention, what is the nature of the restriction implied in calling it external? An external action is a determination of will as exhibited in certain motions of the bodily members which produce certain effects in the material world; not a determination of the will as arising from certain motives and a certain disposition. All that the law can do is to enjoin or forbid determinations of will as exhibited in such motions, etc. It does indeed present a motive, for it enforces its injunctions and prohibitions primarily by fear—by its threat of certain consequences if its commands are disobeyed. This enforcement is not an exercise of physical force in the strict sense, for in this sense no force can produce an action since it cannot produce a determination of will; and the only way in which the law or its administrators employ such force is not in the production but in the prevention of action (as when a criminal is locked up or the police prevent mischievous persons from assaulting us or breaking into our houses). But though, in enforcing its commands by threats, the law is presenting a motive, and thus, according to our distinction, affecting action on its inner side, it does this solely for the sake of the external act. It does not regard the relation of the act to the motive fear as of any intrinsic importance. If the action is performed without this motive ever coming into play under the influence of what the moralist counts higher motives, the purpose of the law is equally satisfied. Indeed, it is always understood that its purpose is most thoroughly served when the threat of pains and penalties has ceased to be necessary, and the obligations correlative to the relations[6] of individuals and of societies are fulfilled from other motives. Its business is to maintain certain conditions of life—to see that certain actions are done which are necessary to the maintenance of those conditions, others omitted which would interfere with them. It has nothing to do with the motive of the actions or omissions, on which, however, the moral value of them depends.

14. It appears, then, that legal obligations—obligations which can possibly form the subject of positive law—can only be obligations to do or abstain from certain acts, not duties of acting from certain motives, or

with a certain disposition. It is not a question whether the law should or should not oblige to anything but performance of outward acts. It simply cannot oblige to anything else, because the only means at its command for obtaining the fulfilment of obligations are (1) threats of pain, and offers of reward, by means of which it is possible indeed to secure the general performance of certain acts, but not their performance from the motive even of fear of the pain threatened or hope of the reward offered, much less from any higher motive; (2) the employment of physical force, (a) in restraining men disposed to violate obligations, (b) in forcibly applying the labour or the property of those who violate obligations to make good the breach, so far as is possible; (as, e.g., when the magistrate forestalls part of a man's wages to provide for a wife whom he has deserted, or when the property of a debtor is seized for the benefit of his creditors.)

15. Only outward acts, then, *can* be matter of legal obligation; but what sort of outward acts *should* be matter of legal obligation? The answer to this question arises out of the above consideration of the means which law employs to obtain the fulfilment of obligations, combined with the view of law as relative to a moral end, i.e., the formation of a society of persons acting from a certain disposition, from interest in the society as such. Those acts only should be matter of legal injunction or prohibition of which the performance or omission, irrespectively of the motive from which it proceeds, is so necessary to the existence of a society in which the moral end stated can be realised that it is better for them to be done or omitted from that unworthy motive which consists in fear or hope of legal consequences than not to be done at all.

16. We distinguish, then, the system of rights actually maintained and obligations actually enforced by legal sanctions ("Recht" or "jus") from the system of relations and obligations which *should be* maintained by such sanctions ("Naturrecht"); and we hold that those actions or omissions should be made obligations which, when made obligations, serve a certain moral end; that this end is the ground or justification or rationale of legal obligation; and that thus we obtain a general rule, of both positive and negative application, in regard to the proper matter or content of legal obligation. For since the end consists in action proceeding from a certain disposition, and since action done from apprehension of legal consequences does not proceed from that disposition, no action should be enjoined or prohibited by law of which the injunction or prohibition interferes with actions proceeding from that disposition, and every ac-

tion should be so enjoined of which the performance is found to produce conditions favourable to action proceeding from that disposition, and of which the legal injunction does not interfere with such action.

17. Does this general rule give any real guidance in the difficulties which practically arise in regard to the province of law—as to what should be required by law, and what left to the inclination of individuals? What cases are there or have there been of enactments which on this principle we can pronounce wrong? Have attempts ever been made by law to enforce acts as virtuous which lose their virtue when done under fear of legal penalties? It would be difficult, no doubt, to find instances of attempts to enforce by law actions of which we should say that the value lies in the disposition from which they are done actions, e.g., of disinterested kindness—because the clear conception of virtue as depending not on outward results but on dispositions is but slowly arrived at, and has never been reflected in law. But without any strictly moral object at all, laws have been made which check the development of the moral disposition. This has been done (a) by legal requirements of religious observance and profession of belief, which have tended to vitiate the religious source of morality; (b) by prohibitions and restraints, unnecessary or which have ceased to be necessary, for maintaining the social conditions of the moral life, and which interfere with the growth of self-reliance, with the formation of a manly conscience and sense of moral dignity—in short, with the moral autonomy which is the condition of the highest goodness; (c) by legal institutions which take away the occasion for the exercise of certain moral virtues (e.g., the Poor-law, which takes away the occasion for the exercise of parental forethought, filial reverence, and neighbourly kindness).

18. Laws of this kind have often been objected to on the strength of a one-sided view of the function of Law; the view, viz., that its only business is to prevent interference with the liberty of the individual. And this view has gained undue favour on account of the real reforms to which it has led. The laws which it has helped to get rid of were really mischievous, but mischievous for further reasons than those conceived of by the supporters of this theory. Having done its work, the theory now tends to become obstructive because in fact advancing civilisation brings with it more and more interference with the liberty of the individual to do as he likes, and this theory affords a reason for resisting all positive reforms––all reforms which involve an action of the state in the way of promoting conditions favourable to moral life. It is one thing to say that the state in

promoting these conditions must take care not to defeat its true end by narrowing the region within which the spontaneity and disinterestedness of true morality can have play; another thing to say that it has no moral end to serve at all, and that it goes beyond its province when it seeks to do more than secure the individual from violent interference by other individuals. The true ground of objection to "paternal government" is not that it violates the "laissez faire" principle and conceives that its office is to make people good, to promote morality, but that it rests on a misconception of morality. The real function of government being to maintain conditions of life in which morality shall be possible, and morality consisting in the disinterested performance of self-imposed duties, "paternal government" does its best to make it impossible by narrowing the room for the self-imposition of duties and for the play of disinterested motives.

19. The question before us, then, is "in what ways and how far do the main obligations enforced and rights maintained by law in all civilised societies contribute to the moral end described; viz., to establish those conditions of life in which a true, i.e., a disinterested or unselfish, morality shall be possible?" The answer to this question will be a theory of the "jus naturae;" i.e., it will explain how far positive law is what it should be, and what is the ground of the duty to obey it; in other words, of political obligation. There are two things from which such a theory must be distinguished. (1) It is not an inquiry into the process by which actual law came to be what it is; nor (2) is it an inquiry how far actual law corresponds to and is derived from the exercise of certain original or natural rights. (1) It is not the former, because the process by which the law of any nation and the law in which civilised nations agree has come to be what it is, has not been determined by reference to that end to which we hold that law ought to be directed and by reference to which we criticise it. That is to say, the process has not been determined by any such conscious reference on the part of the agents in the process. No doubt, a desire for social good as distinct from private pleasure, for what is good on the whole as distinct from what is good for the moment, has been a necessary condition of it, but (a), as an agent in the development of law, this has not reached the form of a conception of moral good according to that definition of it by which the value of law is to be estimated; and (b) in bringing law to its present state it has been indistinguishably blended with purely selfish passions and with the simple struggle for existence.

20. (2) A true theory of "jus naturae," a rationale of law or ideal of what it should be, is not to be had by inquiring how far actual law corresponds to, and is derived from, the exercise of certain original or natural rights, if that is taken to mean that we know, or can ascertain, what rights are natural on grounds distinct from those on which we determine what laws are justifiable, and that then we can proceed to ascertain what laws are justifiable by deduction from such rights. "Natural rights," so far as there are such things, are themselves relative to the moral end to which perfect law is relative. A law is not good because it enforces "natural rights," but because it contributes to the realisation of a certain end. We only discover what rights are natural by considering what powers must be secured to a man in order to the attainment of this end. These powers a perfect law will secure to their full extent. Thus the consideration of what rights are "natural" (in the only legitimate sense) and the consideration what laws are justifiable form one and the same process, each presupposing a conception of the moral vocation of man.

21. The doctrine here asserted, that all rights are relative to moral ends or duties, must not be confused with the ordinary statement that every right implies a duty, or that rights and duties are correlative. This of course is true in the sense that possession of a right by any person both implies an obligation on the part of someone else, and is conditional upon the recognition of certain obligations on the part of the person possessing it. But what is meant is something different, viz., that the claim or right of the individual to have certain powers secured to him by society, and the counter-claim of society to exercise certain powers over the individual, alike rest on the fact that these powers are necessary to the fulfilment of man's vocation as a moral being, to an effectual self-devotion to the work of developing the perfect character in himself and others.

22. This, however, is not the ground on which the claim in question has generally been asserted. Apart from the utilitarian theory, which first began to be applied politically by Hume, the ordinary way of justifying the civil rights of individuals (i.e., the powers secured to them by law as against each other), as well as the rights of the state against individuals, (i.e., the powers which, with the general approval of society, it exercises against them), has been to deduce them from certain supposed prior rights, called natural rights. In the exercise of these natural rights, it has been supposed, men with a view to their general interest established political society. From that establishment is derived both the system of rights and obligations maintained by law as between man and man, and the right of

the state to the submission of its subjects. If the question then is raised, why I ought to respect the legal rights of my neighbours, to pay taxes, or have my children vaccinated, serve in the army if the state requires it, and generally submit to the law, the answer according to this theory will be that if I fail to do so I shall directly or indirectly be violating the natural rights of other men; directly in those cases where the legal rights of my neighbours are also natural rights, as they very well may be (e.g. rights of liberty or personal safety); indirectly where this is not the case, because, although the rights of the state itself are not natural and many rights exercised by individuals would not only not be secured but would not exist at all but for legal enactment, yet the state itself results from a covenant which originally in the exercise of their natural rights men made with each other, and to which all born under the state and sharing the advantages derived from it must be considered parties. There is a natural right, therefore, on the part of each member of a state to have this compact observed, with a corresponding obligation to observe it; and this natural right of all is violated by any individual who refuses to obey the law of the state or to respect the rights, not in themselves natural, which the state confers on individuals.

23. This, on the whole, was the form in which the ground of political obligation, the justification of established rights, was presented throughout the seventeenth century, and in the eighteenth till the rise of the "utilitarian" theory of obligation. Special adaptations of it were made by Hobbes and others. In Hobbes, perhaps (of whom more later), may be found an effort to fit an anticipation of the utilitarian theory of political obligation into the received theory which traced political obligation, by means of the supposition of a primitive contract, to an origin in natural right. But in him as much as anyone the language and framework of the theory of compact is retained, even if an alien doctrine may be read between the lines. Of the utilitarian theory of political obligation more shall be said later. It may be presented in a form in which it would scarcely be distinguishable from the doctrine just now stated, the doctrine, viz., that the ground of political obligation, the reason why certain powers should be recognised as belonging to the state and certain other powers as secured by the state to individuals, lies in the fact that these powers are necessary to the fulfilment of man's vocation as a moral being, to an effectual self-devotion to the work of developing the perfect character in himself and others. Utilitarianism proper, however, recognises no vocation of man but the attainment of pleasure and avoidance of pain. The

only reason why civil rights should be respected—the only justification of them—according to it, would be that more pleasure is attained or pain avoided by the general respect for them; the ground of our consciousness that we ought to respect them, in other words their ultimate sanction, is the fear of what the consequences would be if we did not. This theory and that which I deem true have one negative point in common. They do not seek the ground of actual rights in a prior natural right, but in an end to which the maintenance of the rights contributes. They avoid the mistake of identifying the inquiry into the ultimate justifiability of actual rights with the question whether there is a prior right to the possession of them. The right to the possession of them, if properly so called, would not be a mere power, but a power recognised by a society as one which should exist. This recognition of a power, in some way or other, as that which should be, is always necessary to render it a right. Therefore when we had shown that the rights exercised in political society were derived from prior "natural" rights, a question would still remain as to the ground of those natural rights. We should have to ask why certain powers were recognised as powers which should be exercised, and thus became these natural rights.

24. Thus, though it may be possible and useful to show how the more seemingly artificial rights are derived from rights more simple and elementary, how the rights established by law in a political society are derived from rights that may be called natural, not in the sense of being prior to society but in the sense of being prior to the existence of a society governed by written law or a recognised sovereign, still such derivation is no justification of them. It is no answer to the question why they should be respected; because this question remains to be asked in regard to the most primitive rights themselves. Political or civil rights, then, are not to be explained by derivation from natural rights, but in regard to both political and natural rights, in any sense in which there can be truly said to be natural rights, the question has to be asked, how it is that certain powers are recognised by men in their intercourse with each other as powers that should be exercised, or of which the possible exercise should be secured.

25. I have tried to show in lectures on morals that the conception expressed by the "should be" is not identical with the conception of a right possessed by some man or men, but one from which the latter conception is derived. It is, or implies on the part of whoever is capable of it, the conception of an ideal, unattained condition of himself, as an abso-

lute end. Without this conception the recognition of a power as a right would be impossible. A power on the part of anyone is so recognised by others, as one which should be exercised, when these others regard it as in some way a means to that ideal good of themselves which they alike conceive: and the possessor of the power comes to regard it as a right through consciousness of its being thus recognised as contributory to a good in which he too is interested. No one therefore can have a right except (1) as a member of a society, and (2) of a society in which some common good is recognised by the members of the society as their own ideal good, as that which should be for each of them. The capacity for being determined by a good so recognised is what constitutes personality in the ethical sense; and for this reason there is truth in saying that only among persons, in the ethical sense, can there come to be rights; (which is quite compatible with the fact that the logical disentanglement of the conception of rights precedes that of the conception of the legal person; and that the conception of the moral person; in its abstract and logical form, is not arrived at till after that of the legal person).

Conversely, everyone capable of being determined by the conception of a common good as his own ideal good, as that which unconditionally should be (of being in that sense an end to himself), in other words, every moral person, is capable of rights; i.e., of bearing his part in a society in which the free exercise of his powers is secured to each member through the recognition by each of the others as entitled to the same freedom with himself. To say that he is capable of rights, is to say that he ought to have them, in that sense of "ought" in which it expresses the relation of man to an end conceived as absolutely good, to an end which, whether desired or no, is conceived as intrinsically desirable. The moral capacity implies a consciousness on the part of the subject of the capacity that its realisation is an end desirable in itself, and rights are the condition of realising it. Only through the possession of rights can the power of the individual freely to make a common good his own have reality given to it. Rights are what may be called the negative realisation of this power. That is, they realise it in the sense of providing for its free exercise, of securing the treatment of one man by another as equally free with himself, but they do not realise it positively, because their possession does not imply that in any active way the individual makes a common good his own. The possession of them, however, is the condition of this positive realisation of the moral capacity, and they ought to be possessed because this end (in the sense explained) ought to be attained.

26. Hence on the part of every person ("person" in the moral sense explained) the claim, more or less articulate and reflected on, to rights on his own part is co-ordinate with his recognition of rights on the part of others. The capacity to conceive a common good as one's own and to regulate the exercise of one's powers by reference to a good which others recognise, carries with it the consciousness that powers should be so exercised; which means that there should be rights, that powers should be regulated by mutual recognition. There ought to be rights, because the moral personality—the capacity on the part of an individual for making a common good his own—ought to be developed; and it is developed through rights; i.e., through the recognition by members of a society of powers in each other contributory to a common good and the regulation of those powers by that recognition.

27. In saying that only among "persons" can there come to be rights, and that every "person" should have rights, I have been careful to explain that I use "person" in the moral not merely in the legal sense. In dealing, then, with such phrases as "jura personarum," and, "personal rights," we must keep in view the difference between the legal and ethical sense of the proposition that all rights are personal, or subsist as between persons. In the legal sense, so far as it is true—and it is so only if "person" is used in the sense of Roman law—it is an identical proposition. A person means a subject of rights and nothing more. Legal personality is derived from the possession of right, not *vice versa*. Like other identical propositions, its use is to bring out and emphasise in the predicate what is included in the understood connotation of the subject; to remind us that when we speak of rights we imply the existence of parties, in English phraseology, capable of suing and being sued. In the ethical sense, it means that rights are derived from the possession of personality as = a rational will (i.e., the capacity which man possesses of being determined to action by the conception of such a perfection of his being as involves the perfection of a society in which he lives), in the sense (a) that only among beings possessed of rational will can there come to be rights, (b) that they fulfil their idea, or are justifiable, or such rights as should be rights, only as contributing to realisation of rational will. It is important to bear this distinction in mind in order that the proposition in its ethical sense, which can stand on its own merits, may not derive apparent confirmation from a juristic truism.

28. The moral idea of personality is constantly tending to affect the legal conception of the relation between rights and persons. Thus the

"jura personarum," which properly = either rights arising out of "status," or rights which not only (like all rights) reside in someone having a legal status and are available against others having a legal status, but are exercised over, or in respect of, someone possessed of such status (e.g. a wife or a servant[7]) come to be understood as rights derived from the human personality or belonging to man as man. It is with some such meaning that English writers on law speak of rights to life and liberty as personal rights. The expression might seem pleonastic, since no right can exist except as belonging to a person in the legal sense. They do not use the phrase either pleonastically or in the sense of the Roman lawyers' "jura personarum" above, but in the sense that these rights are immediately derived from, or necessarily attach to, the human personality in whatever that personality is supposed to consist. There is no doubt, however, that historically the conception of the moral person, in any abstract form, is not arrived at till after that of the legal person has been thus disentangled and formulated; and further that the abstract conception of the legal person as the sustainer of rights is not arrived at till long after rights have been actually recognised and established. But the disentanglement or abstract formulation of the conception of moral personality is quite a different thing from the action of the consciousness in which personality consists.

29. The capacity, then, on the part of the individual of conceiving a good as the same for himself and others, and of being determined to action by that conception, is the foundation of rights; and rights are the condition of that capacity being realised. No right is justifiable or should be a right except on the ground that directly or indirectly it serves this purpose. Conversely every power should be a right, i.e., society should secure to the individual every power, that is necessary for realising this capacity. Claims to such powers as are directly necessary to a man's acting as a moral person at all—acting under the conception of a good as the same for self and others—may be called in a special sense personal rights (though they will include more than Stephen includes under that designation); they may also be called, if we avoid misconceptions connected with these terms, "innate" or "natural" rights. They are thus distinguished from others which are (1) only indirectly necessary to the end stated, or (2) are so only under special conditions of society; as well as from claims which rest merely on legal enactment and might cease to be enforced without any violation of the "jus naturae."

30. The objection to calling them "innate" or "natural," when once it is admitted on the one side that rights are not arbitrary creations of law or custom but that there are certain powers which ought to be secured as rights, on the other hand that there are no rights antecedent to society, none that men brought with them into a society which they contracted to form, is mainly one of words. They are "innate" or "natural" in the same sense in which according to Aristotle the state is natural; not in the sense that they actually exist when a man is born and that they have actually existed as long as the human race, but that they arise out of, and are necessary for the fulfilment of, a moral capacity without which a man would not be a man. There cannot be "innate" rights in any other sense than that in which there are innate duties, of which, however, much less has been heard. Because a group of beings are capable each of conceiving an absolute good of himself and of conceiving it to be good for himself as identical with, and because identical with, the good of the rest of the group, there arises for each a consciousness that the common good should be the object of action, i.e., a duty, and a claim in each to a power of action that shall be at once secured and regulated by the consciousness of a common good on the part of the rest. i.e., a right. There is no ground for saying that the right arises out of a primary human capacity, and is thus "innate" which does not apply equally to the duty.

31. The dissociation of innate rights from innate duties has gone along with the delusion that such rights existed apart from society. Men were supposed to have existed in a state of nature, which was not a state of society, but in which certain rights attached to them as individuals, and then to have formed societies by contract or covenant. Society having been formed, certain other rights arose through positive enactment; but none of these, it was held, could interfere with the natural rights which belonged to men antecedently to the social contract or survived it.

Such a theory can only be stated by an application to an imaginary state of things, prior to the formation of societies as regulated by custom or law, of terms that have no meaning except in relation to such societies. "Natural right," as = right in a state of nature which is not a state of society, is a contradiction. There can be no right without a consciousness of common interest on the part of members of a society. Without this there might be certain powers on the part of individuals, but no recognition of these powers by others as powers of which they allow the exercise, nor any claim to such recognition; and without this recognition or claim to recognition there can be no right.

Chapter 2
Spinoza

32. Spinoza is aware of this. In the *Tractatus Politicus*,[8] he says "By the right of nature [*jus naturae*], then, I mean the actual laws or rules of nature in accordance with which all things come to be; that is, the actual power ['potentia'] of nature... Hence everything a man does in accordance with the laws of his nature, he does by the sovereign right of nature, and he has as much right against other things in nature as he has power and strength" (II.4).[9] If only, seeing that the "jus naturae" was mere "potentia", he had denied that it was "jus" at all, he would have been on the right track. Instead of that, however, he treats it as properly "jus," and consistently with this regards all "jus" as mere "potentia;" nor is any "jus humanum" [human law] according to him, guided by or the product of reason. It arises, in the modern phrase, out of the "struggle for existence." As Spinoza says. "... men are led more by blind desire than by reason; and so their natural power, or natural right, must not be defined in terms of reason, but must be held to cover every possible appetite by which they are determined to act, and by which they try to preserve themselves" (II.5).[10] The *jus civile* [civil law] is simply the result of the conflict of natural powers, which = natural rights, which arises from the effort of every man to gratify his passions and "preserve his own being."[11] Man is simply a pars naturae [part of nature], the most crafty of the animals. "In so far as men are tormented by anger, envy, or any passion involving hatred, they are divided and at odds with one another; and are the more to be feared because they are more powerful, more cunning and astute, than other creatures. But men are by nature subject to these passions in the highest degree... so men are by nature enemies" (II.14).[12] Universal hostility means universal fear, and fear means weakness. It follows that in the state of nature there is nothing fit to be called "potentia" or consequently "jus;" I therefore conclude that the right of nature peculiar to human beings can scarcely be conceived save where men hold rights as a body, and thus have the power to defend their possession of territories which they can inhabit and cultivate, to protect themselves, to repel all force, and to live in accordance with the common judgement of all. For (by Section 13 of this Chapter) the more men there be that

unite in this way, the more right they collectively possess;... (II.15).[13]
The collective body, i.e., has more "jus in naturam" [right in nature], i.e.,
potentiam, than any individual could have singly (II. 13). In the advantage of this increased "jus in naturam" the individual shares. On the other
hand, where men hold rights as a body, and are all guided as if by one
mind, then, of course, (by Section 13 of this Chapter) each of them has
the less right the more the rest together exceed him in power; that is, his
only real right against other things in nature is what the corporate right
allows him. In other matters he must carry out every command laid upon
him by the common decision; or (by Section 4 of this Chapter) be compelled to do so by right (II.16).[14] This "jus" by which the individual's
actions are now to be regulated, is still simply "potentia." "This corporate right, which is defined by the power of a people, is generally called
sovereignty..." (II.17).[15] It is not to be considered anything different from
"jus naturae." It is simply the "naturalis potentia" of a certain number of
men combined; "of a people which is guided as if by one mind" (III.2).[16]
Thus in the "status civilis" [civil state] the "jus naturae" of the individual
in one sense disappears, in another does not. It disappears in the sense
that the individual member of the state has no mind to act or power to act
against the mind of the state. Anyone who had such a mind or power
would not be a member of the state. He would be an enemy against whose
"potentia" the state must measure its own. On the other hand, in "statu
civili," just as much as in "statu naturali," "man acts in accordance with
the laws of his own nature and pursues his own advantage" (III.3).[17] He
exercises his "naturalis potentia" for some natural end of satisfying his
wants and preserving his life as he did or would do outside the "status
civilis." Only in "status civilis" these motives on the part of individuals
so far coincide as to form the "one mind" [una veluti mens] (II.16). which
directs the "power of the people" [multitudinis potentia] (II.17). According
to this view any member of a state will have just so much jus, i.e., potentia, against other members as the state allows him. If he can exercise any
"jus" or "potentia" against another "on his own judgement" [ex suo
ingenio] (III.3), he is so far not a member of the state and the state is so
far imperfect. If he could exercise any "jus" or "potentia" against the
state itself, there would be no state, or, which is the same, the state would
not be *sui juris* [autonomous].

33. Is there then no limit to the "jus" which the state may exercise?
With Spinoza this is equivalent to the question, is there no limit to the

"potentia" which it can exercise? As to this, he suggests three considerations.

(1) Its power is weakened by any action against right reason, because this must weaken the "union of minds" [animorum unio] on which it is founded. ... "[T]he right of a commonwealth is determined by the power of a people guided as if by one mind; but this union of minds is quite inconceivable unless the commonwealth does its best to achieve those conditions which sound reason declares to be for the good of all men" (III.7).[18]

(2) The "right" or "power" of the state depends on its power of affecting the hopes and fears of individual citizens. "Subjects are under the control of the commonwealth, and not possessed of their own right, only in so far as they fear its power or its threats, or in so far as they love the political order (by Section 10 of the previous Chapter). It follows that all actions which no one can be induced to do by rewards or threats fall outside the right of the commonwealth" (III.8).[19] Whatever cannot be achieved by rewards and threats is beyond the power and therefore beyond the "right" of the state. Examples are given in the same section.

(3) "Commands which arouse the indignation of a great number of subjects hardly fall within the right of the commonwealth. "Severities of a certain kind lead to conspiracies against the state, and thus weaken it;"... what is true of each citizen, or of each man in the state of nature is true of a commonwealth also; the greater its cause for fear it has, the less is it possessed of own right" (III.9).[20]

Just so far then as there are certain things which the state cannot do, or by doing which it lessens its power, so far there are things which it has no "right" to do.

34. Spinoza proceeds to consider the relation of states or sovereign powers to each other. Here the principle is simple. They are to each other as individuals in the state of nature, except that they will not be subject to the same weaknesses. For since (by Section 2 of this Chapter) the right of the sovereign is simply the right of nature itself, two states are in the same relation to one another as two men in the condition of nature; with this exception, that a commonwealth can guard itself against being subjugated by another, as a man in the state of nature cannot do. For, of course, a man is overcome by sleep every day, is often afflicted by disease of body or mind, and is finally prostrated by old age; in addition, he is subject to other troubles against which a commonwealth can make itself secure (III.11).[21] In other words "...two commonwealths are en-

emies by nature. For men in the state of nature are enemies...; and so all who retain the right of nature, and are not united in a single common-wealth, remain enemies" (III.13).[22] "Rights to make war" [jura belli] are simply the powers of any one state to attack or defend itself against an-other. "Rights to maintain peaceful relations" [jura pacis], on the other hand, do not appertain to any single state, but arise out of the agreement of two at least. They last as long as the agreement, the "foedus," lasts; and this lasts as long as the fear or hope, which led to its being made, continues to be shared by the states which made it. As soon as this ceases to be the case, the agreement is necessarily at an end, "[and a state] can-not be accused of treachery or perfidy because it breaks faith as soon as its reason for fear or hope is removed. For in this respect each contract-ing party was on precisely the same footing; if it could be the first to free itself from fear it would gain possession of its own right, and would use it as its own judgement dictated" (III.14).[23]

35. It would seem to follow from the above that a state can do no wrong, in the sense that there are no rights that it can violate. The same principle is applicable to it as to the individual; "there is no sin in the state of nature; or rather,...if anyone sins, it is against himself, and not against others... [the law of nature] forbids absolutely nothing that is within human power" (II.18).[24] A state is to any other state, and to its subjects, as one individual against another in "statu naturali." A wrong, a "peccatum," consists in a violation by individuals of the "commune de-cretum" [common decree]. There can be no "peccare" on the part of the "commune decretum" itself. But I do not assert that everything which I say is done in the best way. It is one thing to cultivate a field by right, and another to cultivate it in the best way; it is one thing, I say, to defend and preserve oneself, to give judgement and so on by right, another to defend and preserve oneself in the best way, and to give the best judgement. In consequence, it is one thing to rule and have charge of public affairs by right, another to rule and direct public affairs in the best way. So now that I have dealt with the right of commonwealths in general, it is time for me to discuss their best condition (V.1).[25] Hence a further considera-tion "of the best condition of commonwealths" [de optimo cujusque im-perii statu]. This is guided by reference to the "finis status civilis [pur-pose of the political order]," which is "pax vitaeque securitas" [peace and security of life]. Accordingly that is the best government under which men live in harmony and of which the rights are kept inviolate. Where this is not the case the fault lies with the government, not with any "wick-

edness of its subjects" [subditorum malitia]. "For citizens are not born, but made. Besides, man's natural passions are not the same everywhere..." (V.2).[26]

The end is not fully attained where men are merely kept in order by fear. Such a state of things is not peace but merely absence of war. "For peace is not absence of war, but a virtue based on strength of mind;[27] since... obedience is the steadfast will to do what the general decree of the commonwealth requires" (V.4).[28]

The "peace," then, which it is the end of the state to obtain, consists in rational virtue; in a common mind, governed by desire on the part of each individual for perfection of being in himself and others. The harmony of life, too, which is another way of expressing its object, is to be understood in an equally high sense. The life spoken of is one "characterised primarily by reason, the true virtue and life of the mind" (V.5).[29]

The "imperium" [sovereignty] which is to contribute to this end must clearly be one "established by a free people, and not... a tyranny acquired over a people by the right of war" (V.6).[30] Between the two forms of "imperium" there may be no essential difference in respect of the "jus" which belongs to each, but there is the greatest in respect of the ends which they serve as well as in the means by which they have to be maintained.

36. This conclusion of Spinoza's doctrine of the state does not seem really consistent with the beginning. At the outset no motives are recognised in men but such as render them "natura hostes" [natural enemies]. From the operation of these motives the state is supposed to result. Each individual finds that the war of all against all is weakness for all. Consequently the desire on the part of each to strengthen himself, which is a form of the universal effort "to preserve his own being" [suum esse conservare] (II.5), leads to combination, it being discovered that "nothing is more useful to man than man" (*Ethic*, IV.18, Schol.).[31] But we are expressly told that the civil state does not bring with it other motives than those operative "in statu naturali." "The fact is that man acts in accordance with the laws of his own nature and pursues his own advantage in both the natural and the political order."[32] But then it appears that there supervenes or may supervene on such motives, "the steadfast will to do what the general decree of the commonwealth requires,"[33] and that not of a kind which seeks to carry out the "commune decretum" as a means of escaping pain or obtaining pleasure, for it is said to arise from the "animi fortitudo" which rests on reason ("related to the mind in so far

as it thinks" [ad mentem refertur quatenus intelligit], *Ethic*, III.59, Schol.) and includes "generositas" defined as above. It is also said that the true object of "imperium" is "vitam concorditer transigere" [living in harmony] or "vitam colere" [improving life] in a sense of vita in which it is "characterised primarily by reason" [maxime ratione definitur] (V.5). And as the "imperium" established for this end is one which is "established by a free people" [multitudo libera instituit] (V.6), it seems[34] to be implied that there is a desire for such an end on the part of the people. It is not explained how such desires should arise out of the conflict of "naturales potentiae" or out of the impulses which render men "natura hostes." On the other hand, if the elements of them already exist in the impulses which lead to the formation of the "status civilis," the reasons for saying that men are "natura hostes" disappear, and we get a different view of "jus" whether "naturale" or "civile" from that which identifies it simply with "potentia." Some power of conceiving and being interested in a good *as common*, some identification of the "esse" of others with "suum esse" which every man, as Spinoza says, seeks to preserve and promote, must be supposed in those who form the most primitive social combinations if these are to issue in a state directed to such ends and maintained by such a "steadfast will" [constans volutas] as Spinoza describes. And it is the interest of men in a common good, the desire on the part of each which he thinks of others as sharing, for a good which he conceives to be equally good for them, that transforms mere "potentia" into what may fitly be called "jus," i.e., a power claiming recognition as exercised or capable of being exercised for the common good.

37. If this qualification of "potentia" which alone renders it "jus" had been apprehended by Spinoza, he would have been entitled to speak of a "jus naturale" [natural law] as preceding the "jus civile," i.e., of claims to the recognition of powers and the actual customary recognition of such, as exercised for a common good, preceding the establishment of any regular institutions or general laws for securing their exercise. As it is, the term "jus naturale" is with him really unmeaning. If it means no more than "potentia," why call it "jus?" "Jus" might have a meaning distinct from that of "potentia" in the sense of a power which a certain "imperium" enables one man to exercise as against another. This is what Spinoza understands by "jus civile." But there is no need to qualify it as "civile," unless "jus" may be employed with some other qualification and with a distinctive meaning. But the "jus naturale", as he understands it, has no meaning other than that of "potentia", and his theory as it stands

would have been more clearly expressed if instead of "jus naturale" and *jus civile* he had spoken of "potentia" and "*jus*", explaining that the latter was a power on the part of one man against others, maintained by means of an "imperium" which itself results from a combination of "powers." He himself in one passage shows a consciousness of the impropriety of speaking of "jus" except with reference to a community: "the right, of nature peculiar to human beings can scarcely be conceived save where men hold rights as a body, and thus have the power to defend their possession of territories which they can inhabit and cultivate, to protect themselves, to repel all force, and to live in accordance with the common judgement of all" (II.15).[35] He takes no notice, however, of any forms of community more primitive than that of the state. The division into the "status naturalis" and the "status civilis" he seems to treat as exhaustive, and the "status naturalis" he regards, after the manner of his time, as one of pure individualism, of simple detachment of man from man, or of detachment only modified by conflict. Such a "status naturalis" lacks both the natural and the rational principles of social development (the natural principle, i.e., the interest in others arising primarily from family ties, and the rational principle, i.e., the power of conceiving a good consisting in the more perfect being of the individual and of those in whom he is interested), no process could be traced[36] to the "status civilis". The two "status" stand over against each other with an impassable gulf between. "Citizens are not born but made" (V.2).[37] They are so made, he seems to hold, by the action of the "imperium" upon them. But how is the "imperium" to be made? Men must first be, if not "civiles," yet something very different from what they are in the "status naturalis," between which and the "status civilis" Spinoza recognises no middle term, before any "imperium" which could render them "civiles" could be possible.

38. The cardinal error of Spinoza's *Politik* is the admission of the possibility of a right in the individual apart from life in society; apart from the recognition by members of a society of a correlative claim upon and duty to each other, as all interested in one and the same good. The error was the error of his time, but with Spinoza it was confirmed by his rejection of final causes. The true conception of "right" depends on the conception of the individual as being what he really is in virtue of a function which he has to fulfil relatively to a certain end, that end being the common well being of a society. A "right" is an ideal attribute ("ideal" in the sense of not being sensibly verifiable, not reducible to any perceivable fact or facts) which the individual possesses so far as this func-

tion is in some measure freely fulfilled by him—i.e., fulfilled with reference to or for the sake of the end—and so far as the ability to fulfil it is secured to him through its being recognised by the society as properly belonging to him. The essence of right lies in its being not simply a power producing sensible effects, but a power relative to an insensible function and belonging to individuals only in so far as each recognises that function in himself and others. It is not in so far as I *can* do this or that that I have a right to do this or that, but so far as I recognise myself and am recognised by others as able to do this or that for the sake of a common good, or so far as in the consciousness of myself and others I have a function relative to this end. Spinoza, however, objects to regard anything as determined by relation to a final cause. He was not disposed therefore to regard individuals as being what they are in virtue of functions relative to the life of society, still less as being what they are in virtue of the recognition by each of such functions in himself and others. He looked upon man, like everything else in nature, as determined by material and efficient causes, and as himself a material and efficient cause. But as such he has no "rights" or "duties" but only "powers."

39. It was because Plato and Aristotle conceived the life of the πόλις [state] so clearly as the τέλος [end] of the individual, relation to which makes him what he is the relation in the case of the πολίτης [citizen] proper being a conscious or recognised relation—that they laid the foundation for all true theory of "rights." It is true that they have not even a word for "rights." The claims which in modern times have been advanced on behalf of the individual against the state under the designation "natural rights" are most alien from their way of thinking. But in saying that the πόλις was a "natural" institution and that man was φύσει πολιτικός [political by nature] Aristotle, according to the sense which he attached to πόλις was asserting the doctrine of "natural rights" in the only sense in which it is true. He regards the state (πόλις) as a society of which the life is maintained by what its members do for the sake of maintaining it by functions consciously fulfilled with reference to that end, and which in that sense imposes duties; and from which at the same time its members derive the ability, through education and protection, to fulfil their several functions, and which in that sense confers rights. It is thus that the πολίτης μετέχει τοῦ ἄρχειν καὶ τοῦ ἄρχεσθαι [the citizen participates both in ruling and in being ruled]. Man, being φύσει πολίτης [by nature a citizen]–being already in respect of capacities and tendencies a member of such a society, existing only in κοινωνίαι [associations] which

contain its elements has "naturally" the correlative duties and rights which the state imposes and confers. Practically it is only the Greek man that Aristotle regards as φύσει πολίτης, but the Greek conception of citizenship once established was applicable to all men capable of a common interest. This way of conceiving the case, however, depends on the teleological view of man and the forms of society in which he is found to live, i.e., on the view of men as being what they are in virtue of non-sensible[38] functions and of certain forms of life determined by relation to more perfect forms which they have the capacity or tendency to become.

40. Spinoza, like Bacon, found the assumption of ends which things were meant to fulfil in the way of accurate inquiry into what things are (materially) and do. He held Plato and Aristotle cheap as compared with Democritus and Epicurus (*Epist.* LX.13). Accordingly he considers the individual apart from his vocation as a member of society, the state apart from its office as enabling the individual to fulfil that vocation. Each so considered is merely a vehicle of so much power (natural force). On the other hand, he recognises a difference between a higher and lower, a better and worse, state of civil society, and a possibility of seeking the better state because it is understood to be better. And this is to admit the possibility of the course of human affairs being affected by the conception of a final cause. It is characteristic of Spinoza that while he never departs from the principle "homo naturae pars" (11.5), he ascribes to him the faculty of understanding the order of nature, and of conforming to it or obeying it in a new way on account of that understanding. In other words, he recognised the distinction called by Kant the distinction between determination according to law and determination according to the consciousness of law; though in his desire to assert the necessity of each kind of determination he tends to disguise the distinction and to ignore the fact that, if rational determination (or the determination by a conception of a law) is a part of nature, it is so in quite a different sense from determination merely according to laws of nature. As he puts it, the clear understanding that we are parts of nature, and of our position in the universe of things, will yield a new character. We shall only then desire what is ordained for us and shall find rest in the truth, in the knowledge of what is necessary. This he regards as the highest state of the individual, and the desire to attain it he evidently considers the supreme motive by which the individual should be governed. The analogue in political life to this highest state of the individual is the direction of the

"imperium" by a "libera multitudo" [free people] to the attainment of "pax vitaeque securitas" (V.2), in the high sense which he attaches to those words in *Tractatus Politici*, Ch. V.[39]

41. The conclusion then is that Spinoza did really, though not explicitly, believe in a final cause determining human life. That is to say, he held that the conception of an end consisting in the greater perfection of life on the part of the individual and the community might, and to some extent did, determine the life of the individual and the community. He would have said no doubt that this end, like every good, existed only in our consciousness; that it was "nothing positive in things considered in themselves" (*Ethics*, IV, Preface);[40] but an existence of the end in human consciousness, determining human action, is a sufficiently real existence, without being "positivum in rebus" [positive in things]. But he made the mistake of ignoring the more confused and mixed forms in which the conception of this end operates; of recognising it only in the forms of the philosophic "amor Dei" [love of God], or in the wisdom of the exceptional citizen, whom alone he would admit ratione duci [is guided by reason]. And in particular he failed to notice that it is the consciousness of such an end to which his powers may be directed that constitutes the individual's claim to exercise them as rights, just as it is the recognition of them by a society as capable of such direction which renders them actually rights; in short that, just as according to him nothing is good or evil but thinking makes it so, so it is only thinking that makes a might a right—a certain conception of the might as relative to a social good on the part at once of the person or persons exercising it and of a society which it affects.

Chapter 3
Hobbes

42. All the more fruitful elements in Spinoza's political doctrine are lacking in that of Hobbes', but the principle of the two theories is very much the same. Each begins with the supposition of an existence of human individuals, unaffected by society, and each struggling for existence against the rest so that men are "natura hostes" [natural enemies]. Each conceives "jus naturale" [natural law] as = "potentia naturalis" [natural power]. But Spinoza carries out this conception much more consistently. He does not consider that the natural right, which is might, ceases to exist or becomes anything else when a multitude combine their natural rights or mights in an "imperium" [sovereignty]. If the ostensible "imperium" comes into collision with the powers of individuals, single or combined, among those who have hitherto been subject to it and proves the weaker, it *ipso facto* ceases to be an "imperium." Not having superior power, it no longer has superior right to the "subditi" [subjects]. It is on this principle, as we have seen, that he deals with the question of limitations to the right of a sovereign. Its rights are limited because its powers are so. Exercised in certain ways and directions they defeat themselves. Thus as he puts it in *Epist.* L (where he points out his difference from Hobbes), "the Supreme Power in a State has no more right over a subject than is proportionate to the power by which it is superior to the subject."[41] Hobbes on the other hand supposes his sovereign power to have an absolute right to the submission of all its subjects, singly or collectively, irrespectively of the question of its actual power against them. This right he considers it to derive from a covenant by which individuals, weary of the state of war, have agreed to devolve their personae, in the language of Roman law, upon some individual or collection of individuals which is henceforward to represent them, and to be considered as acting with their combined powers. This covenant being in the nature of the case irrevocable, the sovereign derives from it an indefeasible right to direct the actions of all members of the society over which it is sovereign.

43. The doctrine may be found in *Leviathan*, Part II, Chapter 17. In order "to erect such a common power, as may be able to defend them

from the invasion of foreigners, and the injuries of one another," men "confer all their power and strength upon one man, or upon one assembly of men," i.e. "appoint one man, or assembly of men, to bear their person... This is more than consent, or concord; it is a real unity of them all, in one and the same person, made by covenant of every man, in such matter, as if every man should say to every man, "I authorise, and give up my right of governing myself, to this man, or to this assembly of men, on this condition, that thou give up thy right to him, and authorise all his actions in like manner." This done, the multitude so united in one person is called a Commonwealth, in Latin *civita*s...which, (to define it), is one person, of whose acts a great multitude, by mutual covenant one with another, have made themselves everyone the author, to the end he may use the strength and means of them all, as he shall think expedient, for their peace and common defence. And he that carrieth this person, is called sovereign, and said to have sovereign power; and everyone besides, his subject."

44. In order to understand the form in which the doctrine is stated, we have to bear in mind the sense in which "persona" is used by the Roman lawyers, as = either a complex of rights, or the subject (or possessor) of those rights, whether a single individual or a corporate body. In this sense of the word, a man's person is separable from his individual existence as a man. "Unus homo sustinet plures personas" [Each man has many personas]. A magistrate, e.g., would be one thing in respect of what he is in himself, another thing in respect of his persona or complex of rights belonging to him as a magistrate, and so too a monarch. On the same principle, a man remaining a man as before, might devolve his persona, the complex of his rights, on another. A son, when by the death of his father according to Roman law he was delivered from "patria potestas" [fatherly authority] and became in turn head of a family, acquired a persona which he had not before the persona which had previously belonged to the father. Again, to take a modern instance, the fellows of a college, as a corporation, form one persona, but each of them would bear other "persons," if, e.g., they happened to be magistrates, or simply in respect of their rights as citizens. Thus "one person" above = one sustainer of rights; while in the second passage, "carrieth this person," it rather = the rights sustained.

45. Hobbes expressly states that the sovereign "person" may be an *assembly* of men, but the natural associations of the term, when the sov-

ereign is spoken of as a person, favour the development of a monarchical doctrine of sovereignty.

Sovereign power is attained either by acquisition or institution. By acquisition, when a man makes his children and their children, or a conqueror his enemies, to submit under fear of death; by institution, when men agree among themselves to submit to some man or assembly "on confidence to be protected by him against all others." Hobbes speaks (II.17, end) as if these were two ways by which a commonwealth and a sovereign defined as above could be brought into existence, but clearly a sovereign by acquisition is not a sovereign in the sense explained. He does not "carry a person... of whose acts a great multitude by *mutual covenant* one with another, have made themselves everyone the author, to the end he may use the strength and means of them all, as he shall think expedient, for their peace and common defence." And what Hobbes describes in the sequel (Ch.18) are, as he expressly says, rights of sovereigns by institution; but he seems tacitly to assume that every sovereign may claim the same, though he could hardly have supposed that the existing sovereignties were in their origin other than sovereignties by acquisition.

> A commonwealth is said to be instituted, when a multitude of men covenant, everyone with everyone, that to whatsoever man or assembly of men, shall be given by the major part the right to represent the person of them all... every one, as well he that voted for it, as he that voted against it, shall authorise all the actions and judgements of that man or assembly of men, in the same manner as if they were his own, to the end to live peaceably amongst themselves, and to be protected against other men (Ch. 18).

Here a distinction is drawn between the covenant of all with all to be bound by the act of the majority in appointing a sovereign, and that act of appointment itself which is not a covenant of all with all. The natural conclusion would be that it was no violation of the covenant if the majority afterwards transferred the sovereign power to other hands. But in the sequel Hobbes expressly makes out such a transference to be a violation of the original compact. This is an instance of his desire to vindicate the absolute right of a "de facto" monarch.

46. Throughout these statements we are moving in a region of fiction from which Spinoza keeps clear. Not only is the supposition of the devolution of wills or powers on a sovereign by a covenant historically a

fiction (about that no more need be said); the notion of an obligation to observe this covenant, as distinct from a compulsion, is inconsistent with the supposition that there is no right other than power prior to the act by which the sovereign power is established. If there is no such right antecedent to the establishment of the sovereign power, neither can there be any after its establishment except in the sense of a power on the part of individuals which the sovereign power enables them to exercise. This power, or "jus civile," cannot itself belong to the sovereign, who enables individuals to exercise it. The only right which can belong to the sovereign is the "jus naturale,"[42] consisting in the superiority of his power, and this right must be measured by the inability of the subjects to resist. If they *can* resist, the right has disappeared. In a successful resistance, then, to an ostensibly sovereign power, there can on the given supposition be no wrong done to that power. To say that there is, would be a contradiction in terms. Is such resistance, then, a violation of the "jus civile" as between the several subject citizens? In the absence of a sovereign power, no doubt, the "jus civile" (according to the view in question, which makes it depend on the existence of an "imperium") would cease to exist. But then a successful resistance would simply show that there was no longer such a sovereign power. It would not itself be a violation of "jus civile," but simply a proof that the conditions of "jus civile" were no longer present. It might at the same time be a step to re-establishing them if, besides being a proof that the old "imperium" no longer exists, it implied such a combination of powers as suffices to establish a new one.

47. No obligation, then, as distinct from compulsion, to submit to an ostensibly sovereign power can consistently be founded on a theory according to which right either = simple power, or only differs from it, in the form of "jus civile," through being a power which an "imperium" enables individuals to exercise as against each other. Hobbes could not, indeed, have made out his doctrine (of the[43] absolute submission to the sovereign) with any plausibility if he had stated with the explicitness of Spinoza that "jus naturale" = "naturalis potentia." That it is so is implied in the account of the state of things preceding the establishment of sovereignty as one of "bellum omnium contra omnes" [war of all against all]; for where there is no recognition of a common good, there can be no right in any other sense than power. But where there are no rights but natural powers, no obligatory covenant can be made. In order, however, to get a sovereignty, to which there is a perpetual obligation of submission, Hobbes has to suppose a covenant of all with all, preceding the

establishment of sovereignty, and to the observance of which, therefore, there cannot be an obligation in the sense that the sovereign punishes for the non-observance (the obligation corresponding to "jus civile" in Spinoza's sense), but which no one can ever be entitled to break. As the obligatoriness of this covenant, then, cannot be derived from the sovereignty which is established through it, Hobbes has to ascribe it to a "law of nature" which enjoins "that men perform their covenants made." (*Lev.*, I.15) Yet in the immediate sequel of this passage he says expressly, "the nature of justice consisteth in keeping of valid covenants, but the validity of covenants begins not but with the constitution of a civil power, sufficient to compel men to keep them; and then it is also that propriety begins." On this principle the covenant by which a civil power is for the first time constituted cannot be a valid covenant. The men making it are not in a position to make a valid covenant at all. The "law of nature," to which alone Hobbes can appeal according to his principles, as the source of the obligatoriness of the covenant of all with all, he defines as a "precept or general rule," found out by reason, by which a man is forbidden to do that, which is destructive of his life, or taketh away the means of preserving the same; and to omit that, by which he thinketh it may be best preserved" (I.14). When a law of nature, however, is said to command or forbid, we must not understand those terms in that sense which, according to Hobbes, could only be derived from the establishment of an "imperium." This "law of nature," therefore, is merely an expression in a general form of the instinct by which, as Spinoza says, every living creature "seeks to preserve his own being" [in suo esse perseverare conatur] as guided by a calculation of consequences (for no meaning but this can be given to "reason" according to Hobbes). The prohibition, then, by this law of nature of a breach of that covenant of all with all, by which a sovereign power is supposed to be established, can properly mean nothing more than that it is everyone's interest to adhere to it. This however could only be a conditional prohibition conditional, in particular, on the way in which the sovereign power is exercised. Hobbes tries to show that it must always be for the advantage of all to obey it, because not to do so is to return to the state of universal war; but a successful resistance to it must be *ipso facto* an establishment of a new combined power which prevents the "bellum omnium contra omnes" from returning. At any rate an obligation to submit to the established "imperium" measured by the self-interest of each in doing so, is quite a different thing from the obligation which Hobbes describes in terms only appropriate (according to his own showing) to contracts between individuals enforced by a sovereign power.

48. It would seem that Hobbes' desire to prove all resistance to established sovereignty unjustifiable leads him to combine inconsistent doctrines. He adopts the notion that men are "natura hostes," that "jus naturale" = mere power, because it illustrates the benefit to man's estate derived from the establishment of a supreme power and the effects of the subversion of such power once established, which he assumes to be equivalent to a return to a state of nature. But this notion does not justify the view that a rebellion, which is strong enough to succeed, is wrong. For this purpose he has to resort to the representation of the sovereign as having a right, distinct from power, founded on a contract of all with all, by which sovereignty is established. This representation is quite alien to Spinoza, with whom sovereignty arises, it is true, when "many are united," [plures in unum conveniunt] but in the sense of combining their powers, not of contracting. But after all, the fiction of this contract will not serve the purpose which Hobbes wants it to serve. The sovereignty established by the contract can only have a *natural* right to be maintained inviolate, for all other right presupposes it and cannot be presupposed by it. If this natural right means mere power, then upon a successful rebellion it disappears. If it means anything else, it must mean that there are natural rights of men other than their mere power, which are violated by its subversion. But if there are such rights, there must equally be a possibility of collision between the sovereign power and these natural rights, which would justify a resistance to it.

49. It may be asked whether it is worth while to examine the internal consistency of a theory which turns upon what is admitted to be historically a fiction the supposition of a contract of all with all. There are fictions and fictions however. The supposition that some event took place which as a matter of history did not take place may be a way of conveying an essentially true conception of some moral relation of man. The great objection to the representation of the right of a sovereign power over subjects, and the rights of individuals which are enforced by this "imperium," as having arisen out of a contract of all with all, is that it conveys a false notion of rights. It is not merely that the possibility of such a contract being made presupposes just that state of things—a *régime* of recognised and enforced obligations—which it is assumed to account for. Since those who contract must already have rights, the representation of society with its obligations as formed by contract implies that

individuals have certain rights, independently of society and of their functions as members of a society, which they bring with them to the transaction. But such rights abstracted from social function and recognition could only be powers or (according to Hobbes' definition) liberties to use powers, which comes to the same; i.e., they would not be rights at all; and from no combination or devolution of them could any right in the proper sense, anything more than a combined power, arise.

50. Thus, the only logical development of that separation of right from social duty which is implied in the doctrine of "social contract" is that of Spinoza. Happily the doctrine has not been logically developed by those whose way of thinking has been affected by it. The reduction of political right—the right of the state over its subjects—to superior power, has not been popularly accepted, though the general conception of *national* right seems pretty much to identify it with power. Among the enlightened, indeed, there has of late appeared a tendency to adopt a theory very like Spinoza's, without the higher elements which we noticed in Spinoza; to consider all right as a power attained in that "struggle for existence" to which human "progress" is reduced. But for one person, who, as a matter of speculation, considers the right of society over him to be a disguised might, there are thousands who, as a matter of practice, regard their own right as independent of that correlation to duty without which it is merely a might. The popular effect of the notion that the individual brings with him into society certain rights which he does not derive from society—which are other than claims to fulfil freely (i.e., for their own sake) certain functions towards society—is seen in the inveterate irreverence of the individual towards the state in the assumption that he has rights against society irrespectively of his fulfilment of any duties to society, that all "powers that be" are restraints upon his natural freedom which he may rightly defy as far as he safely can.

Chapter 4
Locke

51. It was chiefly Rousseau who gave that cast to the doctrine of the origin of political obligation in contract in which it best lends itself to the assertion of rights apart from duties on the part of individuals, in opposition to the counter-fallacy which claims rights for the state irrespectively of its fulfilment of its function as securing the rights of individuals. It is probably true that the *Contrat Social* had great effect on the founders of American independence, an effect which appears in the terms of the Declaration of Independence and in preambles to the constitutions of some of the original American states. But the essential ideas of Rousseau are to be found in Locke's *Treatise of Government*,[44] which was probably well known in America for half a century before Rousseau was heard of.[45] Locke again constantly appeals to Hooker's first book on *Ecclesiastical Polity*,[46] and Grotius[47] argues in exactly the same strain.

Hooker, Grotius, Hobbes, Locke, and Rousseau only differ in their application of the same conception; viz. that men live first in a state of nature, subject to a law of nature, also called the law of reason; that in this state they are in some sense free and equal; that "finding many inconveniences" in it they covenant with each other to establish a government—a covenant which they are bound by the "law of nature" to observe—and that out of this covenant the obligation of submission to the "powers that be" arises. Spinoza alone takes a different line: he does not question the state of nature or the origin of government in a combination of men who find the state of nature "inconvenient;" but he regards this combination as one of powers directed to a common end and constituting superior force, not as a covenant which men are bound by the law of nature to observe.

52. The common doctrine is so full of ambiguities that it readily lends itself to opposite applications. In the first place "state of nature" may be understood in most different senses. The one idea common to all the writers who suppose such a state to have preceded that of civil society is a negative one. It was a state which was *not* one of political society, one in which there was no civil government; i.e., no supreme power, exercised by a single person or plurality of persons, which could compel

obedience on the part of all members of a society and was recognised as entitled to do so by them all, or by a sufficient number of them to secure general obedience. But was it one of society at all? Was it one in which men had no dealings with each other except in the way of one struggling to make another serve his will and to get for himself what the other had, or was it one in which there were ties of personal affection and common interest, and recognised obligations, between man and man? Evidently among those who spoke of a state of nature there were very various and wavering conceptions on this point. They are apt to make an absolute opposition between the state of nature and the political state, and to represent men as having suddenly contracted themselves out of one into the other. Yet evidently the contract would have been impossible unless society in a form very like that distinctively called political had been in existence beforehand. If political society is to be supposed to have originated in a pact at all, the difference between it and the preceding state of nature cannot with any plausibility be held to have been much more than a difference between a society regulated by written law and officers with defined power and one regulated by customs and tacitly recognised authority.

53. Again, it was held that in a state of nature men were "free and equal." This is maintained by Hobbes as much as by the founders of American independence. But if freedom is to be understood in the sense in which most of these writers seem to understand it, as a power of executing, of giving effect to, one's will, the amount of freedom possessed in a state of nature, if that was a state of detachment and collision between individuals, must have been very small. Men must have been constantly thwarting each other and (in the absence of that "jus in naturam" [right in nature], as Spinoza calls it, which combination gives) thwarted by powers of nature. In such a state those only could be free, in the sense supposed, who were *not* equal to the rest, who in virtue of superior power could use the rest. But whether we suppose an even balance of weaknesses, in subjection to the crushing forces of nature, or a dominion of few over many by means of superior strength, in such a state of nature no general pact would be possible. No equality in freedom is possible except for members of a society of whom each recognises a good of the whole which is also his own, and to which the free cooperation of all is necessary. But if such society is supposed in the state of nature—and otherwise the "pact" establishing political society would be impossible--it is already in principle the same as political society.

54. It is not always certain whether the writers in question considered men to be actually free and equal in the state of nature, or only so according to the "law of nature," which might or might not be observed. (Hobbes represents the freedom and equality in the state of nature as actual, and this state as being for that reason "bellum omnium contra omnes" [a war of all against all]). They all, however, implicitly assume a *consciousness* of the law of nature in the state of nature. It is thus not a law of nature in the sense in which we commonly use the term. It is not a law according to which the agents subject to it act necessarily but without consciousness of the law. It is a law of which the agent subject to it has a consciousness, but one according to which he may or may not act; i.e., one according to which he *ought* to act. It is from it that the obligation of submission to civil government, according to all these writers, is derived. But in regard to such a law, two questions have to be asked: firstly, how can the consciousness of obligation arise without recognition by the individual of claims on the part of others—social claims in some form or other—which may be opposed to his momentary inclinations? And secondly, given a society of men capable of such a consciousness of obligation, constituting a law according to which the members of the society are free and equal, in what does it differ from a political society? If these questions had been fairly considered, it must have been seen that the distinction between a political society and a state of nature, governed by such a law of nature, was untenable; that a state of things out of which political society could have arisen by compact must have been one in which the individual regarded himself as a member of a society which has claims on him and on which he has claims, and that such society is already in principle a political society. But the ambiguity attending the conception of the "law of nature" prevented them from being considered. When the writers in question spoke of a law of nature, to which men in the state of nature were subject, they did not make it clear to themselves that this law, as understood by them, could not exist at all without there being some recognition or consciousness of it on the part of those subject to it. The designation of it as "law of nature" or "law of God" helped to disguise the fact that there was no imponent of it, in the sense in which a law is imposed on individuals by a political superior. In the absence of such an imponent, unless it is either a uniformity in the relations of natural events or an irresistible force and it is not represented in either of these ways in juristic writings it can only mean a recognition of obligation arising in the consciousness of the individual from his relations to soci-

ety. But this not being clearly realised, it was possible to represent the "law of nature" as antecedent to the laws imposed by a political superior, without its being observed that this implied the antecedence of a condition of things in which the result supposed to be obtained through the formation of political society—the establishment, viz. of reciprocal claims to freedom and equality on the part of members of a society-already existed.

55. In fact, the condition of society in which it could properly be said to be governed by a law of nature, i.e., by an obligation of which there is no imponent but the consciousness of man, an obligation of which the breach is not punished by a political superior, is not antecedent to political society but one which it gradually tends to produce. It is the radical fault of the theory which finds the origin of political society in compact that it has to reverse the true process. To account for the possibility of the compact of all with all it has to assume a society subject to a law of nature, prescribing the freedom and equality of all. But a society governed by such a law as a law of nature, i.e., with no imponent but man's consciousness, would have been one from which political society would have been a decline; one in which there could have been no motive to the establishment of civil government. Thus this theory must needs be false to itself in one of two ways. Either it is false to the conception of a "law of nature," with its prescription of freedom and equality as governing the state of things prior to the compact by which political society is established, only introducing the law of nature as the ground of the obligatoriness of that compact but treating the state of nature as one of universal war in which no reciprocal claims of any sort were recognised (so Hobbes); or just so far as it realises the conception of a society governed by a law of nature, as equivalent to that spontaneous recognition by each of the claims of all others, without which the covenant of all with all is in fact unaccountable, it does away with any appearance of necessity for the transition from the state of nature to that of political society and tends to represent the latter as a decline from the former. This result is seen in Rousseau; but to a great extent Rousseau had been anticipated by Locke. The broad differences between Locke and Hobbes in their development of a common doctrine, are (1) that Locke denies that the state of nature is a state of war, and (2) that Locke distinguishes the act by which political society is established from that by which the government, legislative and executive, is established, and is consequently able

to distinguish the dissolution of the political society from the dissolution of the government (*Civ. Gov.* XIX, §211).

56. The "state of nature," and the "state of war"... are so far distant as a state of peace, good will, mutual assistance, and preservation, and a state of enmity, malice, violence, and mutual destruction are one from another. Men living together according to reason, without a common superior on earth, with authority to judge between them, is properly the state of nature. But force, or a declared design of force upon the person of another, where there is no common superior on earth to appeal to for relief, is the state of war...(*Civ. Gov.* III, §19). In the state of nature, however, when the state of war has once begun, there is not the same means of terminating it as in civil society.

The right of war may belong to a man, "though he be in society and a fellow subject," when his person or property is in such immediate danger that it is impossible to appeal for relief to the common superior. "But when the actual force is over, the state of war ceases between those that are in society...because then there lies open the remedy of appeal for the past injury, and to prevent future harm..." In the state of nature, when the state of war has once begun it continues until the aggressor offers peace and reparation. The state of war, though not proper to the state of nature, is a frequent incident of it, and to avoid it "is one great reason of men's putting themselves into society..." (ibid. §21). The state of nature is not one that is altogether over and done with. "All[48] rulers of independent governments all through the world are in a state of nature..." The members of one state in dealing with those of another are in a state of nature, and the law of nature alone binds them, "for truth and keeping of faith belongs to men, as men, and not as members of society" (*Civ. Gov.* II, §14). "All men are naturally in that state, and remain so, till by their own consents they make themselves members of some politic society..." (ibid. §15).

57. The antithesis, as put above, between the state of nature and the state of war can only be maintained on the supposition that the "law of nature," is observed in a state of nature. Locke does not explicitly state that this is the case. If it were so, it would not appear how the state of war should arise in the state of nature. But he evidently thought of the state of nature as one in which men recognised the law of nature, though without fully observing it. He quotes with approval from Hooker language which implies that not only is the state of nature a state of equality but that in it there is such consciousness of equality with each other on the part of

men that they recognise the principle "do as you would be done by" (*Civ. Gov.* II. §5). With Hobbes, in the supposed state of nature the "law of nature" is emphatically *not* observed, and hence it is a state of war. As has been pointed out above, a "law of nature" in the sense in which these writers use the term, as a law which obliges but yet has no imponent in the shape of a sovereign power, is, as Locke says (§136), "nowhere to be found but in the minds of men;" it can only have its being in the consciousness of those subject to it. If therefore we are to suppose a state of nature in which such a law of nature exists, it is more consistent to conceive it in Locke's way than in that of Hobbes'; more consistent to conceive it as one in which men recognise duties to each other than as a "bellum omnium contra omnes."

58. As to the second point, from his own conception of what men are in the state of nature, and of the ends for which they found political societies, Locke derives certain necessary limitations of what the supreme power in a commonwealth may rightfully do. The prime business of the political society, once formed, is to establish the legislative power. This is "sacred and unalterable in the hands where the Community have once placed it" (*Civ. Gov.* XI. §134); "unalterable," that is, as we gather from the sequel, by anything short of an act of the community which originally placed it in these hands. But as men in a state of nature have "no arbitrary power" over each other (which must mean that according to the "law of nature" they have no such power), so they cannot transfer any such power to the community nor it to the legislature. No legislature can have the right to destroy, enslave or designedly impoverish the subjects. And as no legislature can be entitled to do anything which the individual in the state of nature would not by the law of nature be entitled to do, so its great business is to declare the law of nature in general terms and administer it by known authorised judges. The state of nature, Locke seems to think, would have done very well, but for the inconvenience of every man being judge in his own case of what the law of nature requires. It is to remedy this inconvenience by establishing (1) a settled law, received by common consent, (2) a known and indifferent judge, (3) a power to enforce the decisions of such a judge, that political society is formed.

Hence a legislature violates the "trust that is put in it" by society unless it observes the following rules: (1) it is to govern "by promulgated established laws," not to be varied to suit particular interests; (2) these laws are to be designed only for the good of the people; (3) it must not raise taxes but by consent of the people through themselves or their deputies; (4) it "neither must nor can transfer the power of making laws to anybody else or place it anywhere but where the people have" (*Civ. Gov.* XI, §142).

59. Thus "the Legislative being only a fiduciary power to act for certain ends, there remains still in the people a supreme power to remove or alter the legislature…" Subject to this ultimate "sovereignty" (a term which Locke does not use) of the people, the legislative is necessarily the supreme power, to which the executive is subordinate. An appearance to the contrary can only arise in cases where (as in England) the supreme executive power is held by a person who has also a share in the legislative. Such a person may "in a very tolerable sense be called supreme." It is not, however, to him as supreme legislator (which he is not, but only a participator in supreme legislation) but to him as supreme executor of the law that oaths of allegiance are taken. It is only as executing the law that he can claim obedience, his executive power being, like the power of the legislative, a fiduciary trust, placed in him" to enforce obedience to law and that only (*Civ. Gov.* XIII, §151). This distinction of the supreme power of the people from that of the[49] supreme executive, corresponding to a distinction between the act of transferring individual powers to a society and the subsequent act by which that society establishes a particular form of government, enables Locke to distinguish what Hobbes had confounded, the dissolution of government and the dissolution of political society.

60. He gets rid of Hobbes' notion, that because the "covenant of all with all," by which a sovereignty[50] is established, is irrevocable, therefore the government once established is unalterable. He conceives the original pact merely as an agreement to form a civil society, which must indeed have a government, but not necessarily always the same government. The pact is a transfer by individuals of their natural rights to a society, and can only be cancelled through the dissolution of the society by foreign conquest. The delegation by the society of legislative and executive powers to a person or persons is a different matter. The society always retains the right, according to Locke, of resuming the powers thus delegated, and must exercise the right in the event either of the legislative being altered, (placed in different hands from those originally intended), of a collision between its executive and legislative officers, or of a breach between different branches of the legislature (when as in England there are such different branches), or when legislative and ex-

ecutive or either of them "act contrary to their trust." He thus in effect vindicates the right of revolution, ascribing to a "sovereign people" the attributes which Hobbes assigned to a "person" single or corporate on which the people forming a society were supposed by an irrevocable act to have devolved their powers. In other words, he considered the whole civil society in all cases to have the rights which Hobbes would only have allowed it to possess where the government was not a monarchy or aristocracy but a democracy; i.e., where the supreme "person" on to which all devolve their several "personae" is an "assembly of all who will come together." As such a democracy did not then exist in Europe, any more than it does now, except in some Swiss cantons, the practical difference between the two views was very great. Both Locke and Hobbes wrote with a present political object in view, Hobbes wishing to condemn the Rebellion, Locke to justify the Revolution. For practical purposes, Locke's doctrine is much the better; but if Hobbes' translation of the irrevocability of the covenant of all with all into the illegitimacy of resistance to an established government in effect entitles any tyrant[51] to do as he likes, on the other hand, it is impossible upon Locke's theory to pronounce when resistance to a "de facto" government is legitimate or otherwise. It would be legitimate according to him when it is an act of the "sovereign people" (not that Locke uses the phrase), superseding a government which has been false to its trust. But this admitted, all sorts of questions arise as to the means of ascertaining what is and what is not an act of the "sovereign people."

  61. The rapid success of the Revolution without popular disorder prevented Locke's theory from becoming of importance, but in the presence of such sectarian enthusiasm as existed in Hobbes' time it would have become dangerous. It would not any more than that of Hobbes justify resistance to "the powers that be" on the part of any body of men short of the civil society acting as a whole, i.e., by a majority. The sectaries of the time of the Rebellion, in pleading a natural or divine right to resist the orders of the government, would have been as much condemned by Locke's theory as by that of Hobbes'. But who can say when any popular action by which established powers, legislative or executive, are resisted or altered is an act of the "sovereign people," of the civil society acting as a whole or no? Where government is democratic, in Hobbes' sense, i.e., vested in an assembly of all who will come together, the act of the "sovereign people" is unmistakeable. It is the act of the majority of such an assembly. But in such a case the difficulty cannot arise. There can be

no withdrawal by the sovereign people of power from its legislative or executive representatives, since it has no such representatives. In any other case it would seem impossible to say whether any resistance to or deposition of an established legislative or executive is the act of the majority of the society or no. Any sectary or revolutionary may plead that he has the "sovereign people" on his side. If he fails, it is not certain that he has them not on his side; for it may be that, though he has the majority of the society on his side, yet the society has allowed the growth within it of a power which prevents it from giving effect to its will. On the other hand, if the revolution succeeds, it is not certain that it had the majority on its side when it began, though the majority may have come to acquiesce in its result. In short, on Locke's principle that any particular government derives its authority from an act of the society, and the society by a like act may recall the authority, how can we ever be entitled to say that such an act has been exercised?

62. It is true that there is no greater difficulty about supposing it to be exercised in the dissolution than in the establishment of a government, indeed not so much; but the act of first establishing a government is thrown back into an indefinite past. It may easily be taken for granted without further inquiry into the conditions of its possibility. On the other hand, as the act of legitimately dissolving a government or superseding one by another has to be imagined as taking place in the present, the inquiry into the conditions of its possibility cannot well be avoided. If we have once assumed with Hobbes and Locke that the authority of government is derived from a covenant of all with all—either directly or mediately by a subsequent act in which the covenanted society delegates its powers to a representative or representatives—it will follow that a like act is required to cancel it, and the difficulties of conceiving such an act under the conditions of the present are so great, that Hobbes' view of the irrevocability of the original act by which any Government was established has much to say for itself. If the authority of any government––its claim on our obedience—is held to be derived not from an original, or from any, covenant but from the function which it serves in maintaining those conditions of freedom which are conditions of the moral life, then no act of the people in revocation of a prior act need be reckoned necessary to justify its dissolution. If it ceases to serve this function, it loses its claim on our obedience. It is a $\pi\alpha\rho\acute{\epsilon}\kappa\beta\alpha\sigma\iota\varsigma$ [corruption]. (Here again the Greek theory, deriving the authority of government not from consent but from the end which it serves, is sounder than the modern).

Whether or no any particular government has on this ground lost its claim and may be rightly resisted is a question, no doubt, difficult for the individual to answer with certainty. In the long run, however, it seems generally if not always to answer itself. A government no longer serving the function described—which, it must be remembered, is variously served according to circumstances—brings forces into play which are fatal to it. But if it is difficult upon this theory for the individual to ascertain, as a matter of speculation, whether resistance to an established government is justified or no, at any rate upon this theory such a justification of resistance is possible. Upon Locke's theory, the condition necessary to justify it—viz., an act of the whole people governed—is one which, anywhere except in a Swiss canton, would be impossible to fulfil. For practical purposes Locke comes to a right result by ignoring this impossibility. Having supposed the reality of one impossible event—the establishment of government by compact or by act of a society founded on compact—he cancels this error in the result by supposing the possibility of another transaction equally impossible viz. the collective act of a people dissolving its government.

63. It is evident from the chapter (XIX) on the "dissolution of government" that he did not seriously contemplate the conditions under which such an act could be exercised. What he was really concerned about was to dispute "the right divine to govern wrong," on the part of a legislative as much as on the part of an executive power; to maintain the principle that government is only justified by being for the good of the people, and to point out the difference between holding that some government is necessarily for the good of the people and holding that any particular government is for their good a difference which Hobbes had ignored. In order to do this, starting with the supposition of an actual deed on the part of a community establishing a government, he had to suppose a reserved right on the part of the community by a like deed to dissolve it. But in the only particular case in which he contemplates a loss by the legislature of its representative character he does not suggest the establishment of another by an act of the whole people. He saw that the English Parliament in his time could not claim to be such as it could be supposed that the covenanting community originally intended it to be. "It often comes to pass," he says, "in governments, where part of the legislative consists of representatives chosen by the people, that in tract of time this representation becomes very unequal and disproportionate to the reasons it was first established upon . . . The bare name of a town,

of which there remains not so much as the ruins, where scarce so much housing as a sheep-coat; or more inhabitants than a shepherd is to be found, sends as many representatives to the grand assembly of lawmakers, as a whole county numerous in people, and powerful in riches. This, strangers stand amazed at, and everyone must confess needs a remedy; though most think it hard to find one, because the constitution of the legislative being the original and supreme act of the society, antecedent to all positive laws in it, and depending, wholly on the people, no inferior power can alter it. And therefore the people, when the legislative is once constituted, having in such a government as we have been speaking of, no power to act as long as the government stands; this inconvenience is thought incapable of a remedy" (Chapter XIII, §157). The only remedy which he suggests is not an act of the sovereign people, but an exercise of prerogative on the part of the executive, in the way of redistributing representation, which would be justified by "salus populi suprema est lex" [the good of the people is the highest law].

Chapter 5
Rousseau

64. That "sovereignty of the people," which Locke looks upon as held in reserve after its original exercise in the establishment of government, only to be asserted in the event of a legislature proving false to its trust, Rousseau supposes to be in constant exercise. Previous writers had thought of the political society or commonwealth, upon its formation by compact, as instituting a sovereign. They differed chiefly on the point whether the society afterwards had or had not a right of displacing an established sovereign. Rousseau does not think of the society, *civitas* or commonwealth, as thus instituting a sovereign, but as itself in the act of its formation becoming a sovereign and ever after continuing so.

65. In his conception of a state of nature, Rousseau does not differ from Locke. He conceives the motive for passing out of it, however, somewhat differently and more after the manner of Spinoza. With Locke the motive is chiefly a sense of the desirability of having an impartial judge, and efficient enforcement, of the law of nature. According to Rousseau, some pact takes place when men find the hindrances to their preservation in a state of nature too strong for the forces which each individual can bring to bear against them. This recalls Spinoza's view of the "jus in naturam" [right in nature] as acquired by a combination of the forces of individuals in civil society.

66. The "problem of which the social contract is a solution" Rousseau states thus: "To find a form of association which protects with the whole common force the person and property of each associate, and in virtue of which everyone, while uniting himself to all, only obeys himself and remains as free as before" (*Contrat Social*, I, vi). The terms of the contract which solves this problem Rousseau states thus: "Each of us throws into the common stock his person and all his faculties under the supreme direction of the general will and we accept each member as an indivisible part of the whole...There results from this act of association, in place of the several persons of the several contracting parties, a collective moral body, composed of as many members as there are voices in the assembly which body receives from this act its unity, its common self, its life, and its will...It is called by its members a *state* when it is passive, a *sover-*

eign when it is active, a *power* when compared with similar bodies. The associates are called collectively a *people*, severally *citizens* as sharing in the sovereign authority, *subjects* as submitted to the laws of the state (I, b). Each of them is under an obligation in two relations, "as a member of the sovereign body towards the individuals, and as a member of the state towards the sovereign." All the subjects can by a public vote be placed under a particular obligation towards the sovereign, but the sovereign cannot thus incur an obligation towards itself. It cannot impose any law upon itself which it cannot cancel. Nor is there need to restrict its powers in the interest of the subjects. For the sovereign body, being formed only of the individuals which constitute it, can have no interest contrary to theirs. "From the mere fact of its existence, it is always all that it ought to be" (since, from the very fact of its institution, all merely private interests are lost in it). On the other hand, the will of the individual (his particular interest as founded upon his particular desires) may very well conflict with that general will which constitutes the sovereign. Hence the social pact necessarily involves a tacit agreement, that anyone refusing to conform to the general will shall be forced to do so by the whole body politic; in other words, "shall be forced to be free," since the universal conformity to the general will is the guarantee to each individual of freedom from dependence on any other person or persons (I, vii).

67. The result to the individual may be stated thus. He exchanges the natural liberty to do and get what he can a liberty limited by his relative strength for a liberty at once limited and secured by the general will; he exchanges the mere possession of such things as he can get, a possession which is the effect of force for a property founded on a positive title, on the guarantee of society. At the same time he becomes a moral agent. Justice instead of instinct becomes the guide of his actions. For the moral slavery to appetite he substitutes the moral freedom which consists in obedience to a self-imposed law. Now for the first time it can be said that there is anything which he *ought* to do, as distinguished from that which he is *forced* to do (I, viii).

68. Such language makes it clear that the sovereignty of which Rousseau discusses the origin and attributes, is something essentially different from the supreme coercive power which previous writers on the "jus civile" [civil law] had in view. A contemporary of Hobbes had said that:

> There's on earth a yet auguster thing,
> Veiled though it be, than Parliament and King.

It is to this "auguster thing," not to such supreme power as English lawyers held to be vested in "Parliament and King," that Rousseau's account
of the sovereign is really applicable. What he says of it is what Plato or
Aristotle might have said of the θεῖος νοῦς [divine intelligence], which
is the source of the laws and discipline of the ideal polity and what a
follower of Kant might say of the "pure practical reason," which renders
the individual obedient to a law of which he regards himself, in virtue of
his reason, as the author, and causes him to treat humanity equally in the
person of others and in his own always as an end, never merely as a
means. But all the while Rousseau himself thinks that he is treating of the
sovereign in the ordinary sense; in the sense of some power of which it
could be reasonably asked how it was established in the part where it
resides, when and by whom and in what way it is exercised. His reader
more or less familiar with the legal conception of sovereignty but not at
all with that of practical reason or of a "general will"—a common ego,
which wills nothing but what is for the common good—is pretty sure to
retain the idea of supreme coercive power as the attribute of sovereignty
and to ignore the attribute of pure disinterestedness, which, according to
Rousseau, must characterise every act that can be ascribed to the sovereign.

69. The practical result is a vague exaltation of the prerogatives of the
sovereign people, without any corresponding limitation of the conditions under which an act is to be deemed that of the sovereign people.
The justifiability of laws and acts of government, and of the rights which
these confer, comes to be sought simply in the fact that the people wills
them, not in the fact that they represent a true "volonté générale" [gen-
eral will], an impartial and disinterested will for the common good. Thus
the question of what really needs to be enacted by the state in order to
secure the condition under which a good life is possible, is lost sight of in
the quest for majorities; and as the will of the people in any other sense
than the measure of what the people will tolerate is really unascertainable in the great nations of Europe, the way is prepared for the sophistries
of modern political management, for manipulating electoral bodies, for
influencing elected bodies, and procuring plébiscites.

70. The incompatibility between the ideal attributes which Rousseau
ascribes to the sovereign and any power that can actually be exercised by

any man or body of men becomes clearer as we proceed. He expressly distinguishes "sovereignty" from power, and on the ground of this distinction holds that it cannot be alienated, represented, or divided. "Sovereignty being simply the exercise of the general will can never be alienated, and the sovereign, who is only a collective being, can only be represented by himself. Power can be transmitted, but not will" (II, i). In order to the possibility of a representation of the general will, there must be a permanent accord between it and the individual will or wills of the person or persons representing it. But such *permanent* accord is impossible (I. b). Again, a general will is from the nature of the case indivisible. It is commonly held to be divided, not, indeed, in respect of its source, but in respect of the objects to which its acts are directed, e.g. into legislative and executive powers; into rights of taxation, of war, of justice, etc. But this supposed division of sovereign powers or rights implies that "what are only emanations from the sovereign authority are taken to be parts of it" (II, ii). The only exercise of sovereign power, properly so called, is in legislation, and there is no proper act of legislation except when the whole people comes to a decision with reference to the whole people. Then the matter decided on is as general as the will which decides on it; and this is what constitutes a law (II, vi). By this consideration several questions are answered. Whose office is it to make laws? It is that of the general will, which can neither be alienated nor represented. Is the prince above the law? The answer is, "he is a member of the state, and cannot be so." Can the law be unjust? No one can be unjust to himself; therefore not the whole people to the whole people. How can we be free and yet subject to the laws? The laws are the register of our own will (I. b). Laws, in short, are properly those general "conditions of civil association" which the associates impose on themselves. Where either of the specified conditions is lacking, where either it is not the universal will from which an ordinance proceeds or it is not the whole people to which it relates, it is not a law but a decree, not an act of sovereignty but of magistracy (I. b).

71. This leads to a consideration of the nature and institution of magistracy or government (III, i). The government is never the same as the sovereign. The two are distinguished by their functions, that of the one being legislative, that of the other executive. Even where the people itself governs, its acts of government must be distinguished from its acts of sovereignty, the former having a particular, the latter a general, reference. Government is the exercise according to law of the executive power,

and the "prince" or "magistrate" is the man or body of men charged with this administration; "a body intermediary between the subjects and the sovereign, charged with the execution of the laws, and with the maintenance of civil and political freedom" (I. b). Where all or most of the citizens are magistrates, or charged with the supreme functions of government, we have a democracy; where a few, an aristocracy; where one is so charged, a monarchy (III, iii). The differences depend, not as Hobbes and others had supposed, on the quarter where the sovereignty resides—for it must always reside in the whole body of people—but on that in which government resides. The idea of government is that the dominant will of the prince should be the general will or law, that it should be simply the public force by which that general will is brought to bear on individuals or against other states, serving the same purpose in the state as the union of soul and body in the individual (III, i); and this idea is most likely to be satisfied under a democracy. There, the general will (if there *is* a general will, which the democracy is no guarantee for there being, according to Rousseau's distinction between the "volonté générale" and "volonté de tous" [will of all], of which more hereafter) cannot fail to coincide with the dominant will of the government. The prevalence of particular interests may prevent there being a will at all of the kind which Rousseau would count general or truly sovereign, but they cannot be more prevalent in the magistracy, constituted by the whole people, than in the same people acting in the way of legislation. In a democracy, therefore, the will of the sovereign, so far as there is a sovereign in the proper sense, necessarily finds expression in the will of the magistracy. On the other hand, though under either of the other forms of government there is danger of collision between sovereign and government, yet the force of the government is greater than in a democracy. It is greatest when the government is a monarchy because under all other forms there is more or less discrepancy between the individual wills of the several persons composing the government, as directed to the particular good of each, and the corporate will of the government of which the object is its own efficiency, and under a monarchy this source of weakness is avoided (III, ii). As there is more need of force in the government in proportion to the number of subjects whose particular wills it has to control, it follows that monarchy is best suited to the largest, democracy to the smallest, states (III, iii).

72. As to the institution of government, Rousseau maintains strenuously that it is not established by contract. "There is only one contract in

the state. viz. that of the original association; and this excludes every other. No other public contract can be imagined which would not be a violation of the first" (III, xvi). Even when government is vested in an hereditary body, monarchic or aristocratic, this is merely a provisional arrangement, made and liable to be reversed by the sovereign, whose officers the governors are. The act by which government is established is twofold, consisting first of the passing of a law by the sovereign, to the effect that there shall be a government; secondly of an act in execution of this law, by which the governors—the "magistrates" are appointed. But it may be asked, "how can the latter act, being one not of sovereignty, but of magistracy (for it has a particular reference in the designation of the governors), be performed when as yet there is no government?" The answer is that the people resolves itself from a sovereign body into a body of magistrates, as the English Parliament resolves itself constantly from a legislative body into a committee. In other words, by a simple act of the general will a democracy is for the time established, which then proceeds either to retain the government in its own hands, or place it in those of an officer or officers according to the form in which the sovereign has decided to establish the government (III, xvii). Acts similar to that by which the government was originally constituted need to be periodically repeated in order to prevent the government from usurping the function of the sovereign, i.e. the function of legislation (could this usurpation occur under a democracy?) In order that the sovereignty may not fall into abeyance, it must be exercised, and it can only be exercised in assemblies of the whole people. These must be held periodically, and at their opening two questions ought to be submitted; one, whether it pleases the sovereign to maintain the present form of government; the other, whether it pleases the people to leave the administration in the hands of those at present charged with it (III, xviii). Such assemblies are entitled to revise and repeal all previously enacted laws. A law not so repealed the sovereign must be taken tacitly to confirm, and it retains its authority. But as the true sovereign is not any law but the general will, no law, even the most fundamental, can be exempt from liability to repeal. Even the social pact itself might legitimately be dissolved, by agreement of all the citizens assembled (I. b). (Whether unanimity is necessary for the purpose is not specified.) Without such assemblies there can be no exercise of the general will (which, as before stated, cannot be represented), and consequently no freedom. The English people, e.g., is quite mistaken in thinking itself free. It is only free while the election of members of Parliament is going on. As soon as they are elected, it is in bondage, it is nothing. In the short moments of its freedom it makes such a bad use of it that it well deserves to lose it" (III, xv).

73. It appears from the above that, according to Rousseau, the general will, which is the true sovereign, can only be exercised in assemblies of the whole people. On the other hand, he does not hold that an act of such an assembly is necessarily an act of the general will. After telling us that the "general will is always right, and always tends to the public good," he adds, "but it does not follow that the deliberations of the people have always the same rectitude...There is often a great difference between the will of all and the general will. The latter only looks to the common interest; the other looks to private interests, and is only a sum of the wills of individuals" (II, iii). Again (II, iv), "that which generalises the will is not so much the number of voices as the common interest which unites them." He holds apparently that in the assembly of the whole people, if they had sufficient information, and if no minor combinations of particular interests were formed within the entire body, the difference between the wills of individuals would neutralise each other, and the vote of the whole body would express the true general will. But in fact in all assemblies there is at least a liability to lack of information and to the formation of cliques; and hence it cannot be held that the vote of the assembly necessarily expresses the "general will." Rousseau, however, does not go so far as to say that unless the law is actually such as contributes to the common good, it is not an expression of the general will. The general will, according to him, always aims at or wills the common good, but is liable to be mistaken as to the means of attaining it. "It is always right, but the judgement which guides it is not always enlightened. . . Individuals see the good which they reject; the public wills the good which it does not see" (II, vi). Hence the need of a guide in the shape of a great lawgiver. Apparently, however, the possible lack of enlightenment on the part of the "general will" does not, in Rousseau's view, prevent its decisions from being for the public good. In discussing the "limits of the sovereign power" he maintains that there can be no conflict between it and the natural right of the individual, because, "although it is only that part of his power, his goods, his freedom, of which the use is important to the community that the individual transfers to the sovereign by the social pact, yet the sovereign alone can be judge of the importance;" and the sovereign "cannot lay on the subjects any constraint which is not for the good of the community." "Under the law of reason" (which is thus

identified with the general will) "nothing is done without a cause, any more than under the law of nature" (II, iv).

74. But though even an unenlightened "general will" is the general will still, and (as we are left to infer) cannot in its decisions do otherwise than promote the public good, Rousseau distinctly contemplates the possibility of the "general will" being so overpowered by particular interests that it finds no expression in the votes of a popular assembly, though the assembly be really one of a whole people, and the vote of the majority is duly taken (IV, i). In such cases it is not that the "general will" is "annihilated or corrupted; it is always constant, unalterable, and pure." Even in the individual whose vote is governed by his private interest the "general will" is not extinct, nor is he unaware either of what the public good requires or of the fact that what is for the public good is also for his own. But his share in the public evil to which he knows that his vote will contribute, seems nothing by the side of the special private good which he hopes to gain. By his vote, in short, he does not answer the question, "is so and so for the advantage of the state?" But, "is it for the advantage of this particular man or party?" (I. b).

75. The test of the dominance of the general will in assemblies of the people is an approach to unanimity. "Long debates, discussions, tumult, indicate the ascendancy of particular interests and the decline of the state" (IV, ii). Rousseau, however, does not venture to say that absolute unanimity in the assembly is necessary to an expression of the general will, or to give a law a claim upon the obedience of the subjects. This would have been to render effectual legislation impossible. Upon the theory, however, of the foundation of legitimate sovereignty in consent—the theory that the natural right of the individual is violated unless he is himself a joint imponent of the law which he is called to obey, it is not easy to see what rightful claim there can be to the submission of a minority. Rousseau so far recognises the difficulty that he requires unanimity in the original compact (IV, ii). If among those who are parties to it there are others who oppose it, the result is simply that the latter are not included in it. "They are strangers among the citizens." But this does not explain *how* they are to be rightfully controlled, on the principle that the only rightful control is founded on consent; or, if they are not controlled, what is the value of the "social compact." How can the objects of the pact be attained while those who are bound by it have these "strangers" living among them who are not bound by it, and who, not being bound by it cannot be rightfully controlled? The difficulty must recur with each

generation of the descendants of those who were parties to the original pact. The parties to the pact, it is true, have no right to resist the general will, because the pact is *ex hypothesi* to the effect that each individual, in all things of common concern, will take the general will for his own. The true form, therefore, of the question upon which each party to the pact should consider himself to be voting in the assembly is, as Rousseau puts it, not "is the proposed measure what I wish for, or what I approve, or no?" but "is it in conformity with the general will?" If, having voted upon this question, he finds himself in a minority, he is bound to suppose that he is mistaken in his views of the general will, and to accept the decision of the majority as the general will which, by the pact, he is bound to obey. So far all is consistent; though how the individual is to be answered if he pleads that the vote of the assembly has been too much biased by particular interest to be an expression of the "general will," and that therefore it is not binding on him, does not appear.

76. But after the first generation of those who were parties to the supposed original compact, what is to settle whether anyone is a party to it or no? Rousseau faces the question, but his only answer is that "when once the state is instituted, consent is implied in residence; to dwell on the territory is to submit to the sovereignty" (IV, ii). This answer, however, will scarcely stand examination. Rousseau himself does not consider that residence in the same region with the original parties to the pact renders those so resident also parties to it. Why should it do so, when the pact has descended to a later generation? It may be argued of course that everyone residing in a settled society, which secures him in his rights of person and property, has the benefit of the society from the mere fact of his residence in it, and is therefore morally bound to accept its laws. But this is to abandon the doctrine of obligation being founded on consent. Residence in a territory governed by a certain sovereign can only be taken to imply consent to the rule of that sovereign, if there is any real possibility of relinquishing it, and this there can scarcely ever be.

77. Rousseau certainly carried out the attempt to reconcile submission to government with the existence of natural rights antecedent to the institution of government, by the hypothesis of a foundation of government in consent, more consistently than any other writer; and his result shows the hopelessness of the attempt. To the consistency of his theory he sacrifices every claim to right on the part of any state except one in which the whole body of citizens directly legislates, i.e., on the part of nearly all states then or now existing; and finally he can only justify the

control of the minority by the majority in any state whatever by a subterfuge. It does not follow, however, because the doctrine of natural rights and the consequent conception of government as founded on compact are untenable, that there is no truth in the conception of the state or sovereign as representing a "general will," as authorised or entitled to obedience on that account. It is this conception, as the permanently valuable thing in Rousseau, that we have now further to consider.

78. The first remark upon it which suggests itself is that, as Rousseau puts the matter, there may be an independent political society in which there is no sovereign power at all, or in which, at any rate, it is not exercised. The sovereign is the "general will." But the general will can only be exercised through the assembly of a whole people. The necessary conditions of its exercise, then, in Rousseau's time, were only fulfilled in the Swiss cantons and (perhaps) in the United Provinces. In England they were fulfilled in a way during the time of a general election. But even where these conditions were fulfilled, it did not follow that the "general will" was put in force. It might be overpowered, as in the Roman *comitia*, by particular interests. Is it then to be understood that, according to Rousseau, either there could be independent states without any sovereignty in actual exercise, or that the European states of his time, and equally the great states of the present day (for in none of these is there any more exercise of the general will than in the England of his time) are not properly states at all?

79. We may try to answer this question by distinguishing sovereign "de facto" from sovereign "de jure," and saying that what Rousseau meant was that the general will, as defined by him and as exercised under the conditions which he prescribes, was the only sovereign "de jure," but that he would have recognised in the ordinary states of his time a sovereign "de facto;" and that in the same way, when he describes the institution of government as arising out of a twofold act consequent on the original pact (an act in which the sovereign people first decides that there shall be a government and then, not as a sovereign people, but as a democratic magistracy, decides in what hands the government shall be placed) he does not conceive himself to be describing what has actually taken place, but what is necessary to give a government a moral title to obedience. Whether Rousseau himself had this distinction in view is not always clear. At the outset he states his object thus: "Man is born free, and everywhere he is in fetters. How has this change come about? I do not know. What can render it legitimate? That is a question which I deem

myself able to answer" (I, i). The answer is the account of the establishment of a sovereign by social pact. It might be inferred from this that he
considered himself in the sequel to be delineating transactions to the
actual occurrence of which he did not commit himself, but which, if they
did occur, would constitute a duty as distinct from a physical necessity of
submission on the part of subjects to a sovereign, and to which some
equivalent must be supposed, in the shape of a tacit present convention
on the part of the members of a state if their submission is to be matter of
duty as distinct from physical necessity or is to be explained as a matter
of right by the ostensible sovereign. This, however, would merely be an
inference as to his meaning. His actual procedure is to describe transactions, by which the sovereignty of the general will was established, and
by which it in turn established a government, as if they had actually taken
place. Nor is he content with supposing a tacit consent of the people as
rendering subjection legitimate. The people whose submission to law is
to be "legitimate" must actually take part in sovereign legislative assemblies. It is very rarely that he uses language which implies the possibility
of a sovereign power otherwise constituted. He does indeed speak[52] of
the possibility of a prince (in the special meaning of the term, as representing the head of the executive) usurping sovereignty, and speaks of
the sovereignty thus usurped as existing "de facto," not "de jure;" but in
no other connection (so far as I have observed) does he speak of anything short of the "volonté générale" exercised through the vote of an
assembled people as sovereign at all. And the whole drift of his doctrine
is to show that no sovereign, otherwise constituted, had any claim on
obedience. There was no state in Europe at his time in which his doctrine
would not have justified rebellion, and even under existing representative systems the conditions are not fulfilled which according to him are
necessary to give laws the claim on our obedience which arises from
their being an expression of the general will. The only system under
which these conditions could be fulfilled would be one of federated self-
governing communes, small enough to allow each member an active share
in the legislation of the commune. It is probably the influence of Rousseau
that has made such a system the ideal of political enthusiasts in France.

Chapter 6
Sovereignty and the General Will

80. The questions then arise (1) whether there is any truth in Rousseau's conception of sovereignty as founded upon a "volonté générale" in its application to actual sovereignty. Does anything like such a sovereignty exist in the societies properly called political? (2) Is there any truth in speaking of a sovereignty "de jure" founded upon the "volonté générale?" (3) If there is, are we to hold with Rousseau that this "will" can only be exercised through the votes of a sovereign people?

81. (1) The first question is one which, if we take our notions of sovereignty from such writers as Austin, we shall be at first disposed decidedly to negative. Austin is considered a master of precise definition. We may begin, therefore, by looking to his definition of sovereignty and the terms connected with it. His general definition of law runs as follows: "A law, in the most general and comprehensive acceptation in which the term, in its literal meaning, is employed, may be said to be a rule laid down for the guidance of an intelligent being by an intelligent being having power over him." These rules are of two kinds: laws of God, and Human law. We are only concerned with the latter. Human laws are again distinguished into two classes, according as they are or are not established by political superiors. "Of the laws or rules set by men to men, some are established by *political* superiors, sovereign and subject; by persons exercising supreme and subordinate *government*, in independent nations, or independent political societies…the aggregate of the rules established by political superiors, is frequently styled *positive* law, or law existing *by position*" (I, 88-9). This is distinguished from "positive morality." Laws are further explained as a species of commands. A command is "a signification of desire," distinguished by the fact that "the party to whom it is directed is liable to evil from the other, in case he does comply not with the desire" (I, 91). This liability to evil forms the sanction of the command. Where a command "obliges *generally* to acts or forbearances of a *class*, a command is a law or rule" (I, 95). Every positive law, or every law simply and strictly so called, is set by a sovereign person, or a sovereign body of persons, to a member or members of the independent political society wherein that person or body is sover-

eign or supreme. Or (changing the expression) it is set by a monarch, or sovereign number, to a person or persons in a state of subjection to its author. Even though it sprung directly from another fountain or source, it is a positive law, or a law strictly so called, by the institution of that present sovereign in the character of political superior. Or (borrowing the language of Hobbes) "the legislator is he, not by whose authority the law was first made, but by whose authority it continues to be a law." (I, 225-6)

> The notions of sovereignty and independent political society may be expressed concisely thus. If a *determinate* human superior, *not* in a habit of obedience to a like superior, receive *habitual* obedience from the *bulk* of a given society that determinate superior is sovereign in that society and the society (including the superior) is a society political and independent. (I, 226)
>
> In order that a given society may form a society political and independent, the two distinguishing marks which I have mentioned above must unite. The *generality* of the given society must be in a *habit* of obedience to a *determinate* and *common* superior; whilst that determinate person, or determinate body of persons, must *not* be habitually obedient to a determinate person or body. It is the union of that positive, with this negative mark, which renders that certain superior sovereign or supreme, and which renders that given society (including that certain superior) a society political and independent. (I, 227)

82. It may be remarked in passing that, according to the above, while every law implies a sovereign, from whom directly or indirectly (through a subordinate political superior) it proceeds, it is not necessary to a sovereign that his commands should take the form of laws, as opposed to "particular or occasional commands" (I, 95). A superior might signify his desires only in the form of such particular and occasional commands, and yet there might be a habit of obedience to him, and he might not be habitually obedient to any other person or body; in which case he would be a "sovereign."

83. Austin's doctrine seems diametrically opposite to one which finds the sovereign in a "volonté générale," because (a) it only recognises sovereignty in a *determinate* person or persons, and (b) it considers the essence of sovereignty to lie in the power, on the part of such determinate

person or persons, to put compulsion without limit on subjects, to make them do exactly as it pleases.[53] The "volonté générale," on the other hand, it would seem, cannot be identified with the will of any determinate person or persons; it can, indeed, according to Rousseau, only be expressed by a vote of the whole body of subject citizens, but when you have got them together there is no certainty that their vote does express it; and it does not—at any rate necessarily—command any power of compulsion, much less unlimited power. Rousseau expressly contemplates the possibility of the executive power conflicting with and overbearing the "general will." Indeed according to his view it was the ordinary state of things, and though this view may be exaggerated, no one could maintain that the "general will," in any intelligible sense of the words, had always unlimited force at its command.

84. The two views thus seem mutually exclusive, but perhaps it may be by taking each as complementary to the other that we shall gain the truest view of sovereignty, as it actually exists. In those states of society in which obedience is habitually rendered by the bulk of society to some determinate superior, single or corporate, who in turn is independent of any other superior, the obedience is so rendered because this determinate superior is regarded as expressing or embodying what may properly be called the general will, and is virtually conditional upon the superior being so regarded. It is by no means an unlimited power of compulsion that the superior exercises, but one dependent in the long run, or dependent for the purpose of insuring an *habitual* obedience, upon conformity to certain convictions on the part of the subjects as to what is for their general interest. As Maine says (*Early History of Institutions,* p. 359), "The vast mass of influences, which we may call for shortness moral, perpetually shapes, limits, or forbids the actual direction of the forces of society by its Sovereign." Thus, quite apart from any belief in the right of revolution, from the view that the people in any state are entitled to an ultimate sovereignty, or are sovereign "de jure," and may withdraw either legislative or executive power from the hands in which it has been placed in the event of its being misused, it may fairly be held that the ostensible sovereign—the determinate person or persons to whom we can point and say that with him or them lies the ultimate power of exacting habitual obedience from the people is only able to exercise this power in virtue of an assent on the part of the people, nor is this assent reducible to the fear of the sovereign felt by each individual. It is rather a common desire for certain ends specially the "pax vitaeque secuitas" ["peace and

security of life"] to which the observance of law or established usage contributes, and in most cases implies no conscious reference on the part of those whom it influences to any supreme coercive power at all. Thus when it has been ascertained in regard to any people that there is some determinate person or persons to whom in the last resort they pay habitual obedience, we may call this person or persons sovereign if we please, but we must not ascribe to him or them the real power which governs the actions and forbearances of the people, even those actions and forbearances (only a very small part) which are prescribed by the sovereign. This power is a much more complex and less determinate, or rather less easily determinable, thing; but a sense of possessing common interests, a desire for common objects on the part of the people, is always the condition of its existence. Let this sense or desire which may properly be called general will cease to operate, or let it come into general conflict with the sovereign's commands, and the habitual obedience will cease also.

85. If, then, those who adopt the Austinian definition of a sovereign mean no more than that in a thoroughly developed state there must be some determinate person or persons with whom in the last resort lies the recognised power of imposing laws and enforcing their observance, over whom no legal control can be exercised, and that even in the most thorough democracy where laws are passed in the assembly of the whole people, it is still with determinate persons, viz. a majority of those who meet in the assembly, that this power resides, they are doubtless right. So far they only need to be reminded that the thoroughly developed state, as characterised by the existence of such definite sovereignty, is even among civilised people but imperfectly established. It is only perfectly established (1) where customary or "common" or "judge-made" law, which does not proceed from any determinate person or persons, is either superseded by express enactments that do proceed from such person or persons, or (as in England) is so frequently trenched upon by statute law that it may fairly be said only to survive upon sufferance, or to be itself virtually enacted by the sovereign legislature and (2) where no question of right can be raised between local legislatures or authorities and the legislature claiming to be supreme (as in America before the war of secession, and as might perhaps be found to be the case in Germany now, if on certain educational and ecclesiastical matters the Imperial legislature came to be at issue with the local legislatures). But though the organisation of the state, even in civilised and independent nations, is not every-

where complete, it no doubt involves the residence with a determinate person or persons, or a body or bodies, of supreme i.e., legally uncontrolled power to make and enforce laws. The term "sovereign," having acquired this definite meaning, Rousseau was misleading his readers when he ascribed sovereignty to the "general will." He could only be understood as meaning, and in fact understood himself to mean, that there was no legitimate sovereign except in the most thorough democracy, as just described.

86. But the Austinians, having found their sovereign, are apt to regard it as a much more important institution than, if it is to be identified with a determinate person or persons, it really is; they are apt to suppose that the sovereign, with the coercive power (i.e., the power of operating on the fears of the subjects) which it exercises, is the real determinant of the habitual obedience of the people at any rate of their habitual obedience in respect of those acts and forbearances which are prescribed by law. But, as we have seen, this is not the case. It then needs to be pointed out that if the sovereign power is to be understood in this fuller, less abstract sense if we mean by it the "real determinant of the habitual obedience of the people," we must look for its sources much more widely and deeply than the "analytical jurists" do; that it can no longer be said to reside in a determinate person or persons, but in that impalpable congeries of the hopes and fears of a people bound together by common interests and sympathy, which we call the general will.

87. It may be objected that this view of the "general will," as that on which habitual obedience to the sovereign really depends, is at best only applicable to "self-governing" communities, not to those under a despotic sovereign. The answer is that it is applicable in all forms of society where a sovereign in the sense above defined (as a determinate person or persons with whom in the last resort lies the recognised power of imposing laws and enforcing their observance) really exists, but that there are many where there cannot fairly be said to such sovereign at all; in other words, that in all organised communities the power which practically commands the habitual obedience of the people in respect of those acts and forbearances which are enjoined by law or authoritative custom, is one dependent on the general will of the community, but this power is often not sovereign in the sense in which the ruler of an independent state is sovereign. It may very well be that there is at the same time another power merely coercive, a power really operating on people simply through their fears to which obedience is rendered and which is not

in turn representative of a general will; but where this is the case we shall find that such power is only in contact with the people, so to speak, at one or two points; that their actions and forbearances, as determined by law and custom, are in the main independent of it; that it cannot in any proper sense be said to be a sovereign power over them; at any rate, not in the sense in which we speak of King, Lords, and Commons as sovereign in England.

88. Maine has pointed out (*Early History of Institutions*, Lecture XIII) that the great despotic empires of ancient times, excluding the Roman, of which more shall be said directly and modern empires in the East, were in the main tax-collecting institutions. They exercise coercive force over their subjects of the most violent kind for certain purposes, at certain times, but they do not impose laws as distinct from "occasional or particular commands," nor do they judicially administer or enforce a customary law. In a certain sense the subjects render them habitual obedience, i.e., they habitually submit when the agents of the empire descend on them for taxes and recruits, but in the general tenor of their lives their actions and forbearances are regulated by authorities with which the empire never interferes with which probably it could not interfere without destroying itself. These authorities can scarcely be said to reside in a determinate person or persons at all, but so far as they do so, they reside mixedly in priests, or exponents of customary religion, in heads of families acting within the family, and in some village-council acting beyond the limits of the family. Whether in such a state of things we are to consider that there is a sovereign power at all, and, if so, where it is to be considered to reside, are chiefly questions of words. If complete uncontrolledness by a stronger power is essential to sovereignty, the local authorities just spoken of are not sovereign. The conquering despot could descend on them and sweep them away, leaving anarchy in their place, and he does compel them to be put in exercise for a particular purpose, that of raising tribute or sometimes recruits. On the other hand, these authorities, which represent a general will of the communities, form the power which determines such actions and forbearances of the individual as do not proceed from natural inclination. The military ruler, indeed, is sovereign in the sense of possessing irresistible coercive power, but in fact this power is only exercised within narrow limits, and not at all in any legislative or judicial way. If exercised beyond these limits and in conflict with customary law, the result would be a general anarchy. The truest way of expressing the state of the case is to say that, taking the

term "sovereign" in the sense which we naturally associate with it and in which it is used by modern European writers on sovereignty, there is under such conditions no sovereign, but that the practical regulation of life, except during intervals of military violence and anarchy, rests with authorities representing the general will, though these are to a certain extent interfered with by an alien force.

89. The same account is applicable to most cases of foreign dominion over a people with any organised common life of their own. The foreign power is not sovereign in the sense of being a maker or maintainer of laws. Law-making, under such conditions, there is properly none. The subject people inherits laws, written or unwritten, and maintains them for itself, a certain shelter from violence being afforded by the foreign power. Such, in the main, was the condition of North Italy, for instance, under Austrian domination. Where this is the case, the removal of the coercive power of the foreigner need not involve anarchy, or any violation of established rights (such as Hobbes supposes to follow necessarily from the deposition of an actual sovereign). The social order does not depend on the foreign dominion and may survive it. The question whether in any particular case it actually can do so must depend on the possibility of preventing further foreign aggression, and on the question whether there is enough national unity in the subject people to prevent them from breaking up into hostile communities when the foreign dominion is removed.

90. It is otherwise where the foreign power is really a law-making and maintaining one, and is sovereign in that proper sense, as was the Roman Empire. But just so far as the Roman Empire was of this sovereign, i.e., law-making and maintaining, character, it derived its permanence, its hold on the "habitual obedience" of its subjects, from the support of the "general will." As the empire superseded customary or written laws of conquered countries, it conferred rights of Roman citizenship, a much more perfect system of protection in action and acquisition than the conquered people had generally possessed before. Hence, while nothing could be further removed from what Rousseau would have counted liberty than the life of the citizens of the Roman Empire, for they had nothing to do with making the laws which they obeyed, yet probably no political system was ever more firmly grounded on the good-will of the subjects, none in the maintenance of which the subjects felt a stronger interest. The British power in India exercises a middle function between that of the Roman Empire and that of the mere tax-collecting and recruit-raising

empire with which the Roman Empire has just been contrasted. It presents itself to the subject people in the first place as a tax-collector. It leaves the customary law of the people mostly untouched. But if only to a very small extent a law-making power, it is emphatically a law-maintaining one. It regulates the whole judicial administration of the country, but applies its power generally only to enforce the customary law which it finds in existence. For this reason an "habitual obedience" may fairly be said to be rendered by the Indian people to the English government, in a sense in which it could not be said to be rendered to a merely tax-collecting military power; but the habitual obedience is so rendered only because the English government presents itself to the people, not merely as a tax-collector, but as the maintainer of a customary law, which, on the whole, is the expression of the "general will." The same is true in principle of those independent states which are despotically governed, in which, i.e., the ultimate legislative power does not reside, wholly or in part, with an assembly representing the people, or with the people themselves; e.g. Russia. It is not the absolute coercive power of the Czar which determines the habitual obedience of the people. This coercive power, if put to the test as a coercive power, would probably be found very far from absolute. This habitual obedience is determined by a system of law, chiefly customary, which the administration controlled by the Czar enforces against individuals but which corresponds to the general sense of what is equitable and necessary. If a despotic government comes into anything like habitual conflict with the unwritten law which represents the general will, its dissolution is beginning.

91. The answer, then, to the question whether there is any truth in Rousseau's conception of sovereignty as founded upon a "volonté générale," in its application to actual sovereignty, must depend on what we mean by "sovereign." The essential thing in political society is a power which guarantees men rights, i.e., a certain freedom of action and acquisition conditionally upon their allowing a like freedom in others. It is but stating the same condition otherwise to speak of a power which guarantees the members of the society these rights, this freedom of action and acquisition, impartially or according to a general rule or law. What is the lowest form in which a society is fit to be called political, is hard to say. The political society is more complete as the freedom guaranteed is more complete, both in respect of the persons enjoying it and of the range of possible action and acquisition over which it extends. A family or a nomad horde could not be called a political society, on account of the nar-

row range of the freedoms which they severally guarantee. The nomad horde might indeed be quite as numerous as a Greek state or as the sovereign canton of Geneva in Rousseau's time; but in the horde the range within which reciprocal freedom of action and acquisition is guaranteed to the individuals is exceedingly small. It is the power of guaranteeing rights, defined as above, which the old writers on sovereignty and civil government supposed to be established by covenant of all with all, translating the common interest which men have in the maintenance of such a power into an imaginary historical act by which they instituted it. It was this power that they had chiefly in view when they spoke of sovereignty.

92. It is to be observed, however, that the power may very well exist and serve its purpose where it is not sovereign in the sense of being exempt from any liability of being interfered with by a stronger coercive power, such as that of a tax-collecting military ruler. The occasional interference of the military ruler is so far a drawback to the efficiency with which freedom of action and acquisition is guaranteed, but does not nullify the general maintenance of rights. On the other hand, when the power by which rights are guaranteed is sovereign (as it is desirable that it should be) in the special sense of being maintained by a person or persons, wielding coercive force not liable to control by any other human force, it is not this coercive force that is the important thing about it or that determines the habitual obedience essential to the real maintenance of rights. That which determines this habitual obedience is a power residing in the common will and reason of men, i.e., in the will and reason of men as determined by social relations, as interested in each other as acting together for common ends. It is a power which this "universal" rational will exercises over the inclinations of the individual, and which only needs exceptionally to be backed by coercive force.

93. Thus, though it may be misleading to speak of the general will as anywhere either actually or properly sovereign, because the term "sovereign" is best kept to the ordinary usage in which it signifies a determinate person or persons charged with the supreme coercive function of the state, and the general will does not admit of being vested in a person or persons, yet it is true that the institutions of political society—those by which equal rights are guaranteed to members of such a society—are an expression of, and are maintained by, a general will. The sovereign should be regarded, not in abstraction as the wielder of coercive force, but in connection with the whole complex of institutions of political society. It is as their sustainer, and thus as the agent of the general will, that the

sovereign power must be presented to the minds of the people if it is to command habitual loyal obedience; and obedience will scarcely be habitual unless it is loyal, not forced. If once the coercive power, which must always be an incident of sovereignty, becomes the characteristic thing about it in its relation to the people governed, this must indicate one of two things; either that the general interest in the maintenance of equal rights has lost its hold on the people, or that the sovereign no longer adequately fulfils its function of maintaining such rights, and thus has lost the support derived from the general sense of interest in supporting it. It may be doubted whether the former is ever really the case; but whatever explanation of the case may be the true one, it is certain that when the idea of coercive force is that predominantly associated with the law-imposing and enforcing power, then either a disruption of the state or a change in the sources of sovereignty must sooner or later take place. In judging, however, whether this is the case, we must not be misled by words. In England, e.g., from the way in which many people speak of "government," we might suppose that it was looked on mainly as the wielder of coercive force, but it would be a mistake on that account to suppose that English people commonly regard the laws of the country as so much coercion, instead of as an institution in the maintenance of which they are interested. When they speak dyslogistically of "government," they are not thinking of the general system of law but of a central administrative agency which they think interferes mischievously with local and customary administration.

94. It is more true to say that law, as the system of rules by which rights are maintained, is the expression of a general will than that the general will is the sovereign. The sovereign, being a person or persons by whom in the last resort laws are imposed and enforced in the long run and on the whole, is an agent of the general will contributes to realise that will. Particular laws may, no doubt, be imposed and enforced by the sovereign, which conflict with the general will not in the sense that if all the subject people could be got together to vote upon them, a majority would vote against them—that might be or might not be—but in the sense that they tend to thwart those powers of action, acquisition, and self-development on the part of the members of the society, which there is always a general desire to extend though the desire may not be enlightened as to the best means to the end, and which it is the business of law to sustain and extend. The extent to which laws of this kind may be intruded into the general "corpus juris" [body of law] without social dis-

ruption it is impossible to specify. Probably there has never been a civilised state in which they bore more than a very small proportion to the amount of law which there was the strongest general interest in maintaining. But, so far as they go, they always tend to lessen the "habitual obedience" of the people, and thus to make the sovereign cease to be sovereign. The hope must be that this will result in the transfer of sovereignty to other hands before a "social disruption" ensues; before the general system of law has been so far perverted as to lose its hold on the people. Of the possibility of a change in sovereignty without any detraction from the law-abiding habits of the people, France has lately given a conspicuous example. Here, however it must be remembered that a temporary foreign conquest made the transition easier.

95. (2) After what has been said, we need not dwell long on the second question raised[54] concerning Rousseau's theory: Is there any truth in speaking of a sovereignty "de jure" founded upon the "volonte générale." It is a distinction which can only be maintained so long as either "sovereign" is not used in a determinate sense, or by "jus" is understood something else than law or right established by law. If by "sovereign" we understand something short of a person or persons holding the supreme law-making and law-enforcing power, e.g. an English king who is often called sovereign, we might say that sovereignty was exercised "de facto" but not "de jure" when the power of such a "sovereign" was in conflict with, or was not sanctioned by, the law as declared and enforced by the really supreme power. Thus an English king, so far as he affected to control the army or raise money without the co-operation of Parliament, might be said to be sovereign "de facto" but not "de jure" only, however, on the supposition that the supreme law-making and law-enforcing power does not belong to him, and thus that he is called "sovereign" in other than the strict sense. If he were sovereign in the full sense "de facto" he could not fail to be so "de jure" i.e. legally. In such a state of things, if the antagonism between king and parliament continued for any length of time, it would have to be admitted that there was no sovereign in the sense of a supreme law-making and law-enforcing power; that sovereignty in this sense was in abeyance, and that anarchy prevailed. Or the same thing might be explained by saying that sovereignty still resided "de jure" with the king and parliament, though not "de facto" exercised by them; but if we use such language, we must bear in mind that we are qualifying "sovereignty" by an epithet which neutralises its meaning as an actually supreme power. If, however, the king succeeded in establishing such a

power on a permanent footing, he would have become sovereign in the full sense, and there would be no ground for saying, as before, that he was not sovereign "de jure," for the qualifications "de jure" and "not de jure" in that sense in which they might be applied to a power which is not supreme, are equally inapplicable to the power of making and enforcing law which is supreme. The monarchs newly established supremacy may be in conflict with laws that were previously in force, but he has only to abolish those laws in order to render it legal. If, then, it is still to be said to be not "de jure" it must be because "jus" is used for something else than law or right established by law viz. either for "natural right" (if we admit that there is such a thing), and "natural right" as not merely = natural power; or for certain claims which the members of the subject community have come to recognise as inherent in the community and in themselves as members of it, claims regarded as the foundation of law, not as founded upon it, and with which the commands of the sovereign conflict. But even according to this meaning of "jus" a sovereign in the strict Austinian sense, that is not so "de jure" is in the long run an impossibility. "Habitual obedience" cannot be secured in the face of such claims.

96. But whether or no in any qualified sense of "sovereign" or "jus," a sovereign that is not so "de jure" is possible, once understand by "sovereign" the determinate person or persons with whom the ultimate law-imposing and law-enforcing power resides, and by "jus" law, it is then obviously a contradiction to speak of a sovereign "de jure" as distinguished from one "de facto." The power of the ultimate imponent of law cannot be derived from or limited by law. The sovereign may no doubt by a legislative act of its own lay down rules as to the mode in which its power shall be exercised, but if it is sovereign in the sense supposed it must always be open to it to alter these rules. There can be no illegality in its doing so. In short, in whatever sense "jus" is derived from the sovereign, in that sense no sovereign can hold his power "de jure." So Spinoza held that "imperium" was "de jure" indeed, but "de jure naturali" ("jus naturale"—natural power), which is the same as "de jure divino"; only powers exercised in subordination to "imperium" are "de jure civili." So Hobbes said that there could be no unjust law. A law was not a law unless enacted by a sovereign, and the just being that to which the sovereign obliges, the sovereign could not enact the unjust, though it might enact the inequitable and the pernicious the "inequitable" presumably meaning that which conflicts with a "law of nature," the "pernicious" that which tends to weaken individuals or society. Rousseau retains the

same notion of the impeccability of the sovereign, but on different grounds. Every act of the sovereign is according to him "de jure," not because all right is derived from a supreme coercive power and the sovereign is that power, but because the sovereign is the general will which is necessarily a will for the good of all. The enactment of the sovereign could as little, on this view, be "inequitable" or "pernicious" as it could be "unjust." But this view necessitates a distinction between the sovereign, thus conceived, and the actually supreme power of making and enforcing law as it exists anywhere but in what Rousseau considered a perfect state. Rousseau indeed generally avoids calling this actually supreme power "sovereign," though he cannot, as we have seen, altogether avoid it; and since, whatever he liked to call it, the existence of such a power in forms which according to him prevented its equivalence to the general will was almost everywhere a fact, his readers would naturally come to think of the actually supreme power as sovereign "de facto," in distinction from something else which was sovereign "de jure." And further, under the influence of Rousseau's view that the only organ of the general will was an assembly of the whole people, they would naturally regard such an assembly as sovereign "de jure," and any other power actually supreme as merely sovereign "de facto." This opposition, however, really arises out of a confusion in the usage of the term "sovereign" out of inability on the one side to hold fast on the other, to the identification of sovereign with "general will," keep it simply to the sense of supreme law-making and law-enforcing power. If "sovereign" = "general will," the distinction of de facto and de jure is inapplicable to it. A certain desire either is or is not the general will. A certain interest is or is not an interest in the common good. There is no sense in saying that such desire or interest is general will "de jure" but not de facto, or *vice versa*. On the other hand, if "sovereign" = supreme law-making and law-enforcing power, the distinction is equally inapplicable to it. If any person or persons have this power at all, they cannot be said to have it merely "de facto" while others have it "de jure."

97. It may be urged with much truth that the actual possession of such power by a determinate person or persons is rather a convenient hypothesis of writers on jurisprudence than an actual fact; and, as we have seen, the actual condition of things at certain times in certain states may conveniently be expressed by saying that there was a sovereign "de facto" that was not so *de jure*, or *vice versa*, but only on the supposition that "sovereign" is not taken necessarily in the full sense of a supreme law-

making and enforcing power. In a state of things that can be so described, however, there is no "sovereignty" at all in the sense of an actually supreme power of making and enforcing law resident in a determinate person or persons. Sovereignty in this sense can, and when it so exists, it is obvious that no other only exist *de facto*; can in the same sense exist *de jure*. It may be denied indeed in particular cases that an actually supreme power of making and enforcing law is exercised de jure, in a sense of that phrase already explained (see Section 95). Reasons were given for doubting whether a power could really maintain its sovereign attributes if conflicting with *jus*, in the same sense thus explained. But supposing that it could, the fact that it was not exercised "de jure" would not entitle us to say that any other person or persons were sovereign *de jure*, without altering the meaning of "sovereign." If any one has supreme power *de facto*, that which any one else has cannot be supreme power. The qualification of a power as held not "de facto" but "de jure" is one which destroys its character as supreme, i.e., as sovereign in the sense before us.

98. It is only through trying to combine under the term "sovereign" the notions of the general will and of supreme power that we are led to speak of the people as sovereign "de jure", if not "de facto." There would be no harm indeed in speaking of the general will as sovereign, if the natural association of "sovereign" with supreme coercive power could be got rid of; but as this cannot be, when once we have pronounced the general will "sovereign," we are pretty sure to identify the general will with a vote of the majority of citizens. A majority of citizens *can* be conceived as exercising a supreme coercive power, but a general will in the sense of an unselfish interest in the common good which in various degrees actuates men in their dealings with each other cannot be so conceived. Thus for the sovereignty in an impalpable and unnatural sense of the general will we get a sovereignty, in the natural and demonstrable sense, of the multitude. But as the multitude is not everywhere supreme, the assertion of its sovereignty has to be put in the form that it is sovereign de jure. The truth which underlies this proposition is that an interest in common good is the ground of political society, in the sense that without it no body of people would recognise any authority as having a claim on their common obedience. It is so far as a government represents to them a common good that the subjects are conscious that they ought to obey it, i.e., that obedience to it is a means to an end desirable in itself or absolutely. This truth is latent in Rousseau's doctrine of the sovereignty

of the general will, but he confounds with it the proposition that no government has a claim on obedience but that which originates in a vote passed by the people themselves who are called on to obey (a vote which must be unanimous in the case of the original compact, carried by a majority in subsequent cases).

99. This latter doctrine arises out of the delusion of natural right. The individual, it is thought, having a right, not derived from society, to do as he likes, can only forego that right by an act to which he is a party. Therefore he has a right to disregard a law unless it is passed by an assembly of which he has been a member and by the decision of which he has expressly or tacitly agreed to be bound. Clearly, however, such a natural right of the individual would be violated under the most popular sovereignty no less than under one purely monarchical, if he happened to object to the decision of the majority; for to say, as Rousseau says, that he has virtually agreed, by the mere fact of residence in a certain territory, to be bound by votes of the majority of those occupying that territory, is a mere trick to save appearances. But in truth there is no such natural right to do as one likes irrespectively of society. It is on the relation to a society to other men recognising a common good—that the individual's rights depend, as much as the gravity of a body depends on relations to other bodies. A right is a power claimed and recognised as contributory to a common good. A right against society, in distinction from a right to be treated as a member of society, is a contradiction in terms. No one therefore has a right to resist a law or ordinance of government, on the ground that it requires him to do what he does not like, and that he has not agreed to submit to the authority from which it proceeds: and if no one person, no number of persons. If the common interest requires it, no right can be alleged against it. Neither can its enactment by popular vote enhance, nor the absence of such vote diminish, its right to be obeyed. Rousseau himself well says that the proper question for each citizen to ask himself in regard to any proposal before the assembly is not, "do I like or approve it?" but, "is it according to the general will?" which is only another way of asking, "is it according to the general interest?" It is only as the organ of this general interest that the popular vote can endow any law with the right to be obeyed; and Rousseau himself, if he could have freed himself from the presuppositions of natural right, might have admitted that, as the popular vote is by no means necessarily an organ of the general interest, so the decree of a monarch or of an aristocratic assembly, under certain conditions, might be such an organ.

100. But, it may be asked, "must not the individual judge for himself whether a law is for the common good?" and if he decides that it is not, is he not entitled to resist it? Otherwise, not only will laws passed in the interest of individuals or classes and against public good, have a claim to our absolute and permanent submission, but a government systematically carried on for the benefit of a few against the many can never be rightfully resisted. To the first part of this question we must of course answer "yes," without qualification. The degree to which the individual judges for himself of the relation between the common good and the laws which cross the path of his ordinary life, is the measure of his intelligent, as distinguished from a merely instinctive, recognition of rights in others and in the state; and on this recognition again depends his practical understanding of the difference between mere powers and rights as exercised by himself. Supposing then the individual to have decided that some command of a "political superior" is not for the common good, how ought he to act in regard to it? In a country like ours, with a popular government and settled methods of enacting and repealing laws, the answer of common sense is simple and sufficient. He should do all he can by legal methods to get the command cancelled, but till it is cancelled he should conform to it. The common good must suffer more from resistance to a law or to the ordinance of a legal authority than from the individual's conformity to a particular law or ordinance that is bad, until its repeal can be obtained. It is thus the social duty of the individual to conform, and he can have no right, as we have seen, that is against his social duty no right to anything or to do anything, that is not involved in the ability to do his duty.

101. But difficulties arise when either (1) it is a case of disputed sovereignty, and in consequence the legal authority of the supposed command is doubtful; or (2) the government is so conducted that there are no legal means of obtaining the repeal of a law; or (3) when the whole system of law and government is so perverted by private interests hostile to the public that there has ceased to be any common interest in maintaining it; or (4)—a more frequent case—when the authority from which the objectionable command proceeds is so easily separable from that on which the general maintenance of social order and the fabric of settled rights depends, that it can be resisted without serious detriment to this order and fabric. In such cases, may there not be a right of resistance based on a "higher law" than the command of the ostensible sovereign?

102. (1) As to cases where the legal authority of the supposed command is doubtful. In modern states the definition of sovereignty—the determination of the person or persons with whom the supreme power of making and enforcing law legally resides—has only been arrived at by a slow process. The European monarchies have mostly arisen out of the gradual conversion of feudal superiority into sovereignty in the strict sense. Great states such as Germany and Italy have been formed by the combination of independent or semi-dependent states. In England the unity of the state goes back much further than anywhere else, but in England it was but gradually that the residence of sovereignty jointly in King, Lords, and Commons came to be practically established, and it is still founded merely on a customary law. In the United States, with a written constitution, it required all Austin's subtlety to detect where sovereignty lay, and he places it where probably no ordinary citizen of the United States had ever thought of it as residing, viz. "in the states' governments as forming one aggregate body: meaning by a state's government, not its ordinary legislature, but the body of citizens which appoints its ordinary legislature, and which, the union apart, is properly sovereign therein." He bases this view on the provision in the constitution, according to which amendments to it are only valid "when ratified by the legislature in three-fourths of the several states, or by convention in three-fourths thereof" (I, p. 268). But no ordinary citizen of the United States probably ever thought of sovereignty except as residing either in the government of his state or in the federal government consisting of Congress and President, or sometimes in one way, sometimes in the other. In other countries, e.g. France, where since Louis XIV the quarter in which sovereignty resides has at any given time been easily assignable, there have since the revolution been such frequent changes in the ostensible sovereign that there might almost at any time have been a case for doubting whether the ostensible sovereign had such command over the habitual obedience of the people as to be a sovereign in that sense in which there is a social duty to obey the sovereign, as the representative of the common interest in social order; whether some prior sovereignty was not really still in force. For these various reasons there have been occasions in the history of all modern states at which men, or bodies of men, without the conscious assertion of any right not founded upon law, might naturally deem themselves entitled to resist an authority which on its part claimed a right—a legally established power—to enforce obedience, and turned out actually to possess the power of doing so.

103. In such cases the truest retrospective account to be given of the matter will often be that at the time there was nothing amounting to a right on either side. A right is a power of which the exercise by the individual or by some body of men is recognised by a society either as itself directly essential to a common good or as conferred by an authority of which the maintenance is recognised as so essential. But in cases of the kind described the authorities, appealed to on each side as justifying respectively compulsion and resistance, often do not command a sufficiently general recognition of their being necessary to the common good to enable them to confer rights of compulsion or resistance. One or other of them may be coming to do so, or ceasing to do so, but rights, though on the one hand they are eternal or at least coeval with human society, on the other hand take time to form themselves in this or that particular subject and to transfer themselves from one subject to another (just as one may hold reason to be eternal, and yet hold that it takes time for this or that being to become rational). Hence in periods of conflict between local or customary, and imperial or written, law, between the constituent powers of a sovereignty, such as King and Parliament in England, of which the relation to each other has not become accurately defined, between a fallen and a rising sovereign in a period of revolution, between federal and state authorities in a composite state, the facts are best represented by saying that for a time there may be no right on either side in the conflict, and that it is impossible to determine precisely the stage at which there comes to be such a right on the one side as implies a definite resistance to right on the other. This of course is not to be taken to mean that in such periods rights in general are at an end. It is merely that right is in suspense on the particular point at issue between the conflicting powers. As we have seen, the general fabric of rights in any society does not depend on the existence of a definite and ascertained sovereignty, in the restricted sense of the words; on the determination of a person or persons in whom supreme power resides, but on the control of the conduct of men according to certain regular principles by a society recognising common interests; and though such control may be more or less weakened during periods of conflict of the kind supposed, it never ceases.

104. It does not follow, however, because there may often not be strictly a right on either side in such periods of conflict that there is not a good and an evil, a better and a worse, on one side or the other. Of this we can only judge by reference to the end, whatever it be, in which we conceive the good of man to consist. There may be clear ground for saying, in

regard to any conflict, that one side rather than the other *ought* to have been taking, not because those on one side were, those on the other were not, entitled to say that they had a right to act as they did, but because the common good of a nation or mankind was clearly promoted by one line of action, not by the other. E.g., in the American war of secession, though it would be difficult to say that a man had not as much a right to fight for his seceding states as for the Union, yet as the special interest of the seceding state was that of maintaining slavery, there was reason for holding that the side of the Union, not that of the seceding states, was the one which ought to be taken. On the other hand, it does not follow that in a struggle for sovereignty the good of man is more served by one of the competing powers than by the other. Good may come out of the conflict without one power contributing more to it than the other. There may thus be as little ground retrospectively for saying that one side or the other ought to have been taken, as that men had a right to take one and not the other. At the same time, as regards the individual, there is no reason for doubting that the better the motive which determines him to take this side or that, the more he is actuated in doing so by some unselfish desire for human good, the more free he is from egotism, and that conceit or opinionatedness which is a form of egotism the more good he will do whichever side he adopts.

105. It is in such cases as we have been considering that the distinction between sovereign de facto and sovereign "de jure" arises. It has a natural meaning in the mouths of those who, in resisting some coercive power that claims their obedience, can point to another determinate authority to which they not only consider obedience due, but to which such obedience in some considerable measure is actually rendered a meaning which it has not when all that can be opposed to sovereign "de facto" is either a "general will," or the mere name of a fallen dynasty exercising no control over men in their dealings with each other. But where this opposition can be used with a natural meaning, it is a truer account of the matter (as we have seen) to say that sovereignty is in abeyance. The existence of competing powers, each affecting to control men in the same region of outward action, and each having partisans who regard it alone as entitled to exercise such control, implies that there is not that unity of supreme control over the outward actions of men which constitutes sovereignty and is necessary to the complete organisation of a state. The state has either not reached complete organisation, or is for the time disorganised the disorganisation being more or less serious according to the

degree to which the everyday rights of men (their ordinary freedom of action and acquisition) are interfered with by this want of unity in the supreme control.

106. In such a state of things, the citizen has no rule of "right" (in the strict sense of the word) to guide him. He is pretty sure to think that one or other of the competing powers has a right to his obedience because, being himself interested (not necessarily selfishly interested) in its support, he does not take account of its lacking that general recognition as a power necessary to the common good which is requisite in order to give it a right. But we looking back may see that there was no such right. Was there then nothing to direct him either way? Simply I should answer, the general rule of looking to the moral good of mankind, to which a necessary means is the organisation of the state, which again requires unity of supreme control, in the common interest, over the outward actions of men. The citizen ought to have resisted or obeyed either of the competing authorities according as by doing so he contributed most to the organisation of the state in the sense explained. It must be admitted that without more knowledge and foresight than the individual can be expected to possess, this rule, if he had recognised it, could have afforded him no sure guidance; but this is only to say that there are times of political difficulty in which the line of conduct adopted may have the most important effect, but in which it is very hard to know what is the proper line to take. On the other side must be set the consideration that the man who brings with him the character most free from egotism to the decision even of those questions of conduct, as to which established rules of right and wrong are of no avail, is most sure on the whole to take the line which yields the best results.

107. We come next to the question of the possible duty of resistance in cases where no law, acknowledged or half-acknowledged, written or customary, can be appealed to against a command (general or particular) contrary to public good; where no counter-sovereignty, in the natural sense of the words, can be alleged against that of the imponent of the law; and where at the same time, from the people having no share, direct or indirect, in the government, there is no means of obtaining a repeal of the law by legal means. I say the "duty" of resistance because, from the point of view here adopted, there can be no "right" unless on the ground that it is for the common good, and if so there is a duty. In writings of the seventeenth and eighteenth centuries, starting with the assumption of natural rights, the question was never put on its proper footing. It was not

asked, "when for the sake of the common good the citizen ought to resist the sovereign?" but, "what sort of injury to person or property gave him a natural right to resist?" Now there is sense in inquiring upon what sort and amount of provocation from government individuals inevitably will resist how (in Spinoza's language) that "indignatio" [indignation] is excited which leads them "in unum conspirare" [to conspire together]; but there is none in asking what gives them a right to resist, unless we suppose a wrong done to society in their persons; and then it becomes a question not of right merely but of duty, whether the wrong done is such as to demand resistance. Now when the question is thus put, no one presumably would deny that under certain conditions there might be a duty of resistance to sovereign power.

108. It is important, however, that instead of discussing the right of a majority to resist we should discuss the duty of resistance as equally possible for a minority and a majority. There can be no right of a written or majority of citizens, as such, to resist a sovereign. If, by law, customary, the majority of citizens possess or share in the sovereign power, then any conflict that may arise between it and any power cannot be a conflict between it and the sovereign. The majority may have a right to resist such a power, but it will not be a right to resist a *sovereign*. If, on the other hand, the majority of citizens have no share by law or custom in the supreme law-making and enforcing power, they never can have a right, simply as a majority to resist that power. In such a case, there may arise a social duty to resist, and the exercise of men's powers in fulfilment of that duty may be sustained by such a general recognition of its being for the public good, as to become a right; but the resistance may be a duty before a majority of the citizens approve it and does not necessarily become a duty when a majority of them do approve it; while that general recognition of its exercise as being for the common good, through which the power of resistance becomes a right, must be something more habitual and sustained and penetrating than any vote of a majority can convey. Incidentally, however, the consideration of the attitude of the mass of the people in regard to a contemplated resistance to established government must always be most important in determining the question whether the resistance should be made. It should be made, indeed if at all not because the majority approve it but because it is for the public good, but account must be taken of the state of mind of the majority in considering whether it is for the public good or no. The presumption must generally be that resistance to a government is not for the public good when

made on grounds which the mass of the people cannot appreciate; and it must be on the presence of a strong and intelligent popular sentiment in favour of resistance that the chance of avoiding anarchy, of replacing the existing government by another effectual for its purpose, must chiefly depend. On the other hand it is under the worst governments that the public spirit is most crushed; and thus in extreme cases there may be a duty of resistance in the public interest, though there is no hope of the resistance finding efficient popular support. (An instance is the Mazzinian outbreaks in Italy.) Its repeated renewal and repeated failure may afford the only prospect of ultimately arousing the public spirit which is necessary for the maintenance of a government in the public interest. And just as there may thus be a duty of resistance on the part of a hopeless minority so on the other side resistance even to a monarchic or oligarchic government is not justified by the fact that a majority, perhaps in some temporary fit of irritation or impatience, is ready to support it, if, as may very well be, the objects for which government subsists—the general freedom of action and acquisition and self-development are likely to suffer from an overthrow of the government in the popular interest.

109. No precise rule, therefore, can be laid down as to the conditions under which resistance to a despotic government becomes a duty. But the general questions which the good citizen should ask himself in contemplating such resistance will be (a) what prospect is there of resistance to the sovereign power leading to a modification of its character or an improvement in its exercise without its subversion? (b) If it is overthrown, is the temper of the people such—are the influences on which the general maintenance of social order and the fabric of recognised rights depend so far separable from it—that its overthrow will not mean anarchy? (c) If its overthrow does lead to anarchy, is the whole system of law and government so perverted by private interests hostile to the public, that there has ceased to be any common interest in maintaining it?

110. Such questions are so little likely to be impartially considered at a time when resistance to a despotic government is in contemplation, and, however impartially considered, are so intrinsically difficult to answer, that it may seem absurd to dwell on them. No doubt revolutionists do and must to a great extent "go it blind." Such beneficent revolutions as there have been could not have been if they did not. But in most of those questions of right and wrong in conduct, which have to be settled by consideration of the probable effects of the conduct, the estimate of effects which regulates our approval or disapproval "upon a retrospec-

tive survey," and according to which we say that an act should or should not have been done, is not one which we could expect the agent himself to have made. The effort to make it would have paralysed his power of action.

111. In the simple cases of moral duty, where there is no real doubt as to the effects of this or that action and danger arises from interested self-sophistication, we can best decide for ourselves whether we ought to act in this way or that by asking whether it is what is good in us—a disinterested or unselfish motive—that moves us to act in this way or that; and in judging of the actions of others, where the issues and circumstances are simple, the moral question, the question of "ought" or "ought not" is often best put in the form, "how far was the action such as could represent a good character?" That indeed is the form in which the question should always be put, when the nature of the case admits it; since, as argued elsewhere, [*Prol. to Ethics* II, ı and ıı] it is only in its relation to character that action is in the full sense good or bad. But where the probable effects of a certain line of action are at the time of taking it very obscure, we cannot be sure that relatively the best character will lead a man to take the line which turns out best in the result, or that because a line of action has turned out well in result, the character of the man who adopted it was good. This being so, in judging of the act retrospectively, we have to estimate it by the result simply, in abstraction from the character of the agent. Thus in looking back upon a revolutionary outbreak we can only judge whether it was vindicated by the result. If in the light of the result it appears that the conditions were not present under which it would have furthered rather than interfered with the true objects of government, we judge that it should not have been made; if otherwise, we approve it—judge that the persons concerned in it were doing their duty in acting as they did. But whether they were really in the full sense of the term doing their duty in acting as they did in a case when the outbreak was successful, or not doing it in a case where it failed, is what we simply cannot tell; for this depends on the state of character which their action represented, and that is beyond our ken.

112. Such is the necessary imperfection under which all historical judgements labour though historians are not apt to recognise it and would be thought much more dull if they did. They would have fewer readers if they confined themselves to the analysis of situations, which may be correctly made, and omitted judgements on the morality of individuals for which, in the proper sense, the data can never be forthcoming. We

scarcely have them for ourselves (except that we know that we are none of us what we should be) still less for our intimate acquaintances; not at all for men whom we only know through history past or present. In regard to them, we can only fall back on the generalisation, that the best man—the man most disinterestedly devoted to the perfecting of humanity, in some form or other, in his own person or that of others—is most likely to act in a way that is good as measured by its results, those results again being estimated with reference to an ideal of character, and that this is so even under circumstances of political complication. Appearances to the contrary, appearances of harm done from good motives, may be met by the considerations (1) that there is often much egotism, in what calls itself conscientiousness, and that the "conscientious" motives which lead to mischievous acts may not be in the highest sense disinterested; (2) that to what we call the consequences of an action many influences contribute besides the action which we call the cause, and if evil seems to clog the consequences of action pure in motive, this may be due to other influences connected with motives less worthy, and that the consequences which in the rough we call bad might have been worse but for the intervention of the purely-motivated action; (3) that the beneficent results are often put to the credit of the actions of selfish men when they should rather be credited to influences more remote and complex, without which those actions would have been impossible or had no good effect, and which have arisen out of unselfish activities. We see the evil in a course of events and lay the blame on someone who should have acted differently, and whom perhaps we take as an instance of how good men cause mischief; but we do not see the greater evil which would otherwise have ensued.

In regard to the questions stated above as those which the good citizen should ask himself in contemplation of a possible rebellion, though they are questions to which it is impossible for a citizen in the heat of a revolutionary crisis to give a sufficient answer, and which in fact can only be answered after the event, yet they represent objects which the good citizen will set before himself at such times; and in proportion to the amount of good citizenship, as measured by interest in these objects, interest in making the best of existing institutions, in maintaining social order and the general fabric of rights, the interest which leads to a *bona fide* estimate of the value of the existing government in its relation to public good will be the good result of the political movement.

Chapter 7
Will, Not Force, is the Basis of the State

113. Looking back on the political theories we have discussed, we may see that they all start with putting the question to be dealt with in the same way and that their errors are very much due to the way in which they put it. They make no inquiry into the development of society and of man through society. They take no account of other forms of community than that regulated by a supreme coercive power, either in the way of investigating their historical origin and connection, or of considering the ideas and states of mind which they imply or which render them possible. They leave out of sight the process by which men have been clothed with rights and duties, and with senses of right and duty, which are neither natural nor derived from a sovereign power. They look only to the supreme coercive power on the one side and to individuals, to whom natural rights are ascribed, on the other, and ask what is the nature and origin of the right of that supreme coercive power as against these natural rights of individuals. The question so put can only be answered by some device for representing the individuals governed as consenting parties to the exercise of government over them. This they no doubt are so long as the government is exercised in a way corresponding to their several wishes, but so long as this is the case, there is no interference with their "natural liberty" to do as they like. It is only when this liberty is interfered with that any occasion arises for an explanation of the compatibility of the sovereign's right with the natural right of the individual; and it is just then that the explanation by the supposition that the right of the sovereign is founded on consent, fails. But the need of the fictitious explanation arises from a wrong way of putting the question the power which regulates our conduct in political society is conceived in too abstract a way on the one side, and on the other are set over against it, as the subjects which it controls, individuals invested with all the moral attributes and rights of humanity. But in truth it is only as members of a society, as recognising common interests and objects, that individuals come to have these attributes and rights, and the power, which in a political society they have to obey is derived from the development and sys-

tematisation of those institutions for the regulation of a common life without which they would have no rights at all.

114. To ask why I am to submit to the power of the state, is to ask why I am to allow my life to be regulated by that complex of institutions without which I literally should not have a life to call my own, nor should be able to ask for a justification of what I am called on to do. For that I may have a life which I can call my own, I must not only be conscious of myself and of ends which I present to myself as mine; I must be able to reckon on a certain freedom of action and acquisition for the attainment of those ends, and this can only be secured through common recognition of this freedom on the part of each other by members of a society, as being for a common good. Without this, the very consciousness of having ends of his own and a life which he can direct in a certain way, a life of which he can make something would remain dormant in a man. It is true that slaves have been found to have this consciousness in high development; but a slave even at his lowest has been partly made what he is by an ancestral life which was not one of slavery pure and simple a life in which certain elementary rights were secured to the members of a society through their recognition of a common interest. He retains certain spiritual aptitudes from that state of family or tribal freedom. This perhaps is all that could be said of most of the slaves on plantations in modern times, but the slavery of the ancient world, being mainly founded on captivity in war, was compatible with a considerable amount of civilisation on the part of the slaves at the time when their slavery began. A Jewish slave, e.g., would carry with him into slavery a thoroughly developed conception of right and law. Slavery moreover, implies the establishment of some regular system of rights in the slave-owning society. The slave, especially the domestic slave, has the signs and effects of this system all about him. Hence such elementary consciousness of rights—of powers that are his own to make the best of—as the born slave may inherit from an ancestral life of freedom, finds a stimulus to its inward development, though no opportunity for outward exercise, in the habits and ideas of civilised life with which a common language enables the slave to become conversant, and which through the sympathy implied in a common language he to some extent makes his own. Thus the appearance in slaves of the conception that self mastery is properly theirs, does not conflict with the proposition that only so far as a certain freedom of action and acquisition is secured to a body of men through their recognition of the exercise of that freedom by each other as being for the com-

mon good, is there an actualisation of the individual's consciousness of having life and ends of his own. The exercise, manifestation, expression of this consciousness through a freedom secured in the way described is necessary to its real existence, just as language of some sort is necessary to the real existence of thought, and bodily movement to that of the soul.

115. The demand, again, for a justification of what one is called on by authority to do presupposes some standard of right, recognised as equally valid for and by the person making the demand and others who form a society with him, and such a recognised standard in turn implies institutions for the regulation of men's dealings with each other, institutions of which the relation to the consciousness of right may be compared, as above, to that of language to thought. It cannot be said that the most elementary consciousness of right is prior to them, or they to it. They are the expression in which it becomes real. As conflicting with the momentary inclinations of the individual, these institutions are a power which he obeys unwillingly; which he has to, or is made to, obey. But it is only through them that the consciousness takes shape and form which expresses itself in the question, "Why should I thus be constrained? By what right is my natural right to do as I like overborne?"

116. The doctrine that the rights of government are founded on the consent of the governed is a confused way of stating the truth that the institutions by which man is moralised by which he comes to do what he sees that he must as distinct from what he would like, express a conception of a common good; that through them that conception takes form and reality; and that it is in turn through its presence in the individual that they have a constraining power over him, a power which is not that of mere fear, still less a physical compulsion, but which leads him to do what he is not inclined to because there is a law that he should.

Rousseau, it will be remembered, speaks of the "social pact" not merely as the foundation of sovereignty or civil government, but as the foundation of morality. Through it man becomes a moral agent; for slavery to appetite he substitutes freedom of subjection to self-imposed law. If he had seen at the same time that rights do not begin till duties begin, and that if there was no morality prior to the pact there could not be rights, he might have been saved from the error which the notion of there being natural rights introduces into his theory. But though he does not seem himself to have been aware of the full bearing of his own conception, the conception itself is essentially true. Setting aside the fictitious representation of an original covenant as having given birth to that common "ego" or general will, without which no such covenant would have been possible, and of obligations arising out of it, as out of a bargain made between one man and another, it remains true that only through a recognition by certain men of a common interest, and through the expression of that recognition in certain regulations of their dealings with each other, could morality originate, or any meaning be gained for such terms as "ought" and "right" and their equivalents.

117. Morality, in the first instance, is the observance of such regulations, and though a higher morality the morality of the character governed by "disinterested motives" i.e., by interest in some form of human perfection comes to differentiate itself from this primitive morality consisting in the observance of rules established for a common good, yet this "outward" morality is the presupposition of the "higher." Morality and political subjection thus have a common source, "*political* subjection" being distinguished from that of a slave, as a subjection which secures rights to the subject. That common source is the rational recognition by certain human beings—it may be merely by children of the same parent—of a common well-being which is their well-being, and which they conceive as their well-being whether at any moment any one of them is inclined to it or no, and the embodiment of that recognition in rules by which the inclinations of the individuals are restrained, and a corresponding freedom of action for the attainment of well-being on the whole is secured.

118. From this common source morality and political subjection in all its forms always retain two elements in common, one consisting in antagonism to some inclination, the other consisting in the consciousness that the antagonism to inclination is founded on reason or on the conception of some adequate good. It is the antagonism to inclination involved in the moral life, as alone we know it, that makes it proper to speak analogically of moral "laws" and "imperatives." It must be remembered, however, that such language *is* analogical, and that there is an essential difference between laws in the strictest sense (laws which are indeed not adequately described as general commands of a political superior, sanctioned by liability to pains which that superior can inflict, but in which a command so sanctioned is an essential element), and the laws of conscience, of which it is the peculiar dignity that they have no external imponent and no sanction consisting in fear of bodily evil. The relation of constraint, in the one case between the man and the externally imposed law, in the other between some particular desire of the man and his

consciousness of something absolutely desirable, we naturally represent in English, when we reflect on it, by the common term "must." "I *must* connect with the main drainage," says the householder to himself, reflecting on an edict of the Local Board. "I *must* try to get A.B. to leave off drinking," he says to himself, reflecting on a troublesome moral duty of benevolence to his neighbour. And if the "must" in the former case represents in part the knowledge that compulsion may be put on the man who neglects to do what he "must," which is no part of its meaning in the second, on the other hand the consciousness that the constraint is for a common good, which wholly constitutes the power over inclination in the second case, must always be an element in that obedience which is properly called obedience to law, or civil or political obedience. Simple fear can never constitute such obedience. To represent it as the basis of civil subjection is to confound the citizen with the slave, and to represent the motive which is needed for the restraint of those in whom the civil sense is lacking and for an occasional reinforcement of the law abiding principle in others, as if it were the normal influence in habits of life of which the essential value lies in their being independent of it. How far in any particular act of conformity to law the fear of penalties may be operative, it is impossible to say. What is certain is that a habit of subjection founded upon such fear could not be a basis of political or free society to which it is necessary, not indeed that everyone subject to the laws should take part in voting them, still less that he should consent to their application to himself, but that it should represent an idea of common good, which each member of the society can make his own so far as he is rational, i.e. capable of the conception of common good, however much particular passions may lead him to ignore it and thus necessitate the use of force to prevent him from doing that which, so far as influenced by the conception of common good, he would willingly abstain from.

119. Whether the legislative and administrative agencies of society can be kept in the main free from bias by private interests and true to the idea of common good without popular control; whether again, if they can, that "civil sense," that appreciation of common good, on the part of the subjects, which is as necessary to free or political society as the direction of law to the maintenance of common good, can be kept alive without active participation of the people in legislative functions, is a question of circumstances which perhaps does not admit of unqualified answer. The views of those who looked mainly to the highest develop-

ment of political life in a single small society have to be modified if the object sought for is the extension of political life to the largest number of people. The size of modern states renders necessary the substitution of a representative system for one in which the citizens shared directly in legislation, and this so far tends to weaken the active interest of the citizens in the commonwealth, though the evil may partly be counteracted by giving increased importance to municipal or communal administration. In some states, from the want of homogeneity or facilities of communication, a representative legislature is scarcely possible. In others, where it exists, a great amount of power, virtually exempt from popular control, has to be left with what Rousseau would have called the "prince or magistrate." In all this there is a lowering of civil vitality as compared with that of the ancient, and perhaps of some exceptionally developed modern, commonwealths. But perhaps this is a temporary loss that we have to bear as the price of having recognised the claim to citizenship as the claim of all men. Certainly all political ideals, which require active and direct participation by the citizens in the functions of the sovereign state, fail us as soon as we try to conceive their realisation on the wide area even of civilised mankind. It is easy to conceive a better system than that of the great states of modern Europe, with their national jealousies, rival armies and hostile tariffs, but the condition of any better state of things would seem to be the recognition of some single constraining power, which would be even more remote from the active co-operation of the individual citizen than is the sovereign power of the great states at present.

120. These considerations may remind us how far removed from any foundation in their own will the requirements of the modern state must seem to be to most of those who have to submit to them. It is true that the necessity which the state lays upon the individual is for the most part one to which he is so accustomed that he no longer kicks against it; but what is it, we may ask, but an external necessity, which he no more lays on himself than he does the weight of the atmosphere or the pressure of summer heat and winter frosts, that compels the ordinary citizen to pay rates and taxes, to serve in the army, to abstain from walking over the squire's fields or snaring his hares, or fishing in preserved streams, to pay rent, or respect those artificial rights of property which only the possessors of them have any obvious interest in maintaining, or even (if he is one of the "proletariate") to keep his hands off the superfluous wealth of his neighbour, when he has none of his own to lose? Granted that there

are good reasons of social expediency for maintaining institutions which thus compel the individual to actions and forbearances that are none of his willing, is it not abusing words to speak of them as founded on a conception of general good? A conception does not float in the air. It must be somebody's conception. Whose conception, then, of general good is it that these institutions represent? Not that of most of the people who conform to them, for they do so because they are made to, or have come to do so habitually from having been long made to; (i.e. from being frightened at the consequences of not conforming, not consequences which follow from not conforming in the ordinary course of nature, but of consequences which the state inflicts, artificial consequences.) But when a man is said to obey an authority from interest in a common good, some other good is meant than that which consists in escaping the punishment which the authority would inflict on disobedience. Is the conception of common good alleged, then, a conception of it on the part of those who founded or maintain the institutions in question? But is it not certain that private interests have been the main agents in establishing, and are still in maintaining, at any rate all the more artificial rights of property? Have not our modern states again, in nearly every case, been founded on conquest, and are not the actual institutions of government in great measure the direct result of such conquest, or, where revolutions have intervened, of violence which has been as little governed by any conception of general good? Supposing that philosophers can find exquisite reasons for considering the institutions and requirements which have resulted from all this self-seeking and violence to be contributory to the common good of those who have to submit to them, is it not trifling to speak of them as founded on or representing a conception of this good, when no such conception has influenced those who established, maintain, or submit to them? And is it not seriously misleading to speak of an obedience to the requirements of the state, when these requirements have so largely arisen out of force directed by selfish motives and when the motive to the obedience is determined by fear, as having a common source with the morality of which it is admitted that the essence is to be disinterested and spontaneous.

121. If we would meet these objections fairly certain admissions, must be made. That idea of a common good which the state fulfils has never been the sole influence actuating those who have been agents in the historical process by which states have come to be formed; and even so far as it has actuated them, it has been only as conceived in some very im-

perfect form that it has done so. This is equally true of those who contribute to the formation and maintenance of states rather as agents, and of those who do so rather as patients. No one could pretend that even the most thoughtful and dispassionate publicist is capable of the idea of the good served by the state to which he belongs, in all its fulness. He apprehends it only in some of its bearings, but it is as a common good that he apprehends it, i.e., not as a good for himself or for this man or that more than another, but for all members equally in virtue of their relation to each other and their common nature. The idea of the common good served by the state on the part of the ordinary citizen, is much more limited in content. Very likely he does not think of it at all in connection with anything that the term "state" represents to him. But he has a clear understanding of certain interests and rights common to himself with his neighbours—if only such as consist in getting his wages paid at the end of the week, in getting his money's worth at the shop, in the inviolability of his own person and his wife's. Habitually and instinctively i.e., without asking the reason why he regards the claim which in these respects he makes for himself as conditional upon his recognising a like claim in others, and thus as in the proper sense a right—a claim of which the essence lies in its being common to himself with others. Without this instinctive recognition he is one of the "dangerous classes," virtually outlawed by himself. With it, though he has no reverence for the "state" under that name, no sense of an interest shared with others in maintaining it, he has the needful elementary conception of a common good maintained by law. It is the fault of the state if this conception fails to make him a loyal subject, if not an intelligent patriot. It is a sign that the state is not a true state that it is not fulfilling its primary function of maintaining law equally in the interest of all, but is being administered in the interest of classes; whence it follows that the obedience which, if not rendered willingly, the state compels the citizen to render, is not one that he feels any spontaneous interest in rendering, because it does not present itself to him as the condition of the maintenance of those rights and interests, common to himself with his neighbours, which he understands.

122. But even if the law which regulates private relations and its administration are so equally applied to all, that all who are capable of a common interest are prompted by that interest to conform to the law, the result is still only the loyal subject as distinct from the intelligent patriot, i.e., as distinct from the man who so appreciates the good which in common with others he derives from the state—from the nation organised in

the form of a self-governing community to which he belongs—as to have a passion for serving it whether in the way of defending it from external attack or developing it from within. The citizens of the Roman Empire were loyal subjects; the admirable maintenance of private rights made them that; but they were not intelligent patriots, and chiefly because they were not, the empire fell. That active interest in the service of the state, which makes patriotism in the better sense, can hardly arise while the individual's relation to the state is that of a passive recipient of protection in the exercise of his rights of person and property. While this is the case, he will give the state no thanks for the protection which he will not specially associate with it, and will only be conscious of it when it descends upon him with some unusual demand for service or payment, and then he will be conscious of it in the way of resentment. If he is to have a higher feeling of political duty, he must take part in the work of the state. He must have a share, direct or indirect, by himself acting as a member or by voting for the members of supreme or provincial assemblies, in making and maintaining the laws which he obeys. Only thus will he learn to regard the work of the state as a whole, and to transfer to the whole the interest which otherwise his particular experience would lead him to feel only in that part of its work that goes to the maintenance of his own and his neighbour's rights.

123. And even then his patriotism will hardly be the passion which it needs to be, unless his judgement of what he owes to the state is quickened by a feeling of which the "patria," the fatherland, the seat of one's home, is the natural object and of which the state becomes the object only so far as it is an organisation of a people to whom the individual feels himself bound by ties analogous to those which bind him to his family—ties derived from a common dwelling-place with its associations, from common memories, traditions and customs, and from the common ways of feeling and thinking which a common language and still more a common literature embodies. Such an organisation of an homogeneous people the modern state in most cases is (the two Austrian states being the most conspicuous exceptions), and such the Roman state emphatically was not.

124. But, it will be said, we are here again falling back on our unproved assumption that the state is an institution for the promotion of a common good. This granted, it is not difficult to make out that in most men at any rate there is a sufficient interest in some form of social well-being, sufficient understanding of the community between their own well-

being and that of their neighbours, to make them loyal to such an institution. But the question is, whether the promotion of a common good, at any rate in any sense appreciable by the multitude, is any necessary characteristic of a state. It is admitted that the outward visible sign of a state is the presence of a supreme or independent coercive power, to which habitual obedience is rendered by a certain multitude of people, and that this power may often be exercised in a manner apparently detrimental to general well-being. It may be the case, as we have tried to show that it is, that a power which is in the main so exercised and is generally felt to be so, is not likely long to maintain its supremacy, but this does not show that a state cannot exist without promotion of the common good of its subjects or that (in any intelligible sense) the promotion of such good belongs to the idea of a state. A short-lived state is not therefore not a state, and if it were, it is rather the active interference with the subjects' well-being, than a failure to promote it, that is fatal to the long life of a state. How, finally, can the state be said to exist for the sake of an end, or to fulfil an idea, the contemplation of which, it is admitted, has had little to do with the actions which have had most to do with bringing states into existence?

125. The last question is a crucial one, which must be met at the outset. It must be noticed that the ordinary conception of organisation, as we apply it in the interpretation of nature, implies that agents may be instrumental in the attainment of an end or the fulfilment of an idea of which there is no consciousness on the part of the organic agents themselves. If it is true on the one hand that the interpretation of nature by the supposition of ends external to it, with reference to which its processes are directed, has been discarded, and that its rejection has been the condition of growth in an exact knowledge of nature, on the other hand the recognition of ends immanent in nature, of ideas realised within it, is the basis of a scientific explanation of life. The phenomena of life are not ideal, in the sense in which the ideal is opposed to that which is sensibly verifiable, but they are related to the processes of material change which are their conditions, as ideas or ideal ends which those processes contribute to realise, because while they determine the processes (while the processes would not be what they are but for relation to them), yet they are *not* those processes *not* identical with any one or number of them, or all of them together. Life does not reside in any of the organs of life or in any or all of the processes of material change through which these pass. Analyse or combine these as you will, you do not detect it as the result of

the analysis or combination. It is a function or end which they realise according to a plan or idea which determines their existence before they exist and survives their disappearance. If it were held, then, that the state were an organised community in the same sense in which a living body is, of which the members at once contribute to the function called life and are made what they are by that function, according to an idea of which there is no consciousness on their part, we should only be following the analogy of the established method of interpreting nature.

126. The objection to such a view would be that it represents the state as a purely natural, not at all as a moral, organism. Moral agency is not merely agency by which an end is attained, or an idea realised or a function fulfilled, but agency determined by an idea on the part of the agent, by his conception of an end or function; and the state would be brought into being and sustained by merely natural, as opposed to moral, agency unless there were a consciousness of ends—and of ends the same in principle with that served by the state itself—on the part of those by whom it is brought into being and sustained. I say "ends the same in principle with that served by the state itself," because if the state arose out of the action of men determined indeed by the consciousness of ends, but ends wholly heterogeneous to that realised by the state, it would not be a moral institution, would not stand in any moral relation to men. Now among the influences that have operated in the formation of states, a large part, it must be admitted, are simply natural. Such are influences of climate, of distribution of mountain and plain, land and water, etc., of all physical demarcations and means of communication. But these, it is clear, are only organic to the formation of states so far as, so to speak, they take a character, which does not belong to them as merely natural, from agencies distinctively human.

127. "Human, if you like," it may be replied, "but not moral, if a moral agency implies any reference to a social or human good, to a good which the individual[55] desires because it is good for others, or for mankind, as well as himself. In the earth-hunger of conquering hordes, in the passions of military despots, in the pride of avarice or vindictiveness which moved such men as Louis XI or Henry VIII to override the semianarchy of feudalism with a real sovereignty, what is there of reference to such good? Yet if we suppose the influence of such motives as these, together with the natural influences just spoken of, to be erased from the history of the formation of states, its distinguishing features are gone."

128. The selfish motives described must not, any more than the natural influences, be regarded in abstraction if we would understand their true place in the formation of states. The pure desire for social good does not indeed operate in human affairs unalloyed by egotistic motives, but on the other hand what we call egotistic motives do not act without direction from an involuntary reference to social good—"involuntary" in the sense that it is so much a matter of course that the individual does not distinguish it from his ordinary state of mind. The most conspicuous modern instance of a man who was instrumental in working great and in some ways beneficial changes in the political order of Europe, from what we should be apt to call the most purely selfish motives, is Napoleon. Without pretending to analyse these motives precisely, we may say that a leading one was the passion for glory; but if there is to be truth in the statement that this passion governed Napoleon, it must be qualified by the farther statement that the passion was itself governed by social influences, operative on him, from which it derived its particular direction. With all his egotism, his individuality was so far governed by the action of the national spirit in and upon him that he could only glorify himself in the greatness of France; and though the national spirit expressed itself in an effort after greatness which was in many ways of a mischievous and delusive kind, yet it again had so much of what may be called the spirit of humanity in it that it required satisfaction in the belief that it was serving mankind. Hence the aggrandisement of France, in which Napoleon's passion for glory satisfied itself, had to take at least the semblance of a deliverance of oppressed peoples, and in taking the semblance to a great extent performed the reality; at any rate in western Germany and northern Italy, wherever the Code Napoléon was introduced.

129. It is thus that actions of men whom in themselves we reckon bad are "overruled" for good. There is nothing mysterious or unintelligible in such "overruling." There is nothing in the effect which we ascribe to the "overruling," any more than in any effect belonging to the ordinary course of nature which there was not in the cause as it really was and as we should see it to be if we fully understood it. The appearance to the contrary arises from our taking too partial and abstract a view of the cause. We look at the action e.g., of Napoleon with reference merely to the selfishness of his motives. We forget how far his motives, in respect of their concrete reality in respect of the actual nature of the ends pursued as distinct from the particular relation in which those ends stood to his personality were made for him by influences with which his selfish-

ness had nothing to do. It was not his selfishness that made France a nation or presented to him continuously an end consisting in the national aggrandisement of France, or at particular periods such ends as the expulsion of the Austrians from Italy, the establishment of a centralised political order in France on the basis of social equality, the promulgation of the civil code, the maintenance of the French system along the Rhine. His selfishness gave a particular character to his pursuit of these ends, and (so far as it did so) did so for evil. Finally it led him into a train of action altogether mischievous. But at each stage of his career, if we would understand what his particular agency really was, we must take account of his ends in their full character, as determined by influences with which his passion for glory no doubt cooperated, but which did not originate with it or with him, and in some measure represented the struggle of mankind towards perfection.

130. And not only must we thus correct our too abstract views of the particular agency of such a man as Napoleon. If we would understand the apparent results of his action we must bear in mind how much besides his particular agency has really gone to produce them, so far as they were good, how much of unnoticed effort on the part of men obscure because unselfish, how much of silent process in the general heart of man. Napoleon was called the "armed soldier of revolution" and it was in that character that he rendered what service he did to men; but the revolution was not the making of him or his likes. Caesar again we have learnt to regard as a benefactor of mankind, but it was not Caesar that made the Roman law through which chiefly or solely the Roman Empire became a blessing. The idiosyncrasy, then, of the men who have been most conspicuous in the production of great changes in the condition of mankind, though it has been an essential element in their production, has been so only so far as it has been overborne by influences and directed to ends, which were indeed not external to the men in question—which on the contrary helped to make them inwardly and spiritually what they really were—but which formed no part of their distinguishing idiosyncrasy. If that idiosyncrasy was conspicuously selfish, it was still not through their selfishness that such men contributed to mould the institutions by which nations have been civilised and developed, but through their fitness to act as organs of impulses and ideas which had previously gained a hold on some society of men, and for the realisation of which the means and conditions had been preparing quite apart from the action

of those who became the most noticeable instruments of their realisation.

131. The assertion, then, that an idea of social good is represented by or realised in the formation of states, is not to be met by pointing to the selfishness and bad passions of men who have been instrumental in forming them, if there is reason to think that the influences, under direction of which these passions became thus instrumental, are due to the action of such an idea. And when we speak thus, we do not refer to any action of the idea otherwise than in the consciousness of men. It may be legitimate, as we have seen, to consider ideas as existing and acting otherwise, and perhaps, on thinking the matter out, we should find ourselves compelled to regard the idea of social good as a communication to the human consciousness a consciousness developing itself in time from an eternally complete consciousness. But here we are considering it as a source of the moral action of men, and therefore necessarily as having its seat in their consciousness, and the proposition advanced is that such an idea is a determining element in the consciousness of the most selfish men who have been instrumental in the formation or maintenance of states; that only through its influence in directing and controlling their actions could they be so instrumental; and that, though its active presence in their consciousness is due to the institutions, the organisation of life, under which they are born and bred, the existence of these institutions is in turn due to the action, under other conditions, of the same idea in the minds of men.

132. It is the necessity of a supreme coercive power to the existence of a state that gives plausibility to the view that the action of merely selfish passions may lead to the formation of states. They have been motive causes, it would seem, in the processes by which this "imperium" has been established; as, e.g., the acquisition of military power by a tribal chieftain, the conquest of one tribe by another, the supersession of the independent prerogatives of families by a tyrant which was the antecedent condition of the formation of states in the ancient world, the supersession of feudal prerogatives by the royal authority which served the same purpose in modern Europe. It is not, however, supreme coercive power, simply as such, but supreme coercive power, exercised in a certain way and for certain ends, that makes a state; viz. exercised according to law, written or customary and for the maintenance of rights. The abstract consideration of sovereignty has led to these qualifications being overlooked. Sovereignty = supreme coercive power, indeed, but

such power as exercised in and over a state, which means with the qualifications specified; but the mischief of beginning with an inquiry into
sovereignty, before the idea of a State has been investigated, is that it
leads us to adopt this abstract notion of sovereignty as merely supreme
coercive power, and then, when we come to think of the state as distinguished by sovereignty, makes us suppose that supreme coercive power
is all that is essential to a state, forgetting that it is rather the state that
makes the sovereign than the sovereign that makes the state. Supposing
one man had been master of all the slaves in one of the states of the
American Union, there would have been a multitude of men under one
supreme coercive power, but the slaves and the master would have formed
no state, because there would have been no recognised[56] rights of slave
against slave enforced by the master, nor would dealings between master
and slaves have been regulated by any law, and in consequence the multitude consisting of slaves and master would not have been a state. The
fact that sovereign power, as implied in the fact of its supremacy, can
alter any laws, is apt to make us overlook the necessity of conformity to
law on the part of the sovereign, if he is to be sovereign of a state. A
power that altered laws otherwise than according to law, according to a
constitution, written or unwritten, would be incompatible with the existence of a state, which is a body of persons, recognised by each other as
having rights, and possessing certain institutions for the maintenance of
those rights. The office of the sovereign, as an institution of such a society, is to protect those rights from invasion, either from without, from
foreign nations, or from within, from members of the society who cease
to behave as such. Its supremacy is the society's independence of such
attacks from without or within. It is an agency of the society, or the society itself acting for this end. If the power, existing for this end, is used on
the whole otherwise than in conformity either with a formal constitution
or with customs which virtually serve the purpose of a constitution, it is
no longer an institution for the maintenance of rights and ceases to be the
agent of a state. We only count Russia a state by a sort of courtesy on the
supposition that the power of the Czar, though subject to no constitu-
tional control is so far exercised in accordance with a recognised tradi-
tion of what the public good requires as to be on the whole a sustainer of
rights.

   It is true that just as in a state, all law being derived from the sovereign, there is a sense in which the sovereign is not bound by any law, so
there is a sense in which all rights are derived from the sovereign and no

power which the sovereign refuses to allow can be a right; but it is only in the sense that, the sovereign being the state acting in a certain capacity, and the state being an institution for the more complete and harmonious maintenance of the rights of its members, a power, claimed as a right, but which the state or sovereign refuses to allow, cannot be really compatible with the general system of rights. In other words, it is true only on supposition that a state is made a state by the function which it fulfils of maintaining the rights of its members as a whole or a system, in such a way that none gains at the expense of another (no one has any power guaranteed to him through another's being deprived of that power). Thus the state, or the sovereign as a characteristic institution of the state, does not create rights, but gives fuller reality to rights already existing. It secures and extends the exercise of powers, which men, influenced in dealing with each other by an idea of common good, had recognised in each other as being capable of direction to that common good, and had already in a certain measure secured to each other in consequence of that recognition. It is not a state unless it does so.

133. It may be said that this is an arbitrary restriction of the term "state." If any other word, indeed, can be found to express the same thing, by all means let it be used instead. But some word is wanted for the purpose, because as a matter of fact societies of men, already possessing rights, and whose dealings with each other have been regulated by customs conformable to those rights, but not existing in the form to which the term "state" has just been applied (i.e., not having a systematic law in which the rights recognised are expressed and harmonised, and which is enforced by a power strong enough at once to protect a society against disturbance within and aggression from without), have come to take on that form. A word is needed to express that form of society both according to the idea of it which has been operative in the minds of the members of the societies which have undergone the change described, (an idea only gradually taking shape as the change proceeded), and according to the more explicit and distinct idea of it which we form in reflecting on the process. The word "state" is the one naturally used for the purpose. The exact degree to which the process must have been carried before the term "state" can be applied to the people in which it has gone on cannot be precisely determined, but as a matter of fact we never apply it except in cases where it has gone some way, and we are justified in speaking of the state according to its idea as the society in which it is completed.

134. It is a mistake then to think of the state as an aggregation of individuals under a sovereign-equally so whether we suppose the individuals as such, or apart from what they derive from society, to possess natural rights, or suppose them to depend on the sovereign for the possession of rights. A state presupposes other forms of community, with the rights that arise out of them, and only exists as sustaining, securing, and completing them. In order to make a state there must have been families of which the members recognised rights in each other (recognised in each other powers capable of direction by reference to a common good); there must further have been intercourse between families, or between tribes that have grown out of families, of which each in the same sense recognised rights in the other. The recognition of a right being very short of its definition, the admission of a right in each other by two parties, whether individuals, families, or tribes, being very different from agreement as to what the right consists in, what it is a right to do or acquire, the rights recognised need definition and reconciliation in a general law. When such a general law has been arrived at, regulating the position of members of a family towards each other and the dealings of families or tribes with each other; when it is voluntarily recognised by a community of families or tribes, and maintained by a power strong enough at once to enforce it within the community and to defend the integrity of the community against attacks from without, then the elementary state has been formed.

135. That, however, is the beginning, not the end, of the state. When once it has come into being, new rights arise in it and further purposes are served by it. New rights arise in it (1) through the claim for recognition on the part of families and tribes living on the same territory with those which in community form the state but living at first in some relation of subjection to them. A common humanity, of which language is the expression, necessarily leads to recognition of some good as common to these families with those which form the state. This is in principle the recognition of rights on their part; and the consequent embodiment of this recognition in the law of the state is their admission as members of it (Instances of this process are found in the states of Greece and the early history of Rome.) (2) The same thing may happen in regard to external communities ("external" territorially), whether these have been already formed into states or no. It may happen through conquest of one by another, through their submission to a common conqueror, as under the Roman empire, or through voluntary combination (as with the Swiss

cantons and the United States of America). However the combination may arise, it results in new rights as between the combined communities within the system of a single state. (3) The extended intercourse between individuals, which formation of the state renders possible, leads to new complications in their dealings with each other, and with it to new forms of right, especially in regard to property-rights as far removed from any obvious foundation on the *suum cuique* principle as that of a college to the great tithes of a parish for which it does nothing. (4) The administration of the state gives rise to rights, to the establishment of powers necessary for its administration. (5) New situations of life may arise out of the extended dealings of man with man which the state renders possible, (e.g. through the crowding of population in certain localities), which make new modes of protecting the people a matter virtually of right. And, as new rights arise in the state once formed, so further purposes are served. It leads to a development and moralisation of man beyond the stage which they must have reached before it could be possible.

136. On this I shall dwell more in my next course of lectures.[57] What I am now concerned to point out is that, however necessary a factor force may have been in the process by which states have been formed and transformed, it has only been such a factor as cooperating with those ideas without which rights could not exist. I say "could not *exist*," not "could not be recognised," because rights are made by recognition. There is no right "but thinking makes it so;" none that is not derived from some idea that men have about each other. Nothing is more real than a right, yet its existence is purely ideal, if by "ideal" is meant that which is not dependent on anything material but has its being solely[58] in consciousness. It is to these ideal realities that force is subordinate in the creation and development of states. The force of conquest from without, the force exercised within communities by such agents as the early Greek Tyrants or the royal suppressors of feudalism in modern Europe, has only contributed to the formation of states in so far as its effects have taken a character which did not belong to them as effects of force; a character due to their operation in a moral world, in which rights already existed, resting on the recognition by men of each other as determined, or capable of being determined, by the conception of a common good. It is not indeed true that only a state can produce a state, though modern history might seem to favour that notion. As a matter of fact the formation of modern states through feudalism out of an earlier tribal system has been dependent on ideas derived from the Roman state, if not on institutions

actually handed down from it; and the improvement and development of the state system which has taken place since the French Revolution has been through agencies which all presuppose and are determined by the previous existence of states. But the Greek states, so far as we know, were a first institution of the kind, not a result of propagation from previously existing states. But the action, which brought them into being, was only effectual for its purpose because the idea of right, though only in the form of family or tribal right, was already in operation.[59]

Chapter 8
Has the Citizen Rights Against the State?

137. I propose to pursue the inquiry, begun in my last course, into the nature and functions of the state. In the last course, we were chiefly occupied with criticism. We have seen that no true conception of the rights of individuals against each other or against the state, or of the rights of the state over individuals, can be arrived at, while we look upon the state merely as an aggregation of individuals under a sovereign power that is able to compel their obedience, and consider this power of compelling a general obedience to be the characteristic thing in a state. So long as this view is retained, no satisfactory answer can be given to the question, by what right the sovereign compels the obedience of individuals. It can only be met either by some device for representing the individuals as so consenting to the exercise of sovereign power over them that it is no violation of their individual rights, or by representing the rights of individuals as derived from the sovereign and thus as having no existence against it. But it is obviously very often against the will of individuals that sovereign power is exercised over them; indeed if it were not so, its characteristic as a power of compulsion would be lost; it would not be a sovereign power; and the fact that the majority of a given multitude may consent to its exercise over an unconsenting minority is no justification for its exercise over that minority, if its justification is founded on consent; the representation that the minority virtually consents to be bound by the will of the majority being an obvious fiction. On the other hand, the theory that all right is derived from a sovereign, that it is a power of which the sovereign secures the exercise to the individual, and that therefore there can be no right against that sovereign, conflicts with the primary demands of human consciousness. It implies the identification of "I ought" with "I am forced to." Reducing the "right" of the sovereign simply to a power, it makes it unintelligible that this power should yet represent itself, and claim obedience to itself, as a right. No such theory indeed admits of consistent statement. To say (with Hobbes) that a law may be inequitable or pernicious, though it cannot be unjust, is to admit a criticism of laws, a distinction between those enactments of the sovereign which are what they should be and those which are not. And this is

to recognise the individual's demand for a justification of the laws which he obeys; to admit in effect that there is some rule of right, of which the individual is conscious and to which law ought to conform.

138. It is equally impossible, then, to hold that the right of the sovereign power in a state over its members is dependent on their consent, and, on the other hand, that these members have no rights except such as are constituted and conferred upon them by the sovereign. The sovereign, and the state itself as distinguished by the existence of a sovereign power, presupposes rights and is an institution for their maintenance. But these rights do not belong to individuals as they might be in a state of nature, or as they might be if each acted irrespectively of others. They belong to them as members of a society in which each recognises the other as an originator of action in the same sense in which he is conscious of being so himself (as an "ego" as himself the object which determines the action), and thus regards the free exercise of his own powers as dependent upon his allowing an equally free exercise of his powers to every other member of the society. There is no harm in saying that they belong to individuals as such, if we understand what we mean by "individual," and if we mean by "individual" a self-determining subject conscious of itself as one among other such subjects, and of its relation to them as making it what it is; for then there is no opposition between the attachment of rights to the individuals as such and their derivation from society. They attach to the individual, but only as a member of a society of free agents, as recognising himself and recognised by others to be such a member, as doing and done by accordingly. A right, then, to act unsocially—to act otherwise than as belonging to a society of which each member keeps the exercise of his powers within the limits necessary to the like exercise by all the other members—is a contradiction. No one can say that, unless he has consented to such a limitation of his powers, he has a right to resist it. The fact of his not consenting would be an extinction of all right on his part.

139. The state then presupposes rights, and rights of individuals. It is a form which society takes in order to maintain them. But rights have no being except in a society of men recognising each other as *ίσοι και όμοιοι* [equals]. They are constituted by that mutual recognition. In analysing the nature of any right, we may conveniently look at it on two sides, and consider it as on the one hand a claim of the individual, arising out of his rational nature, to the free exercise of some faculty; on the other, as a concession of that claim by society, a power given to the individual of

putting the claim in force by society. But we must be on our guard against supposing that these distinguishable sides have any really separate existence. It is only a man's consciousness of having an object in common with others, a well-being which is consciously his in being theirs and theirs in being his—only the fact that they are recognised by him and he by them as having this object—that gives him the claim described. There can be no reciprocal claim on the part of a man and an animal each to exercise his powers unimpeded by the other, because there is no consciousness common to them. But a claim founded on such a common consciousness is already a claim conceded; already a claim to which reality is given by social recognition, and thus implicitly a right.

140. It is in this sense that a slave has "natural rights." They are "natural" in the sense of being independent of, and in conflict with, the laws of the state in which he lives, but they are not independent of social relations. They arise out of the fact that there is a consciousness of objects common to the slave with those among whom he lives—whether other slaves or the family of his owner—and that this consciousness constitutes at once a claim on the part of each of those who share it to exercise a free activity conditionally upon his allowing a like activity in the others, and a recognition of this claim by the others, through which it is realised. The slave thus derives from his social relations a real right which the law of the state refuses to admit. The law cannot prevent him from acting and being treated, within certain limits, as a member of a society of persons freely seeking a common good. And as that capability of living in a certain limited community with a certain limited number of human beings, which the slave cannot be prevented from exhibiting, is in principle a capability of living in a community with any other human beings, supposing the necessary training to be allowed; and as every such capability constitutes a right, we are entitled to say that the slave has a right to citizenship to a recognised equality of freedom with any and every one with whom he has to do—and that in refusing him not only citizenship but the means of training his capability of citizenship, the state is violating a right, founded on that common human consciousness which is evinced both by language which the slave speaks and by actual social relations subsisting between him and others. And on the same principle upon which a state is violating natural rights in, it does the same in using force, except under maintaining slavery necessity of self-defence, against members of another community. Membership of any community is so far in principle membership of all communities as

to constitute a right to be treated as a freeman by all other men, to be exempt from subjection to force except for prevention of force.

141. A man may thus have rights as a member of a family or of human society in any other form without being a member of a state at all—rights which remain rights though any particular state or all states refuse to recognise them; and a member of a state, on the ground of that capability of living as a freeman among freemen which is implied in his being a member of a state, has rights as against all other states and their members. These latter rights are in fact during peace recognised by all civilised states. It is the object of "private international law" to reduce them to a system. But though it follows from this that the state does not create rights, it may be still true to say that the members of a state derive their rights from the state and have no rights against it. We have already seen that a right against society, as such, is an impossibility; that every right is derived from some social relation; that a right against any group of associated men depends on association, as *ἴσος καὶ ὅμοιος* [an equal], with them and with some other men. Now for the member of a state to say that his rights are derived from his social relations, and to say that they are derived from his position as member of a state, are the same thing. The state is for him the complex of those social relations out of which rights arise, so far as those rights have come to be regulated and harmonised according to a general law, which is recognised by a certain multitude of persons, and which there is sufficient power to secure against violation from without and from within. The other forms of community which precede and are independent of the formation of the state do not continue to exist outside it, nor yet are they superseded by it. They are carried on into it. They become its organic members, supporting its life and in turn maintained by it in a new harmony with each other. Thus the citizen's rights, e.g., as husband or head of a family or a holder of property, though such rights, arising out of other social relations than that of citizen to citizen, existed when as yet there was no state, are yet to the citizen derived from the state from that more highly developed form of society in which the association of the family and that of possessors who respect each other's possessions are included as in a fuller whole; which secures to the citizen his family rights and his rights as a holder of property, but under conditions and limitations which membership of the fuller whole—the reconciliation of rights arising out of one sort of social capability with those arising out of another—renders necessary. Nor can the citizen have any right against the state, in the sense of a right to act

otherwise than as a member of some society, the state being for its members the society of societies, the society in which all their claims upon each other are mutually adjusted.

142. But what exactly is meant by the citizen's acting "as a member of his state?" What does the assertion that he can have no right to act otherwise than as a member of his state amount to? Does it mean that he has no right to disobey the law of the state to which he belongs, whatever that law may be; that he is not entitled to exercise his powers in any way that the law forbids and to refuse to exercise them in any way that it commands? This question was virtually dealt with before[60] in considering the justifiability of resistance to an ostensible sovereign. The only unqualified answer that can be given to it is one that may seem too general to be of much practical use, viz. that so far as the laws anywhere or at any time in force fulfil the idea of a state, there can be no right to disobey them; or, that there can be no right to disobey the law of the state except in the interest of the state; i.e., for the purpose of making the state in respect of its actual laws more completely correspond to what it is in tendency or idea, viz. the reconciler and sustainer of the rights that arise out of the social relations of men. On this principle there can be no right to disobey or evade any particular law on the ground that it interferes with any freedom of action, any right of managing his children or "doing what he will with his own," which but for that law the individual would possess. Any power which has been allowed to the individual up to a certain time, he is apt to regard as permanently his right. It has, indeed, been so far his right if the exercise of that power has been allowed with any reference to social good but it does not, as he is apt to think, remain his right when a law has been enacted that interferes with it. A man, e.g., has been allowed to drive at any pace he likes through the streets, to build houses without any reference to sanitary conditions, to keep his children at home or send them to work "analphabetic," to buy or sell alcoholic drinks at his pleasure. If laws are passed interfering with any or all of these powers, he says that his rights are being violated. But he only possessed these powers as rights through membership of a society which secured them to him, and of which the only permanent bond consists in the reference to the well-being of its members as a whole. It has been the social recognition grounded on that reference that has rendered certain of his powers rights. If upon new conditions arising, or upon elements of social good being taken account of which had been overlooked before, or upon persons being taken into the reckoning as capable of participat-

ing in the social well-being who had previously been treated merely as means to its attainment—if in any of these ways or otherwise the reference to social well-being suggests the necessity of some further regulation of the individual's liberty to do as he pleases, he can plead no right against this regulation, for every right that he has possessed has been dependent on that social judgement of its compatibility with general well-being which in respect to the liberties in question is now reversed.

143. "Is then," it may be asked, "the general judgement as to the requirements of social well-being so absolutely authoritative that no individual right can exist against it? What if according to this judgement the institution of slavery is so necessary that citizens are prohibited by law from teaching slaves to read and from harbouring runaways? or if according to it the maintenance of a certain form of worship is so necessary that no other worship can be allowed and no opinion expressed antagonistic to it? Has the individual no rights against enactments founded on such accepted views of social well-being?" We may answer, "a right against society as such, a right to act without reference to the needs or good of society is an impossibility since every right depends on some social relation, and a right against any group of associated men depends on association upon some footing of equality with them or with some other men." We saw how the right of the slave really rested on this basis- on a social capacity shown in the footing on which he actually lives with other men. On this principle it would follow, if we regard the state as the sustainer and harmoniser of social relations, that the individual can have no right against the state; that its law must be to him of absolute authority. But in fact, as actual states at best fulfil but partially their ideal function, we cannot apply this rule to practice. The general principle that the citizen must never act otherwise than as a citizen does not carry with it an obligation under all conditions to conform to the law of his state, since those laws may be inconsistent with the true end of the state as the sustainer and harmoniser of social relations. The assertion by the citizen of any right, however, which the state does not recognise must be founded on a reference to an acknowledged social good. The fact that the individual would like to exercise the power claimed as a right does not render the exercise of it a right, nor does the fact that he has been hitherto allowed to exercise it render it a right, if social requirements have newly arisen under changed conditions, or have newly come to be recognised, with which its exercise is incompatible. The reason that the assertion of an illegal right must be founded on reference to acknowledged social

good is that, as we have seen, no exercise of a power, however abstractedly desirable for the promotion of human good it might be, can be claimed as a right unless there is some common consciousness of utility shared by the person making the claim and those on whom it is made. It is not a question whether or no it ought to be claimed as a right; it simply can not be except on this condition. It would have been impossible, e.g., in an ancient state, where the symbol of social union was some local worship, for a monotheistic reformer to claim a right to attempt the subversion of that worship. If a duty to do so had suggested itself, consciousness of the duty could never have expressed itself in the form of a claim of right, in the absence of any possible sense of a public interest in the religious revolution to which the claim could be addressed. Thus just as it is not the exercise of every power, properly claimable as a right, that is a right in the full or explicit sense of being legally established, so it is not every power, of which the exercise would be desirable in an ideal state of things, that is properly claimable as a right. The condition of its being so claimable is that its exercise should be contributory to some social good which the public conscience is capable of appreciating, not necessarily one which in the existing prevalence of private interests can obtain due acknowledgement, but still one of which men in their actions and language show themselves to be aware.

144. Thus to the question, "has the individual no rights against enactments founded on imperfect views of social well-being?" We may answer, "he has no rights against them, founded on any right to do as he likes." Whatever counter-rights he has must be founded on a relation to social well-being, and that a relation of which his fellow-citizens are aware. He must be able to point to some public interest, generally recognised as such, which is involved in the exercise of the power claimed by him as a right to show that it is not the general well-being, even as conceived by his fellow-citizens, but some special interest of a class that is concerned in preventing the exercise of the power claimed. In regard to the right of teaching or harbouring the slave, he must appeal to the actual capacity of the slave for community with other men as evinced in the manner described above, to the recognition of this capacity as shown by the actual behaviour of the citizens in many respects towards the slave, on the addition to social well-being that results from the realisation of this capacity in all who possess it through rights being legally guaranteed to them. In this way he must show that the reference to social well-being, on which is founded the recognition of powers as rights, if fairly and

thoroughly carried out, leads to the exercise of powers in favour of the slave, in the manner described, not to prohibition of that exercise as the supposed law prohibits it. The response which in so doing he elicits from the conscience of fellow-citizens shows that in talking of the slave as "a man and a brother" he is exercising what is implicitly his right, though it is a right which has not become explicit through legal enactments. This response supplies the factor of social recognition which, as we have seen, is necessary in order to render the exercise of any power a right. To have an implicit right, however, to exercise a power which the law disallows is not the same thing as having a right to exercise that right. The right may be claimed without the power being actually exercised so long as the law prohibits its exercise. The question, therefore, would arise whether the citizen was doing his duty as such—acting as a member of the state––if he not merely did what he could for repeal of the law prohibiting the instruction of a slave or the assistance of runaways, but himself in defiance of the law instructed and assisted them. As a general rule, no doubt, even bad laws, laws representing the interests of classes or individuals as opposed to those of the community—should be obeyed. There can be no right to disobey them, even while their repeal is urged on the ground that they violate rights, because the public interest, on which all rights are founded, is more concerned in the general obedience to law than in the exercise of those powers by individuals or classes which the objectionable laws unfairly withhold. The maintenance of a prohibitory duty upon import of certain articles in the interest of certain manufacturers would be no justification for smuggling these articles. The smuggler acts for his private gain, as does the man who buys of him, and no violation of the law for the private gain of the violator, however unfair the law violated, can justify itself by reference to a recognised public good, or be vindicated as a right. On the other hand, there may be cases in which the public interest—not merely according to some remote philosopher's view of it but according to the conceptions which the people are able to assimilate—is best served by a violation of some actual law. It is so in regard to slavery when the public conscience has come to recognise a capacity for right (for exercising powers under control of a reference to general well-being) in a body of men to whom legal rights have hitherto been refused, but when some powerful class in its own interest resists alteration of the law. In such a case a violation of the law on behalf of the slave is not only not a violation in the interest of the violator; the general sense of right on which general observance of law depends being represented by it, there is no danger of its making a breach in the law-abiding habits of the people.

145. "But this," it will be said, "is to assume a condition of things in which the real difficulty of the question disappears. What is to be done when no recognition of the implicit rights of the slave can be elicited from the public conscience; when the legal prohibitions described are supported by the only conceptions of general good of which the body of citizens is capable? Has the citizen still a right to disregard these legal prohibitions? Is the assertion of such a right compatible with the doctrine that social recognition of any mode of action as contributory to the common good is necessary to constitute a right so to act, and that no member of a state can have a right to act otherwise than according to that position?" The question, be it observed, is not as to the right of the slave, but as to the right of the citizen to treat the slave as having rights in a state of which the law forbids his being so treated. The claim of the slave to be free, his right implicit to have rights explicit, i.e., to membership of a society of which each member is treated by the rest as entitled to seek his own good in his own way on supposition that he so seeks it as not to interfere with the like freedom of quest on the part of others, rests, as we have seen, on the fact that the slave is determined by conceptions of a good common to himself with others, as shown by the actual social relations in which he lives. No state law can neutralise this right. The state may refuse him family rights and rights of property but it cannot help his living as a member of a family—acting and being treated as a father, husband, son, or brother—and therefore cannot extinguish the rights which are necessarily involved in his so acting and being so treated. Nor can it prevent him from appropriating things and from associating with others on the understanding that they respect each other's appropriations, and thus possessing and exercising rights of property. He has thus rights which the state neither gives nor can take away, and they amount to or constitute a right to freedom in the sense explained. The state, under which the slave is a slave, refusing to recognise this right, he is not limited in its exercise by membership of the state. He has a right to assert his right to such membership in any way compatible with that susceptibility to the claims of human fellowship on which the right rests. Other men have claims upon him, conditioning his rights, but the state, as such, which refuses to recognise his rights, has no claim on him. The obligation to observe the law, because it is the law, does not exist for him.

146. It is otherwise with the citizen. The slave has a claim upon him to be treated in a certain way, the claim which is properly described as that of a common humanity. But the state which forbids him so to treat the slave has also a claim upon him, a claim which embodies many of the claims that arise out of a common humanity in a form that reconciles them with each other. Now it may be argued that the claim of the state is only absolutely paramount on supposition that in its commands and pro-hibitions it takes account of all the claims that arise out of human fellow-ship; that its authority over the individual is in principle the authority of those claims, taken as a whole; that if, as in the case supposed, its ordi-nances conflict with those claims as possessed by a certain class of per-sons, their authority, which is essentially a conditional or derived author-ity, disappears; that a disregard of them in the interest of the claims which they disregard is really conformity to the requirements of the state ac-cording to its true end or idea, since it interferes with none of the claims or interests which the state has its value in maintaining or protecting, but, on the contrary, forces on the attention of members of the state claims which they hitherto disregarded; and that if the conscience of the citizens is so far mastered by the special private interests which the institution of slavery breeds that it cannot be brought to recognize action on the slave's behalf as contributory to a common good, yet there is no ground under such conditions for considering a man's fellow-citizens to be the sole organs of the recognition which is needed to render his power of action a right; that the needful recognition is at any rate forthcoming from the slaves and from all those acquainted with the action in whom the idea of a good common to each man with others operates freely.

147. This may be truly urged, but it does not therefore follow that the duty of befriending the slave is necessarily paramount to the duty of obeying the law which forbids his being befriended: and if it is possible for the latter duty to be paramount, it will follow, on the principle that there is no right to violate a duty, that under certain conditions the right of helping the slave may be cancelled by the duty of obeying the prohibi-tory law. It would be so if the violation of law in the interest of the slave were liable to result in general anarchy,[61] not merely in the sense of the dissolution of this or that form of civil combination, but of the disap-pearance of conditions under which any civil combination is possible; for such a destruction of the state would mean a general loss of freedom a general substitution of force for mutual good-will in men's dealings

with each other, that would outweigh the evil of any slavery under such limitations and regulations as an organised state imposes on it.

Chapter 9
Private Rights. The Right to Life and Liberty

148. Returning from this digression, we resume our consideration of the nature and functions of the state. In order then to understand this nature, we must understand the nature of those rights which do not come into being with the state but arise out of social relations that may exist where a state is not; it being the first, though not the only, office of the state to maintain those rights. They depend for their existence, indeed, on society a society of men who recognise each other as *ἴσοι καì ὅμοιοι* [equals], as capable of a common well-being, but not on society's having assumed the form of a state. They may therefore be treated as claims of the individual without reference to the form of the society which concedes or recognises them, and on whose recognition, as we have seen, their nature as rights depends. Only it must be borne in mind that the form in which these claims are admitted and acted on by men in their dealings with each other varies with the form of society—that the actual form, e.g., in which the individual's right of property is admitted under a patriarchal *régime* is very different from that in which it is admitted in a state; and that though the principle of each right is throughout the same, it is a principle which only comes to be fully recognised and acted on when the state has not only been formed, but fully developed according to its idea.

149. The rights which may be treated as independent of the state in the sense explained are of course those which are commonly distinguished as *private*, in opposition to *public* rights. "If rights be analysed, they will be found to consist of several kinds. For first they are such as regard a man's own person; secondly such as regard his dominion over the external and sensible things by which he is surrounded; thirdly, such as regard his private relations, as a member of a family; fourthly such as regard his social state or condition, as a member of the community; the first of which classes may be designated as *personal rights*, the second, as *rights of property*, the third, as *rights in private relations*, and the fourth, as *public right*" (Stephen, *Comm.*, I, p. 136).

150. An objection might fairly be made to distinguishing one class of rights as "personal," on the ground that all rights are so; not merely in the legal sense of "person," according to which the proposition is a truism,

since every right implies a person as its subject, but in the moral sense, since all rights depend on that capacity in the individual for being determined by a conception of well-being, as an object at once for himself and for others, which constitutes personality in the moral sense. By personal rights in the above classification are meant rights of life and liberty—i.e., of preserving one's body from the violence of other men, and of using it as an instrument only of one's own will—if of another's, still only through one's own. The reason why these come to be spoken of as "personal" is probably the same with the reason why we talk of a man's "person" in the sense simply of his body. They may however, be reckoned in a special sense personal even by, those who consider all rights personal because the person's possession of a body and its exclusive determination by his own will is the condition of his exercising any other rights—indeed, of all manifestation of personality. Prevent a man from possessing property (in the ordinary sense), and his personality may still remain. Prevent him (if it were possible) from using his body to express a will, and the will itself could not become a reality; he would not be really a person.

151. If there are such things as rights at all, then, there must be a right to life and liberty, or, to put it more properly to free life. No distinction can be made between the right to life and the right to liberty, for there can be no right to mere life, no right to life on the part of a being that has not also the right to direct the life according to the motions of its own will. What is the foundation of this right? The answer is, capacity on the part of the subject for membership of a society, for determination of the will, and through it of the bodily organisation, by the conception of a well-being as common to self with others. This capacity is the foundation of the right, or the right potentially, which becomes actual through the recognition of the capacity by a society, and through the power which the society in consequence secures to the individual of acting according to the capacity. In principle, or intrinsically, or in respect of that which it has it in itself to become, the right is one that belongs to every man in virtue of his human nature (of the qualities that render him capable of any fellowship with any other men), and is a right as between him and any other men; because, as we have seen, the qualities which enable him to act as a member of any one society having the general well-being of its members for its object (as distinct from any special object requiring special talent for its accomplishment) form a capacity for membership of

any other such society; but actually, or as recognised, it only gradually becomes a right of a man, as man, and against all men.

152. At first it is only a right of the man as a member of some one particular society, and a right as between him and the other members of that society, the society being naturally a family or tribe. Then, as several such societies come to recognise, in some limited way, a common well-being and thus to associate on settled terms, it comes to be a right not merely between the members of any one of the societies but between members of the several families or tribes in their dealings with each other not, however, as men, but only as belonging to this or that particular family. This is the state of things in which, if one man is damaged or killed, compensation is made according to the terms of some customary law by the family or tribe of the offender to that of the man damaged or killed, the compensation varying according to the rank of the family. Upon this system-generally through some fusion of family demarcations and privileges, whether through pressure upward of a population hitherto inferior, or through a levelling effected by some external power—there supervenes one in which the relation between citizen and citizen, as such, is substituted for that between family and family, as such. This substitution is one of the essential processes in the formation of the state. It is compatible, however, with the closest limitation of the privileges of citizenship and implies no acknowledgement in man as man of the right to free life ascribed to the citizen as citizen. In the ancient world, the companion of citizenship is everywhere slavery, and it was only actual citizenship, not any such capacity for becoming a citizen as might naturally be held to be implied in civil birth, that was considered to give a right to live; for the exposure of children was everywhere practised[62] (and with the approval of the philosophers), a practice in strong contrast with the principle of modern law that even a child in the womb has a right to live.

153. The influences commonly pointed out as instrumental in bringing about the recognition of rights in the man, as independent of particular citizenship, are: (1) adjudication by Roman praetors of questions at issue between citizens and those who were not so, which led to the formation of the system of "equity," independent of the old civil law and tending gradually to be substituted for it. The existence of such a system, however, presupposes the recognition of rights so far independent of citizenship in a particular state as to obtain between citizens of different states. (2) The doctrine of a "law of nature," applicable to dealings of all

men, popularised by the Stoics. (3) The Christian conception of the universal redemption of a brotherhood, of which all could become members through a mental act within the power of all.

154. The admission of a right to free life on the part of every man, as man, does in fact logically imply the conception of all men as forming one society in which each individual has some service to render, one organism in which each has a function to fulfil. There can be no claim on society, such as constitutes a right, except in respect of a capacity freely (i.e., under determination by conception of the good) to contribute to its good. If the claim is made on behalf of any and every human being, it must be a claim on human society as a whole, and there must be a possible common good of human society as a whole, conceivable as independent of the special conditions of particular societies, to render such a claim possible. We often find, however, that men assimilate a practical idea in respect of one of its implications without doing so in respect of the rest. Thus the idea of the individual's right to free life has been strongly laid hold of in Christendom in what may be called an abstract or negative way but little notice has been taken of what it involves. Slavery is everywhere condemned. It is established that no one has a right to prevent the individual from determining the conditions of his own life. We treat life as sacred even in the human embryo, and even in hopeless idiots and lunatics recognise a right to live—a recognition which can only be rationally explained on either or both of two grounds: (1) that we do not consider either their lives or the society which a man may freely serve to be limited to this earth, and thus ascribe to them a right to live on the strength of a social capacity which under other conditions may become what it is not here; or (2) that the distinction between curable and incurable, between complete and incomplete, social incapacity is so indefinite that we cannot in any case safely assume it to be such as to extinguish the right to live. Or perhaps it may be argued that even in cases where the incapacity is ascertainably incurable, the patient has still a social function (as undoubtedly those who are incurably ill in other ways have) a passive function as the object of affectionate ministrations arising out of family instincts and memories and that the right to have life protected corresponds to this passive social function. The fact, however, that we have almost to cast about in certain cases for an explanation of the established belief in the sacredness of human life shows how deeply rooted that belief is unless where some counter-belief interferes with it.

155. On the other hand, it is equally noticeable that there are counter-beliefs which, under conditions, do neutralise it, and that certain other beliefs, which form its proper complement, have very slight hold on the mind of modern Christendom. It is taken for granted that the exigencies of the state in war, whether the war be necessary or not for saving the state from dissolution, absolutely neutralise the right to live. We are little influenced by the idea of the universal brotherhood of men of mankind as forming one society with a common good, of which the conception may determine the action of its members. In international dealings we are apt to suppose that it can have no place at all. Yet, as has been pointed out, it is the proper correlative of the admission of a right to free life as belonging to man in virtue simply of his human nature. And though this right can only be grounded on the capacity, which belongs to the human nature, for freely fulfilling some function in the social organism, we do very little to give reality to the capacity or to enable it to realise itself. We content ourselves with enacting that no man shall be used by other men as a means against his will, but we leave it to be pretty much a matter of chance whether or no he shall be qualified to fulfil any social function to contribute anything to the common good, and to do so freely (i.e., under the conception of a common good). The only reason why a man should not be used by other men simply as a means to their ends is that he should use himself as a means to an end which is really his and theirs at once. But while we say that he shall not be used as a means, we often leave him without the chance of using himself for any social end at all.

156. Four questions then arise: (1) With what right do the necessities of war override the individual's right of life? (2) In what relation do the rights of states to act for their own interest stand to that right of human society as such, of which the existence is implied in the possession of right by the individual as a member of that society, irrespectively of the laws of particular states? (3) On what principle is it to be assumed that the individual by a certain conduct of his own forfeits the right of free life, so that the state (at any rate for a time) is entitled to subject him to force, to treat him as an animal or a thing? Is this forfeiture ever so absolute and final that the state is justified in taking away his life? (4) What is the nature and extent of the individual's claim to be enabled to realise that capacity for contributing to a social good, which is the foundation of his right to free life?

Chapter 10
The Right of the State Over the Individual in War

157. (1) It may be admitted that to describe war as "multitudinous murder" is a figure of speech. The essence of murder does not lie in the fact that one man takes away the life of another, but that he does this to "gain his private ends" and with "malice" against the person killed. I am not here speaking of the legal definition of murder, but of murder as a term of moral reprobation, in which sense it must be used by those who speak of war as "multitudinous murder." They cannot mean murder in the legal sense, because in that sense only "unlawful killing," which killing in war is not, is murder. When I speak of "malice," therefore, I am not using "malice" in the legal sense. In that sense "malice" is understood to be the attribute of every "wrongful act done intentionally, without just or lawful excuse,"[63] and is ascribed to acts (such as killing an officer of justice, knowing him to be such, while resisting him in a riot) in which there is no ill-will of the kind which we suppose in murder, when we apply the term in its natural sense as one of moral disapproval. Of murder in the moral sense the characteristics are those stated and these are not present in the case of a soldier who kills one on the other side in battle. He has no ill-will to that particular person or to any particular person. He incurs an equal risk with the person whom he kills, and incurs that risk not for the sake of killing him. His object in undergoing it is not private to himself but a service (or what he supposes to be a service) to his country—a good which is his own, no doubt (that is implied in his desiring it), but which he presents to himself as common to him with others. Indeed, those who might speak of war as "multitudinous murder" would not look upon the soldier as a murderer. If reminded that there cannot be a murder without a murderer, and pressed to say who, when a bloody battle takes place, the murderer or murderers are, they would probably point to the authors of the war. It may be questioned, by the way, whether there has ever been a war of which the origination could be truly said to rest with a definite person or persons, in the same way in which the origination of an act which would be called murder in the ordinary sense rests with a

particular person. No doubt there have been wars for which certain assignable individuals were specially blameable, wars which they specially helped to bring about or had special means of preventing (and the more the wickedness of such persons is kept in mind the better); but even in these cases the cause of the war can scarcely be held to be gathered up within the will of any individual, or the combined will of certain individuals, in the same way as is the cause of murder or other punishable acts. When A.B. is murdered, the sole cause lies in some definite volition of C.D. or others, however that volition may have been caused. But when a war "breaks out," though it is not to be considered, as we are too apt to consider it, a natural calamity which could not be prevented, it would be hard to maintain that the sole cause lies in some definite volition on the part of some assignable person or persons, even of those who are most to blame. Passing over this point, however, if the acts of killing in war are not murders (in the *moral* sense, the *legal* being out of the question) because they lack those characteristics on the part of the agent's state of mind which are necessary to constitute a murder, the persons who cause those acts to be committed, if such persons can be pointed out, are not the authors of murder, multitudinous or other. They would only be so if the characteristic of "malice," which is absent on the part of the immediate agent of the act, were present on their part as its ultimate agents. But this is not the case. However selfish their motives, they cannot fairly be construed into ill-will towards the persons who happened to be killed in the war; and therefore, whatever wickedness the persons responsible for the war are guilty of, they are not guilty of "murder" in any natural sense of the term, nor is there any murder in the case at all.

158. It does not follow from this, however, that war is ever other than a great wrong, as a violation on a multitudinous scale of the individual's right to life. Whether it is so or not must be discussed on other grounds. If there is such a thing as a right to life, on the part of the individual man as such, is there any reason to doubt that this right is violated in the case of every man killed in war? It is not to the purpose to allege that in order to a violation of right there must be not only a suffering of some kind on the part of the subject of a right but an intentional act causing it on the part of a human agent. There is of course no violation of right when a man is killed by a wild beast or a stroke of lightning, because there is no right as between a man and a beast or between a man and natural force. But the deaths in a battle are caused distinctly by human agency, and intentional agency. The individual soldier may not have any very distinct

intention when he fires his rifle except to obey orders, but the command-
ers of the army and the statesmen who send it into the field intend the
death of as many men as may be necessary for their purpose. It is true
they do not intend the death of this or that particular person, but no more
did the Irishman who fired into a body of police guarding the Fenian
prisoners. It might fairly be held that this circumstance exempted the
Irishman from the special moral guilt of murder, though according to our
law it did not exempt him from the legal guilt expressed by that term; but
no one would argue that it made the act other than a violation of the right
to life on the part of the policeman killed. No more can the absence, on
the part of those who cause men to be killed in battle, of an intention to
kill this or that specific person, save their act from being a violation of
the right to life.

159. Is there then any condition on the part of the persons killed that
saves the act from having this character? It may be urged that when the
war is conducted according to usages that obtain between civilised nations (not when it is a village-burning war like that between English and
Afghans) the persons killed are voluntary combatants, and *ουδεις
αδικειται εκών* [no one does wrong willingly]. Soldiers, it may be said,
are in the position of men who voluntarily undertake a dangerous employment. If some of them are killed, this is not more a violation of the
human right to life than is the death of men who have engaged to work in
a dangerous coalpit. To this it must be answered that if soldiers did in
fact voluntarily incur the special risk of death incidental to their calling,
it would not follow that the right to life was not violated in their being
killed. It is not a right which it rests with a man to retain or give up at his
pleasure. It is not the less a wrong that a man should be a slave because
he has sold himself into slavery. The individual's right to live is but the
other side of the right which society has in his living. The individual can
no more voluntarily rid himself of it than he can of the social capacity,
the human nature, on which it is founded. Thus, however ready men may
be for high wages to work in a dangerous pit, a wrong is held to be done
if they are killed in it. If provisions which might have made it safe have
been neglected, someone is held responsible. If nothing could make it
safe, the working of the pit would not be allowed. The reason for not
more generally applying the power of the state to prevent voluntary nox-
ious employments, is not that there is no wrong in the death of the individual through the incidents of an employment which he has voluntarily
undertaken, but that the wrong is more effectually prevented by training

and trusting individuals to protect themselves than by the state protecting them. Thus the waste of life in war would not be the less a wrong—
not the less a violation of the right, which subsists between all members
of society, and which none can alienate, that each should have his life
respected by society—if it were the fact that those whose lives are wasted
voluntarily incurred the risk of losing them. But it can scarcely be held to
be the fact. Not only is it impossible, even when war is conducted on the
most civilised methods, to prevent great incidental loss of life (to say
nothing of other injury) among non-combatants; the waste of the life of
the combatants is one which the power of the state compels. This is equally
true whether the army is raised by voluntary enlistment or by conscription. It is obviously so in the case of conscription, but under a system of
voluntary enlistment, though the individual soldier cannot say that he in
particular has been compelled by the government to risk his life, it is still
the case that the state compels the risk of a certain number of lives. It
decrees that an army of such a size shall be raised, though if it can get the
men by voluntary hiring it does not exercise compulsion on the men of a
particular age, and it sends the army into the field. Its compulsive agency
causes the death of the soldiers killed, not any voluntary action on the
part of the soldiers themselves. The action of the soldiers no doubt contributes to the result, for if they all refused to fight there would be no
killing, but it is an action put in motion and directed by the power of the
state, which is compulsive in the sense that it operates on the individual
in the last resort through fear of death.

160. We have then in war a destruction of human life inflicted on the
sufferers intentionally by voluntary human agency. It is true, as we saw,
that it is not easy to say in any case by whose agency in particular. We
may say indeed that it is by the agency of the state, but what exactly does
that mean? The "state" here must = the sovereign power in the state, but
it is always difficult to say by whom that power is wielded, and if we
could in any case specify its present holders, the further question will
arise whether their course of action has not been shaped for them by
previous holders of power. But however widely distributed the agency
may be which causes the destruction of life in war, it is still intentional
human agency. The destruction is not the work of accident or of nature.
If then it is to be other than a wrong, because a violation of the right to
mutual protection of life involved in membership of human society, it
can only be because there is exercised in war some right that is paramount to this. It may be argued that this is the case; that there is no right

to the preservation of life at the cost of losing the necessary conditions of "living well;" that war is in some cases the only means of maintaining these conditions, and that where this is so, the wrong of causing the destruction of physical life disappears in the paramount right of preserving the conditions under which alone moral life is possible.

161. This argument, however, seems to be only available for shifting the quarter in which we might be at first disposed to lay the blame of the wrong involved in war, not for changing the character of that wrong. It goes to show that the wrong involved in the death of certain soldiers does not necessarily lie with the government which sends those soldiers into the field, because this may be the only means by which that government can prevent more serious wrong; it does not show that there is no wrong in their death. If the integrity of any state can only be maintained at the cost of war, and if that state is more than what many so-called states have been—more than an aggregation of individuals or communities under one ruling power—if it so far fulfils the idea of a state, that its maintenance is necessary to the free development of the people belonging to it; then by the authorities or people of that state no wrong is done by the destruction of life which war involves, except so far as they are responsible for the state of things which renders the maintenance of the integrity of the state impossible by other means. But how does it come about that the integrity of such a state is endangered? Not by accident or by forces of nature, but by intentional human agency in some form or other, however complicated; and with that agency lies the wrong-doing. To determine it (as we might be able to do if a horde of barbarians broke in on a civilised state, compelling it to resort to war for its defence) is a matter of small importance: what *is* important to bear in mind (being one of those obvious truths out of which we may allow ourselves to be sophisticated) is that the destruction of life in war is always wrong-doing, whoever be the wrong-doer, and that in the wars, most strictly defensive of political freedom, the wrong-doing is only removed from the defenders of political freedom to be transferred elsewhere. If it is difficult in any case to say precisely where, that is only a reason for more general self-reproach, for a more humbling sense (as the preachers would say) of complicity in that radical (but conquerable because moral) evil of mankind which renders such a means of maintaining political freedom necessary. The language, indeed, which we hear from the pulpit about war being a punishment for the sins of mankind, is perfectly true, but it needs to be accompanied by the reminder that this punishment of sin is simply

a consequence of the sin and itself a further sin, brought about by the action of the sinner, not an external infliction brought about by agencies to which man is not a party.

162. In fact, however, if most wars had been wars for the maintenance or acquisition of political freedom, the difficulty of fixing the blame of them, or at any rate of freeing one of the parties in each case from blame, would be much less than it really is. Of the European wars of the last four hundred years, how many could be fairly said to have been wars in which either or any of the parties were fighting for this end? Perhaps the wars in which the Dutch Republics defended themselves against Spain and against Louis XIV, and that in which Germany shook off the dominion of Napoleon. Perhaps the more recent struggles of Italy and Hungary against Austrian government. Perhaps in the first outset of the war of 1792 the French may be fairly held to have been defending institutions necessary for the development of social freedom and equality. In this war, however, the issue very soon ceased to be one between the defenders of such institutions on the one side, and their assailants on the other, and in most modern wars the issue has not been of this kind at all. The wars have arisen primarily out of the rival ambition of kings and dynasties for territorial aggrandisement, with national antipathies and ecclesiastical ambitions, and the passions arising out of religious partisanship, as complicating influences. As nations have come more and more to distinguish and solidify themselves, and a national consciousness has come definitely to be formed in each, the rival ambitions of nations have tended more and more first to support, then perhaps to supersede, the ambitions of dynasties as causes of war. The delusion has been practically dominant that the gain of one nation must mean the loss of another. Hence national jealousies in regard to colonial extensions, hostile tariffs and the effort of each nation to exclude others from its markets. The explosion of this idea in the region of political economy has had little effect in weakening its hold on men's minds. The people of one nation still hear with jealousy of another nation's advance in commerce, as if it meant some decay of their own. And if the commercial jealousy of nations is very slow in disappearing, their vanity, their desire apart from trade each to become or to seem stronger than the other, has very much increased. A hundred and fifty years ago national vanity could scarcely be said to be an influence in politics. The people under one ruler were not homogeneous enough, had not enough of a corporate consciousness, to develop a national vanity. Now (under the name of patriotism) it has become a

more serious disturber of peace than dynastic ambition. Where the latter is dangerous, it is because it has national vanity to work upon.

163. Our conclusion then is that the destruction of life in war (to say nothing of other evils incidental to it with which we are not here concerned) is always wrong-doing, with whomsoever the guilt of the wrong-doing may lie; that only those parties to a war are exempt from a share in the guilt who can truly plead that to them war is the only means of maintaining the social conditions of the moral development of man, and that there have been very few cases in which this plea could be truly made. In saying this it is not forgotten either that many virtues are called into exercise by war, or that wars have been a means by which the movement of mankind, which there is reason for considering a progress to higher good, has been carried on. These facts do not make the wrong-doing involved in war any less so. If nothing is to be accounted wrong-doing through which final good is wrought, we must give up either the idea of there being such a thing as wrong-doing, or the idea of there being such a thing as final good. If final good results from the world of our experience, it results from processes in which wrong-doing is an inseparable element. Wrong-doing is voluntary action, either (in the deeper moral sense) proceeding from a will uninfluenced by the desire to be good on the part of the agent (which may be taken to include action tending to produce such action) or (in the sense contemplated by the "jus naturae" [law of nature]) it is action that interferes with the conditions necessary to the free-play and development of a good will on the part of others. It may be that, according to the divine scheme of the world, such wrong-doing is an element in a process by which men gradually approximate more nearly to good (in the sense of a good will). We cannot think of God as a moral being without supposing this to be the case. But this makes no difference to wrong-doing in those relations in which it *is* wrong-doing, and with which alone we are concerned, viz., in relation to the will of human agents and to the results which those agents can foresee and intend to produce. If an action, so far as any results go which the agent can have in view or over which he has control, interferes with conditions necessary to the free-play and development of a good will on the part of others, it is not the less wrong-doing because, through some agency which is not his, the effects which he intended and which rendered it wrong-doing, come to contribute to an ulterior good. Nor, if it issues from bad will (in the sense explained), is it less wrong (in the moral sense) because this will is itself, in the view of some higher being,

contributory to a moral good which is not, in whole or part, within the view of the agent. If then war is wrong-doing in both the above senses (as it is always at any rate on the part of those with whom the ultimate responsibility for it lies), it does not cease to be so on account of any good resulting from it in a scheme of providence.

164. "But," it may be asked, "are we justified in saying that it is always wrong-doing on the part of those with whom the ultimate responsibility lies? It is admitted that certain virtues may be evoked by war; that it may have results contributory to the moral progress of mankind; may not the eliciting of these virtues, the production of these results, be contemplated by the originators of war, and does not the origination of war, so far as influenced by such motives, cease to be wrong-doing? It must be admitted that Caesar's wars in Gaul were unprovoked wars of conquest, but their effect was the establishment of Roman civilisation with its equal law over a great part of western Europe in such a way that it was never wholly swept away, and that a permanent influence in the progress of the European polity can be traced to it. May he not be credited with having had, however indefinitely, such an effect as this in view? Even if his wish to extend Roman civilisation was secondary to a plan for raising an army by which he might master the Republic, is he to have no credit for the beneficent results which are admitted to have ensued from the success of that plan? May not a similar justification be urged for English wars in India? Of, again, the establishment of the civil unity of Germany, and the liberation of Christian populations in Turkey are, admitted to have been gains to mankind, is not that a justification of such persons concerned in the origination of the wars that brought about those results as can be supposed to have been influenced by a desire for them?"

165. These objections might be to the purpose if we were attempting the task (generally, if not always, an impossible one) of determining the moral desert, good or ill, of those who have been concerned in bringing this or that war about. Their tendency merely is to distribute the blame of the wrong-doing involved in war, to show how widely ramified is the agency in that wrong-doing, not to affect its character as wrong-doing. If the only way of civilising Gaul was to kill all the people whom Caesar's wars caused to be killed, and if the desire for civilising it was a prevailing motive in Caesar's mind, so much the better for Caesar but so much the worse for the other unassignable and innumerable human agents who brought it about that such an object could only be attained in such a way. We are not, indeed, entitled to say that it could have been brought about

in any other way. It is true to say (if we know what we are about in saving it) that nothing which happens in the world could have happened otherwise than it has. The question for us is whether that condition of things which rendered e.g., Caesar's Gallic wars, with the violation of human rights which they involved the interference in the case of innumerable persons with the conditions under which man can be helpful to man, physical life being the first of these, the *sine qua non* in the promotion of ulterior human welfare, was or was not the work of human agency. If it was (and there is no doubt that it was, for to what merely natural agency could the necessity be ascribed?) then in that ordinary sense of the word "could" in which it expresses our responsibility for our actions, men *could* have brought about the good result without the evil means. They could have done so if they had been better. It was owing to human wickedness—if less on Caesar's part, then so much the more on the part of innumerable others—that the wrong-doing of those wars was the appropriate means to this ulterior good. So in regard to the other cases instanced. It is idle to speculate on other means by which the permanent pacification of India, or unification of Germany or liberation of Christians in European Turkey might have been brought about; but it is important to bear in mind that the innumerable wrong acts involved in achieving them—acts wrong because violations of the rights of those directly affected by them—did not cease to be wrong acts because under the given condition of things the results specified would not have been obtained without them. This given condition of things was not like that (e.g.) which compels the castaways from a shipwreck, so many days from shore and with only so much provision in their boat, to draw lots which shall be thrown overboard. It was a condition of things which human wickedness, through traceable and untraceable channels, brought about. If the individual promoters of wars, which through the medium of multitudinous wrong-doing have yielded good to mankind, have been really influenced by desire for any such good—and much scepticism is justified in regard to such a supposition—then so much less of the guilt of the wrong-doing has been theirs. No nation, at any rate, that has taken part in such wars can fairly take credit for having been governed by such a motive. It has been either a passive instrument in the hands of its rulers or has been animated by less worthy motives, very mixed but of which perhaps a diffused desire for excitement has been the most innocent. On what reasonable ground can Englishmen or Germans or Russians claim that their several nations took part in the wars by which India was pacified, Germany unified, Bulgaria liberated, under the dominant influence of a desire for human good? Rather, if the action of a national conscience in such matters is possible at all, they should take shame for their share in that general human selfishness which rendered certain conditions of human development only attainable by such means.

166. (2) Reverting then to the questions which arose[64] out of the assertion of a right to free life on the part of the individual man as such, it appears that the first must be answered in the negative. No state of war can make the destruction of man's life by man other than a wrong, though the wrong is not always chargeable upon all the parties to a war. The second question is virtually answered by what has been said about the first. In regard to the state according to its idea the question could not arise, for according to its idea the state is an institution in which all rights are harmoniously maintained, in which all the capacities that give rise to rights have free play given to them. No action in its own interest of a state that fulfilled this idea could conflict with any true interest or right of general society, of the men not subject to its law taken as a whole. There is no such thing as an inevitable conflict between states. There is nothing in the nature of the state that, given a multiplicity of states, should make the gain of the one the loss of the other. The more perfectly each one of them attains its proper object of giving free scope to the capacities of all persons living on a certain range of territory, the easier it is for others to do so; and in proportion as they all do so the danger of conflict disappears.

167. On the other hand, the imperfect realisation of civil equality in the full sense of the term in certain states is in greater or less degree a source of danger to all. The presence in states either of a prerogatived class or of a body of people who, whether by open denial of civil rights or by restrictive laws, are thwarted in the free development of their capacities, or of an ecclesiastical organisation which disputes the authority of the state on matters of right and thus prevents the perfect civil fusion of its members with other citizens, always breeds an imagination of there being some competition of interests between states. The privileged class involuntarily believes and spreads the belief that the interest of the state lies in some extension without, not in an improvement of organisation within. A suffering class attracts sympathy from without and invites interference with the state which contains it; and that state responds not by healing the sore but by defending against aggression what it conceives to be its special interests, but which are only special on account of its bad

organisation. Or perhaps the suffering population overflows into another state, as the Irish into America, and there becomes a source not only of internal difficulty but of hostile feeling between it and the state where the suffering population still survives. People, again, who, in matters which the state treats as belonging to itself, take their direction from an ecclesiastical power external to the state under which they live, are necessarily in certain relations alien to that state, and may at any time prove a source of apparently conflicting interests between it and some other state which under the influence of the hostile ecclesiastical power espouses their cause. Remove from European states, as they are and have been during the last hundred years, the occasions of conflict, the sources of apparently competing interests, which arise in one or other of the ways mentioned—either from the mistaken view of state interests which a privileged class inevitably takes or from the presence in them of oppressed populations, or from what we improperly call the antagonism of religious confessions—and there would not be or have been anything to disturb the peace between them. And this is to say that the source of war between states lies in their incomplete fulfilment of their function; in the fact that there is some defect in the maintenance or reconciliation of rights among their subjects.

168. This is equally true in regard to those causes of conflict which are loosely called "religious." These do not arise out of any differences between the convictions of different people in regard to the nature of God or their relations to Him, or the right way of worshipping Him, but either out of some aggression upon the religious freedom of certain people, made or allowed by the powers of the state, which thus puts these people in the position of an alien or unenfranchised class, or else out of an aggression on the rights of the state by some corporation calling itself spiritual but really claiming sovereignty over men's actions in the same relations in which the state claims to determine them. There would be nothing tending to international disturbance in the fact that bodies of people who worship God in the Catholic manner live in a state where the majority worship in the Greek or Protestant manner and alongside of another state where the majority is Catholic but for one or other or both of these circumstances, viz. if the Catholic worship and teaching is interfered with by the Protestant or Greek state, and that Catholics are liable to a direction by a power which claims to regulate men's transactions with each other by a law of its own, and which may see fit (e.g.) to forbid the Catholic subjects in the Greek or Protestant state from being mar-

ried, or having their parents buried, or their children taught the necessary acts, in the manner which the state directs. This reciprocal invasion of right, the invasion of the rights of the state by the church on one side, and on the other the restriction placed by the sovereign upon the subject's freedom, not of conscience (for that is impossible), but of expressing his conscience in word and act—has sometimes caused a state of things in which certain of the subjects of a state have been better affected to another state than to their own, and in such a case there is an element of natural hostility between the states. An obvious instance to give of this relation between states would have been that between Russia and Turkey if Turkey could be considered to have been constituted as a state at all. Perhaps a better instance would be the position of Ireland in the past— its disaffection to England and gravitation, first to France, then to the United States, caused chiefly by Protestant penal laws which in turn were at least provoked by the aggressive attitude of the church towards the English state. Whenever a like invasion of rights still takes place, e.g., in the treatment of the Catholic subjects of Russia in Poland, in the ultramontane movement of resistance to certain requirements of the state among the Catholic subjects of Germany, it tends to international conflict. And what is now a somewhat remote tendency has in the past been a formidable stimulant to war.

169. It is nothing then in the necessary organisation of the state, but rather some defect of that organisation in relation to its proper function of maintaining and reconciling rights, of giving scope to capacities, that leads to a conflict of apparent interests between one state and another. The wrong, therefore, which results to human society from conflicts between states cannot be condoned on the ground that it is a necessary incident of the existence of states. The lost in a higher right, which attaches to wrong cannot be held to be the maintenance of the state as the institution through which alone the freedom of man is realised. It is not the state, as such, but this or that particular state, which by no means fulfils its purpose, and might perhaps be swept away and superseded by another with advantage to the ends for which the true state exists, that needs to defend its interests by action injurious to those outside it. Hence there is no holding that a state is justified in doing whatever its ground for interests seem to require, irrespectively of effects on other men. If those effects are bad, involving either a direct violation of personal rights or obstruction to the moral development of society anywhere in the world, then there is no ultimate justification for the political action that gives

rise to them. The question can only be (as we have seen generally in regard to the wrong-doing of war) where in particular the blame lies. Whether there is any justification for a particular state which in defence of its interests inflicts an injury on some portion of mankind; whether e.g., the Germans in holding Metz, on the supposition that their tenure of such a thoroughly French town necessarily thwarts in many ways the healthy activity of the inhabitants, or the English in carrying fire and sword into Afghanistan for the sake of acquiring a scientific frontier; this must depend (1) on the nature of the interests thus defended, (2) on the impossibility of otherwise defending them, (3) on the question how they came to be endangered. If they are interests of which the maintenance is essential to those ends as a means to which the state has its value, if the state which defends them has not itself been a joint-cause of their being endangered, and if they cannot be defended except at the cost of injury to some portion of mankind, then the state which defends them is clear of the guilt of that injury. But the guilt is removed from it only to lie somewhere else, however wide its distribution may be. It may be doubted, however, whether the second question could ever be answered altogether in favour of a state which finds it necessary to protect its interests at the cost of inflicting an injury on mankind.

170. It will be said, perhaps, that these formal arguments in proof of the wrong-doing involved in war, and of the unjustifiability of the policy which nations constantly adopt in defence of their apparent interests, carry very little conviction; that a state is not an abstract complex of institutions for maintenance of rights, but a nation, a people, possessing such institutions; that the nation has its passions which inevitably lead it to judge all questions of international right from its own point of view, and to consider its apparent national interests as justifying anything; that if it were otherwise, if the cosmopolitan point of view could be adopted by nations, patriotism would be at an end: that whether this be desirable or no, such an extinction of national passions is impossible; that while they continue, wars are as inevitable between nations as they would be between individuals, if individuals were living in what philosophers have imagined to be the state of nature, without recognition of a common superior; that nations in short are in the position of men judging their own causes, which it is admitted that no one can do impartially; and that this state of things cannot be altered without the establishment of a common constraining power, which would mean the extinction of the life of independent states—a result as undesirable as it is unattainable. Projects

of perpetual peace, to be logical, must be projects of all-embracing empire.

171. There is some cogency in language of this kind. It is true that when we speak of a state as a living agency, we mean, not an institution or complex of institutions, but a nation organised in a certain way; and that members of the nation in their corporate or associated action are animated by certain passions, arising out of their association, which, though not egoistic relatively to the individual subjects of them (for they are motives to self-sacrifice), may, in their influence on the dealings of one nation with another, have an effect analogous to that which egoistic passions, properly so called, have upon the dealings of individuals with each other. On the other hand, it must be remembered that the national passion, which in any good sense is simply the public spirit of the good citizen, may take and every day is taking, directions which lead to no collision between one nation and another; (or, to say the same thing negatively, that it is utterly false to speak as if the desire for one's own nation to show more military strength than others were the only or the right form of patriotism); and that though a nation, with national feeling of its own, must everywhere underlie a state, properly so called, yet still, just so far as the perfect organisation of rights within each nation, which entitles it to be called a state, is attained, the occasions of conflict between nations disappear; and again, that by the same process, just so far as it is satisfactorily carried out, an organ of expression and action is established for each nation in dealing with other nations, which is not really liable to be influenced by the same egoistic passions in dealing with the government of another nation as embroil individuals with each other. The love of mankind, no doubt, needs to be particularised in order to have any power over life and action. Just as there can be no true friendship except towards this or that individual, so there can be no true public spirit which is not localised in some way. The man whose desire to serve his kind is not centred primarily in some home, radiating from it to a commune, a municipality, and a nation, presumably has no effectual desire to serve his kind at all. But there is no reason why this localised or nationalised philanthropy should take the form of a jealousy of other nations or a desire to fight them, personally or by proxy. Those in whom it is strongest are every day expressing it in without interfering good works which benefit their fellow-citizens with the men of other nations. Those who from time to time talk of the need of a great war to bring unselfish impulses into play give us reason to suspect that they are too

selfish themselves to recognise the unselfish activity that is going on all round them. Till all the methods have been exhausted by which nature can be brought into the service of man, till society is so organised that everyone's capacities have free scope for their development, there is no need to resort to war for a field in which patriotism may display itself.

172. And in fact, just so far as states are thoroughly formed, the diversion of patriotism into the military channel tends to come to an end. It is a survival from a condition of things in which, as yet, the state, in the full sense, was not; in the sense, namely, that in each territory controlled by a single independent government the rights of all persons, as founded on their capacities for contributing to a common good, are equally established by one system of law. If each separately governed territory were inhabited by a people so organised within itself, there would be nothing to lead to the association of the public spirit of the good citizen with military aggressiveness—an association which belongs properly not to the πολιτεία [constitutional state], but to the δυναστεία [arbitrary oligarchy]. The Greek states, however complete might be the equality of their citizens among themselves, were all δυναστεία in relation to some subject populations, and, as such, jealous of each other. The Peloponnesian war was eminently a war of rival δυναστεία. And those habits and institutions and modes of feeling in Europe of the present day which tend to international conflict, are either survivals from the δυναστεία of the past, or arise out of the very incomplete manner in which as yet, over most of Europe the πολιτεία has superseded the δυναστεία. Patriotism, in that special military sense in which it is distinguished from public spirit, is not the temper of the citizen dealing with fellow-citizens, or with men who are themselves citizens of their several states, but that of the follower of the feudal chief, or of the member of a privileged class conscious of a power, resting ultimately on force, over an inferior population, or of a nation holding empire over other nations.

173. Standing armies, again, though existing on a larger scale now than ever before, are not products of the civilisation of Europe, but of the predominance over that civilisation of the old δυναστεία. The influences which have given rise to and keep up those armies essentially belong to a state of things in which mankind—even European mankind—is not yet thoroughly organised into political life. Roughly summarised, they are these: (1) The temporary confiscation by Napoleon to his own account of the products of the French Revolution, which thus, though founded on a true idea of a citizenship in which not the few only, but all

men, should partake, for the time issued in a δυναστεία over the countries which most directly felt the effects of the revolution. (2) The consequent revival in dynastic forms, under the influence of antagonism to
France, of national life in Germany. (3) The aspiration after national
unity elsewhere in Europe—a movement which must precede the organisation of states on a sound basis, and for the time readily yields itself
to direction by a δυναστεία. (4) The existence over all the Slavonic side
of Europe of populations which are only just beginning to make any
approach to political life—the life of the πολιτεία, or "civitas"—and
still offer a tempting field to the ambition of rival δυναστείαι, Austrian,
Russian, and Turkish (which, indeed, are by no means to be put on a
level, but are alike as not resting on a basis of citizenship). (5) The tenure of a great Indian empire by England, which not only gives it a military character which would not belong to it simply as a state, but brings
it into outward relations with the δυναστείαι just spoken of. This is no
doubt a very incomplete account of the influences which have combined
to "turn Europe into a great camp" (a very exaggerated expression), but
it may serve to show what a fuller account would show more clearly that
the military system of Europe is no necessary incident of the relations
between independent states, but arises from the fact that the organisation
of state-life, even with those peoples that have been brought under its
influence at all, is still so incomplete.

174. The more complete that organisation becomes, the more the
motives and occasions of international conflict tend to disappear, while
the bonds of unity become stronger. The latter is the case, if for no other
reason, yet for this; that the better organisation of the state means freer
scope to the individual (not necessarily to do as he likes, e.g. in the buying and selling of alcohol, but in such development of activity as is good
on the whole). This again means freer intercourse between members of
one state and those of another, and in particular more freedom of trade.
All restrictions on freedom of wholesome trade are really based on special class interests, and must disappear with the realisation of that idea of
individual right, founded on the capacity of every man for free contribution to social good, which is the true idea of the state. And as trade between members of different states becomes freer and more full, the sense
of common interests between them, which war would infringe, becomes
stronger. The bond of peace thus established is sometimes depreciated
as a selfish one, but it need be no more selfish than that which keeps the
peace between members of the same state, who have no acquaintance

with each other. In one case as in the other it may be said that the individual tries to prevent a breach of the peace because he knows that he has more to gain than to lose by it. In the latter case, however, this account of the matter would be, to say the least, insufficient. The good citizen observes the law in letter and in spirit, not from any fear of consequences to himself if he did not, but from an idea of the mutual respect by men for each other's rights as that which should be, which has become habitual with him and regulates his conduct without his asking any questions about it. There was a time, however, when this idea only thus acted spontaneously in regulating a man's action towards his family or immediate neighbours or friends. Considerations of interest were the medium through which a wider range of persons came to be brought within its range. And thus, although considerations of an identity of interests, arising out of trade, may be the occasion of men's recognising in men of other nations those rights which war violates, there is no reason why upon that occasion and through the familiarity which trade brings about an idea of justice, as a relation which should subsist between all mankind as well as between members of the same state, may not come to act on men's minds as independently of all calculation of their several interests as does the idea which regulates the conduct of the good citizen.

175. If the restraining or impelling power of the idea of what is due from members of different nations to each other is weak, it must be observed on the other hand that the individual members of a nation have no such apparent interest in their government's dealing unfairly with another nation as one individual may have in getting the advantage of another. Thus, so far as this idea comes to form part of the habit of men's minds, there ceases to be anything in the passions of the people which a government represents to stimulate the government to that unfairness in dealing with another government to which an individual might be moved by self-seeking passions in dealing with another individual, in the absence of an impartial authority having power over both. If at the same time the several governments are purely representative of the several peoples, as they should become with the due organisation of the state, and thus have no dynastic interests of their own in embroiling one nation with another, there seems to be no reason why they should not arrive at a passionless impartiality in dealing with each other, which would be beyond the reach of the individual in defending his own cause against another. At any rate, if no government can ever get rid of some bias in its

own favour, there remains the possibility of mediation in cases of dispute by disinterested governments. With the abatement of national jealousies and the removal of those[65] deeply-seated causes of war which, as we have seen, are connected with the deficient organisation of states, the dream of an international court with authority resting on the consent of independent states may come to be realised. Such a result may be very remote, but it is important to bear in mind that there is nothing in the intrinsic nature of a system of independent states incompatible with it, but that on the contrary every advance in the organization of mankind into states in the sense explained is a step towards it.

Chapter 11
The Right of the State to Punish

176. (3) We come now to the third of the questions raised[66] in regard to the individual's right to free life the question under what conditions that right may be forfeited; the question, in other words, of the state's right of punishment. The right (i.e. the power secured by social recognition) of free life in every man rests on the assumed capacity in every man of free action contributory to social good ("free" in the sense of determined by the idea of a common good. Animals may and do contribute to the good of man, but not thus "freely"). This right on the part of associated men implies the right on their part to prevent such action as interferes with the possibility of free action contributory to social good. This constitutes the right of punishment the right so far to use force upon a person (treat him as an animal or a thing) as may be necessary to save others from this interference.

177. Under what conditions a person needs to be thus dealt with what particular actions on his part constitute such an interference is a question which can only be answered when we have considered what powers in particular need to be secured to individuals or to officials in order to the possibility of free action of the kind described. Every such power is a right of which the violation—if intended as a violation of a right requires a punishment, of which the kind and amount must depend on the relative importance of the right and of the extent to which its general exercise is threatened. Thus every theory of rights in detail must be followed by, or indeed implies, a corresponding theory of punishment in detail a theory which considers what particular acts are punishable, and how they should be punished. The latter cannot precede the former. All that can be done here is further to consider what general rules of punishment are implied in the principle on which we hold all right of punishment to rest, and how far in the actual practice of punishment that principle has been realised.

178. It is commonly asked whether punishment according to its proper nature is retributive or preventive or reformatory. The true answer is that it is and should be all three. The statement, however, that the punishment of the criminal by the state is retributive, though true in a sense that will be explained directly, yet so readily lends best avoided. It is not itself to

a misunderstanding, that it is perhaps true in the sense that in legal punishment as it should be there survives any element of private vengeance, of the desire on the part of the individual who has received a hurt from another to inflict an equivalent hurt in return. It is true that the beginning of punishment by the state first appears in the form of a regulation of private vengeance, but it is not therefore to be supposed that punishment by the state is in any way a continuation of private vengeance. It is the essence of the former to suppress and supersede the latter, but it only does so gradually, just as rights in actuality are only formed gradually. Private vengeance belongs to the state of things in which rights are not as yet actualised in the sense that the powers which it is for the social good that a man should be allowed to exercise, are not yet secured to him by society. In proportion as they are actualised, the exercise of private vengeance must cease. A *right* of private vengeance is an impossibility for just so far as the vengeance is private, the individual in executing it is exercising a power not derived from society nor regulated by reference to social good, and such a power is not a right. Hence the view commonly taken by writers of the seventeenth and eighteenth centuries, implies an entire misconception of the nature of a right; the view, viz., that there first existed rights of self-defence and self-vindication on the part of individuals in a state of nature and that these came to be devolved on a power representing all individuals, so that the state's right of using force against those men who use or threaten force against other men, is merely the sum or equivalent of the private rights which individuals would severally possess if there were no public equivalent for them. It is to suppose that to have been a right which in truth, under the supposed conditions, would merely have been animal impulse and power and public right (which is a pleonasm, for all right is public) to have resulted from the combination of these animal impulses and powers; to suppose that from a state of things in which "homo homini lupus" [man is no man, but a wolf, to a stranger], by mere combination of wolfish impulses there could result the state of things in which "homo homini deus" [man is but a god to a stranger].

179. In a state of things in which private vengeance for hurt inflicted was the universal practice, there could be no rights at all. In the most primitive society in which rights can exist, it must at least within the limits of the family be suppressed by that authority of the family or its head which first constitutes rights. In such a society it is only on the members of another family that a man may retaliate at pleasure a wrong

done to him, and then the vengeance is not strictly speaking taken by individual upon individual, though individuals may be severally the agent and patient of it, but by family upon family. Just because there is as yet no idea of a state independent of ties of birth, much less of a universal society from relation to which a man derives rights, there is no idea of rights attaching to him as a citizen or as a man but only as a member of a family. That social right, which is at once a right of society over the individual, and a right which society communicates and secures the individual, appears so far only as a control exercised by the family over its members in their dealings with each other, as an authorisation which it gives them in prosecuting their quarrels with members of another family, and at the same time to a certain extent as a limitation on the manner in which feuds between families may be carried on, a limitation generally dependent on some religious authority equally recognised by the families at feud.

180. From this state of things it is a long step to the régime of law in a duly constituted state. Under it the arm of the state alone is the organ through which force may be exercised on the individual; the individual is prohibited from averting violence by violence, except so far as is necessary for the immediate protection of life, and altogether from avenging wrong done to him, on the understanding that the society, of which he is an organ and from which he derives his rights, being injured in every injury to him, duly protects him against injury, and when it fails to prevent such injury from being done, inflicts such punishment on the offender as is necessary for future protection. But the process from the one state of things to the other, though a long one, consists in the further development of that social right[67] which properly speaking was the only right the individual ever had, and from the first, or ever since a permanent family tie existed, was present as a qualifying and restraining element in the exercise of private vengeance so far as that exercise partook at all in the nature of a right. The process is not a continuance of private vengeance under altered forms, but a gradual suppression of it by the fuller realisation of the higher principle which all along controlled it.

181. But it will be asked, how upon this view of the nature of punishment as inflicted by the state it can be considered retributory. If no private vengeance, no vengeance of the injured individual, is involved in punishment, there can be no vengeance in it at all. The conception of vengeance is quite inappropriate to the action of society or the state on the criminal. The state cannot be supposed capable of vindictive pas-

sion. Nor, if the essence of crime is a wrong done to society, does it admit of retaliation upon the person committing it. A hurt done to an individual can be requited by the infliction of a like hurt upon the person who has done it; but no equivalent of wrong done to society can be paid back to the doer of it.

182. It is true that there is such a thing as a national desire for revenge[68] (France and Germany): and, if a state = a nation organised in a certain way why should it not be "capable of vindictive passion?" No doubt there is a unity of feeling among the members of a nation which makes them feel any loss of strength, real or apparent, sustained by the nation in its corporate character, as a hurt or disgrace to themselves, which they instinctively desire to revenge. The corporate feeling is so strong that individuals feel themselves severally hurt in the supposed hurt of the nation. But when it is said that a crime is an offence against the state, it is not meant that the body of persons forming the nation feel any hurt in the sense in which the person robbed or wounded does such a hurt as excites a natural desire for revenge. What is meant is that there is a violation of a system of rights which the nation has, no doubt, an interest in maintaining, but a purely social interest, quite different from the egoistic interest of the individual of which the desire for vengeance is a form. A nation is capable of vindictive feeling, but not so a nation as acting through the medium of a settled, impartial, general law for the maintenance of rights, and that is what we mean when we talk of the state as that against which crimes are committed and which punishes them.

183. It is true that when a crime of a certain sort, e.g., a cold-blooded murder, has been committed, a popular sympathy with the sufferer is excited, which expresses itself in the wish to "serve out" the murderer. This has some resemblance to the desire for personal revenge, but is really quite different, because not egoistic. Indignation against wrong done to another has nothing in common with desire to revenge a wrong done to oneself. It borrows the language of private revenge, just as the love of God borrows the language of sensuous affection. Such indignation is inseparable from the interest in social well-being, and along with it is the chief agent in the establishment and maintenance of legal punishment. Law indeed is necessarily general while indignation is particular in its reference; and accordingly the treatment of any particular crime, so far as determined by law, cannot correspond with the indignation which the crime excites, but the law merely determines the general category under which the crime falls, and fixes certain limits to the punishment

that may be inflicted under that category. Within those limits discretion is left to the judge as to the sentence that he passes, and his sentence is in part influenced by the sort of indignation which, in the given state of public sentiment, the crime is calculated to excite; though generally much more by his opinion as to the amount of terror required for the prevention of prevalent crime. Now what is it in punishment that this indignation demands? If not the sole foundation of public punishment, it is yet inseparable from that public interest on which the system of rights, with the corresponding system of punishments protective of rights, depends. In whatever sense then this indignation demands retribution in punishment, in that sense retribution would seem to be a necessary element in punishment. It demands retribution in the sense of demanding that the criminal should have his due, should be dealt with according to his deserts, should be punished justly.

184. This is quite a different thing from an equivalence between the amount of suffering inflicted by the criminal and that which he sustains in punishment. The amount of suffering which is caused by any crime is really as incalculable as that which the criminal endures in punishment, whatever the punishment. It is only in the case of death for murder that there is any appearance of equivalence between the two sufferings, and in this case the appearance is quite superficial. The suffering involved in death depends almost entirely on the circumstances, which are absolutely different in the case of the murdered man and in that of the man executed for murder. When a man is imprisoned with hard labour for robbery there is not even an appearance of equivalence of suffering between the crime and the punishment. In what then does the justice of a punishment, or its correspondence with the criminal's deserts consist? It will not do to say that these terms merely represent the result of an association of ideas between a crime and the penalty which we are accustomed to see inflicted on it; that society has come to attach certain penalties to certain actions as a result of the experience (1) of suffering and loss caused by those acts, and (2) of the kind of suffering of which the expectation will deter men from doing them; and that these penalties having become customary, the onlookers and the criminal himself, when one of them is inflicted, feel that he has got what was to be expected, and call it his due or desert or a just punishment. If this were the true account of the matter, there would be nothing to explain the difference between the emotion excited by the spectacle of a just punishment inflicted or the demand that it should be inflicted, on the one side, and on the other that excited by the

sight of physical suffering following according to the usual course of things upon a physical combination of circumstances or the expectation that such suffering will follow. If it is said that the difference is explained by the fact that in one case both the antecedent (the criminal act) and the consequent represent voluntary human agency, while in the other they do not, we reply. Just so, but for that reason the conception of a punishment as just differs wholly from any conception of it that could result either from its being customary or from the infliction of such punishment having been commonly found a means for protecting us against hurt.

185. The idea of punishment implies on the side of the person punished at once a capacity for determination by conception of a common or public good, or in other words a practical understanding of the nature of rights as founded on relations to such public good, and an actual violation of a right or omission to fulfil an obligation, the right or obligation being one of which the agent might have been aware and the violation or omission one which he might have prevented. On the side of the authority punishing, it implies equally a conception of right founded on relation to public good, and one which, unlike that on the part of the criminal, is realised in act; a conception of which the punitive act, as founded on a consideration of what is necessary for the maintenance of rights, is the logical expression. A punishment is unjust if either element is absent; if either the act punished is not a violation of known rights or an omission to fulfil known obligations of a kind which the agent might have prevented, or the punishment is one that is not required for the maintenance of rights, or (which comes to the same thing) if the ostensible rights for the maintenance of which the punishment is required are not real rights, are not liberties of action or acquisition which there is any real public interest in maintaining.

186. When the specified conditions of just punishment are fulfilled, the person punished himself recognises it as just, as his due or desert, and it is so recognised by the onlooker who thinks himself into the situation. The criminal, being susceptible to the idea of public good, and through it of rights, though this idea has not been strong enough to regulate his actions, sees in the punishment its natural expression. He sees that the punishment is his own act returning on himself, in the sense that it is the necessary outcome of his act in a society governed by the conception of rights—a conception which he appreciates and to which he does involuntary reverence.

It is the outcome of his act or his act returning upon himself in a different way from that in which a man's act returns on himself when, having misused his body, he is visited according to physical necessity by painful consequences. The cause of the suffering which the act entails in the one case is the relation of the act to a society governed by the conception of rights, in the other it is not. For that reason, the painful consequence of the act to the doer in the one case is, in the other is not, properly a punishment. We do indeed commonly speak of the painful consequences of imprudent or immoral acts ("immoral" as distinct from "illegal") as a punishment of them, but this is either metaphorically or because we think of the course of the world as regulated by a divine sovereign, whom we conceive as a maintainer of rights like the sovereign of a state. We may think of it as divinely regulated, and so regulated with a view to the realisation of moral good, but we shall still not be warranted in speaking of the sufferings which follow in the course of nature upon certain kinds of conduct as punishments, according to the distinctive sense in which crime is punished, unless we suppose the maintenance of rights to be the object of the moral government of the world—which is to put the cart before the horse; for, as we have seen, rights are relative to morality, not morality to rights (the ground on which certain liberties of action and acquisition should be guaranteed as rights being that they are conditions of the moral perfection of society).

While there would be reason, then, as against those who say that the punishment of crime is merely preventive, in saying that it is also retributive, if the needed correction of the "merely preventive" doctrine could not be more accurately stated, it would seem that the truth can be more accurately stated by the proposition that punishment is not justified unless it is just, and that it is not just unless the act punished is an intentional violation of real right or neglect of real obligation which the agent could have avoided (i.e., unless the agent knowingly and by intentional act interferes with some freedom of action or acquisition which there is a public interest in maintaining) and unless the future maintenance of rights requires that the criminal be dealt with as he is in the punishment.[69]

187. It is clear, however, that this requirement that punishment of crime should be just may be covered by the statement that in its proper nature it is preventive if the nature of that which is to be prevented by it is sufficiently defined. Its proper function is in the interest of rights that are genuine (in the sense explained), to prevent actions of the kind described by associating in the mind of every possible doer of them a cer-

tain terror with the contemplation of the act such terror as is necessary on the whole to protect the rights threatened by such action. The whipping of an ill-behaved dog is preventive, but not preventive in the sense in which the punishment of crime is so because (1) the dog's ill conduct is not an intentional violation of a right or neglect of a known obligation, the dog having no conception of right or obligation, and (2) for the same reason the whipping does not lead to the association of terror in the minds of other dogs with the violation of rights and neglect of obligations. To shoot men down who resist a successful *coup d'état* may be effectually preventive of further resistance to the government established by the *coup d'état*, but it does not satisfy the true idea of punishment because the terror produced by the massacre is not necessary for the protection of genuine rights—rights founded on public interest. To hang men for sheep-stealing, again, does not satisfy the idea; because, though it is a genuine right that sheep-stealing violates, in a society where there was any decent reconciliation of rights no such terror as is caused by the punishment of death would be required for protection of the right. It is because the theory that punishment is "merely preventive" favours the notion that the repetition of any action which any sufficient body of men find inconvenient may justifiably be prevented by any sort of terror that may be convenient for the purpose, that it requires to be guarded by substituting for the qualifying "merely" a statement of what it is which the justifiable punishment prevents and why it prevents it.

188. But does our theory, after all has been said about the wrongness of punishment that is not just, afford any standard for the apportionment of just punishment, any criterion of the amount of interference with a criminal's personal rights that is appropriate to his crime, except such as is afforded by a prevalent impression among men as to what is necessary for their security? Can we construe it so as to afford such a criterion without at the same time condemning a great deal of punishment which yet society could be never brought to dispense with? Does it really admit of being applied at all in the presence of the admitted impossibility of ascertaining the degree of moral guilt of criminals, as depending on their state of character or habitual motives? How, according to it, can we justify punishments inflicted in the case of "culpable negligence," e.g. when an engine-driver by careless driving, for which we think very little the worse of him, is the occasion of a bad accident, and is heavily punished in consequence?

189. It is true that there can be no *a priori* criterion of just punishment, except of an abstract and negative kind. We may say that no punishment is just, unless the rights which it serves to protect are powers on the part of individuals or corporations of which the general maintenance is necessary to the well-being of society on the whole and unless the terror which the punishment is calculated to inspire is necessary for their maintenance. For a positive and detailed criterion of just punishment we must wait till a system of rights has been established in which the claims of all men, as founded on their capacities for contributing to social well-being, are perfectly harmonised, and till experience has shown the degree and kind of terror with which men must be affected in order to the suppression of the antisocial tendencies which might lead to the violation of such a system of rights. And this is perhaps equivalent to saying that no complete criterion of just punishment can be arrived at till punishment is no longer necessary; for the state of things supposed could scarcely be realised without bringing with it an extinction of the tendencies which state-punishment is needed to suppress. Meanwhile there is no method of approximation to justice in punishment but that which consists in gradually making the system of established rights just, i.e., in harmonising the true claims of all men, and in discovering by experience the really efficient means of restraining tendencies to violation of rights. An intentional violation of a right must be punished, whether the right violated is one that should be a right or no, on the principle that social well-being suffers more from violation of any established right, whatever the nature of the right, than from the establishment as a right of a power which should not be so established; and it can only be punished in the way which for the time is thought most efficient by the maintainers of law for protecting the right in question by associating terror with its violation. This, however, does not alter the moral duty, on the part of the society authorising the punishment, to make its punishments just by making the system of rights which it maintains just. The justice of the punishment depends on the justice of the general system of rights; not merely on the propriety with reference to social well-being of maintaining this or that particular right which the crime punished violates, but on the question whether the social organisation in which a criminal has lived and acted is one that has given him a fair chance of not being a criminal.

190. We are apt to think that the justice of a punishment depends on some sort of equality between its magnitude and that of the crime punished, but this notion arises from a confusion of punishment as inflicted

by the state for a wrong done to society with compensation to the individual for damage done him. Neither a crime nor its punishment admits of strictly quantitative measurement. It may be said, indeed, that the greater the crime the heavier should be its punishment, but this is only true if by the "heavier punishment" is understood that with which most terror is associated in the popular imagination, and if the conception of the "greater crime" is taken on the one hand to exclude any estimation of the degree of moral guilt, and, on the other hand, to be determined by an estimate not only of the importance in the social system of the right violated by the crime but of the amount of terror that needs to be associated with the crime in the general apprehension in order to its prevention. But when its terms are thus understood, the statement that the greater the crime the heavier should be its punishment, becomes an identical proposition. It amounts to this that the crime which requires most terror to be associated with it in order to its prevention should have most terror thus associated with it.

191. But why do the terms "heavier punishment" and "greater crime" need to be thus understood? Why should not the "greater crime" be understood to mean the crime implying most moral wickedness, or partly this, partly the crime which violates the more important kind of right? Why should a consideration of the amount of terror that needs to be associated with it in order to its prevention enter into the determination of the "greater crime" at all? Why again should not the "heavier punishment" mean simply that in which the person punished actually suffers most pain? Why should it be taken to mean that with which most terror is associated upon the contemplation? In short, is not the proposition in question at once true and significant in the sense that the crime which implies most moral depravity, or violates the most important right (such as the right to life), or which does both, should be visited with the punishment that involves most pain to the sufferer?

192. The answer is: As regards heaviness of punishment, it is not in the power of the state to regulate the amount of pain which it causes to the person whom it punishes. If it could only punish justly by making this pain proportionate in each case to the depravity implied in the crime, it could not punish justly at all. The amount of pain which any kind of punishment causes to the particular person depends on his temperament and circumstances, which neither the state nor its agent, the judge, can ascertain. But if it could be ascertained, and if (which is equally impossible) the amount of depravity implied in each particular crime could be

ascertained likewise, in order to make the pain of the punishment proportionate to the depravity, a different punishment would have to be inflicted in each case according to the temperament and circumstances of the criminal. There would be an end to all general rules of punishment.

193. In truth, however, the state in its capacity as the sustainer of rights (and it is in this capacity that it punishes) has nothing to do with the amount of moral depravity in the criminal, and the primary reference in punishment, as inflicted by the state, is not to the effect of the punishment on the person punished but to its effect on others. The considerations determining its amount should be prospective rather than retrospective. In the crime a right has been violated. No punishment can undo what has been done, or make good the wrong to the person who has suffered. What it can do is to make less likely the doing of a similar wrong in other cases. Its object, therefore, is not to cause pain to the criminal for the sake of causing it, nor chiefly for the sake of preventing him, individually, from committing the crime again, but to associate terror with the contemplation of the crime in the mind of others who might be tempted to commit it. And this object, unlike that of making the pain of the punishment commensurate with the guilt of the criminal, is in the main attainable. The effect of the spectacle of punishment on the onlooker is independent of any minute inquiry into the degree to which it affects the particular criminal. The attachment of equal penalties to offences that are alike in respect of the importance of the rights which they violate, and in respect of the ordinary temptations to them, will on the whole lead to the association of an equal amount of terror with the prospect of committing the like offences in the public mind. When the circumstances indeed of two criminals guilty of offences alike in both the above respects are very greatly and obviously different so different as to make the operation of the same penalty upon them very conspicuously different, then the penalty may be varied without interfering with its terrific effect on the public mind. We will suppose, e.g., that a fraud on the part of a respectable banker is equivalent, both in respect of the rights which it violates and of the terror needed to prevent the recurrence of like offences, to a burglary. It will not follow because the burglary is punished by imprisonment with hard labour that hard labour should be inflicted on the fraudulent banker likewise. The infliction of hard labour is in everyone's apprehension so different to the banker from what it is to the burglar, that its infliction is not needed in order to equalise the terror

which the popular imagination associates with the punishment in the two cases.

194. On the same principle may be justified the consideration of extenuating circumstances in the infliction of punishment. In fact, whether under that name or another, they are taken account of in the administration of criminal law among all civilised nations. "Extenuating circumstances" is not a phrase in use among our lawyers, but in fact consideration of them does constantly, with the approval of the judge, convert what would otherwise have been conviction for murder into conviction for manslaughter, and, when there has been conviction for murder, leads to commutation of the sentence. This fact is often taken to show that the degree of moral depravity on the part of the criminal, the question of his character and motive, is and must be considered in determining the punishment due to him. In truth, however, "extenuating circumstances" may very well make a difference in the kind of terror which needs to be associated with a crime in order to the future protection of rights, and under certain conditions the consideration of them may be sufficiently justified on this ground. Suppose a theft by a starving man, or a hare shot by an angry farmer whose corn it is devouring. These are crimes, but crimes under such extenuating circumstances that there is no need to associate very serious terror with them in order to the protection of essential rights of property. In the latter case the right which the farmer violates is one which perhaps might be disallowed altogether without interference with any right which society is interested in maintaining. In the former case the right violated is a primary and essential one—one which, where there are many starving people, is in fact pretty sure to be protected by the most stringent penalties. And it might be argued that on the principle stated this is as it should be; that so far from the hunger of the thief being a reason for lightening his punishment, it is a reason for increasing it, in order that the special temptation to steal when far gone in hunger may, if possible, be neutralised by a special terror associated with the commission of the crime under those conditions. But this would be a one-sided application of the principle. It is not the business of the state to protect one order of rights specially, but all rights equally. It ought not therefore to protect a certain order of rights by associating special terror with the violation of them when the special temptation to their violation itself implies a violation of right in the persons of those who are so tempted, as is the case when a general danger to property arises from the fact that many people are on the edge of starvation. The attempt to do so is at

once ineffectual and diverts attention from the true way of protecting the endangered right, which is to prevent people from falling into a state of starvation. In any tolerably organised society the condition of a man, ordinarily honest and industrious, who is driven to theft by hunger, will be so abnormal that very little terror needs to be associated with the crime as so committed in order to maintain the sanctity of property in the general imagination. Suppose again a man to be killed in a quarrel arising out of his having tampered with the fidelity of his neighbour's wife. In such a case "extenuating circumstances" may fairly be pleaded against the infliction of the extremest penalty because the extremest terror does not need to be associated with homicide, as committed under such conditions, in order to the general protection of human life, and because the attempt so to associate it would tend, so far as successful, to weaken the general sense of the wrong—the breach of family right—involved in the act which, in the case supposed, provokes the homicide.

195. "After all," it may be said, "this is a farfetched way of explaining the admission of extenuating circumstances as modifying the punishment of crime. Why so strenuously avoid the simpler explanation, that extenuating circumstances are taken into account because they are held to modify the moral guilt of the crime? Is not their recognition a practical proof that punishment of a crime by the state represents the moral disapproval of the community? Does it not show that, however imperfectly the amount of punishment inflicted on a crime may in fact correspond to its moral wickedness, it is generally felt that it ought to do so?"

196. The answer is that there are two reasons for holding that the state neither can nor should attempt to adjust the amount of punishment which it inflicts on a crime to the degree of moral depravity which the crime implies. (1) That the degree of moral depravity implied in any crime is unascertainable. It depends on the motive of the crime, and on this as part of the general character of the agent; on the relation in which the habitual set of his character stands to the character habitually set on the pursuit of goodness. No one can ascertain this in regard to himself. He may know that he is always far from being what he ought to be; that one particular action of his represents on the whole, with much admixture of inferior motives, the better tendency; another, with some admixture of better motives, the worse. But any question in regard to the degree of moral goodness or badness in any action of his own or of his most intimate friend is quite unanswerable. Much less can a judge or jury answer such a question in regard to an unknown criminal. We may be sure in-

deed that every ordinary crime—nay, perhaps even that of the "disinterested rebel"—implies the operation of some motive which is morally bad, for though it is not necessarily the worst men who come into conflict with established rights, it probably never can be the best; but the degree of badness implied in such a conflict in any particular case is quite beyond our ken, and it is this degree that must be ascertained if the amount of punishment which the state inflicts is to be proportionate to the moral badness implied in the crime. (2) The notion that the state should, if it could, adjust the amount of punishment which it inflicts on a crime to the moral wickedness of the crime rests on a false view of the relation of the state to morality. It implies that it is the business of the state to punish wickedness as such. But it has no such business. It cannot undertake to punish wickedness, as such, without vitiating the disinterestedness of the effort to escape wickedness and thus checking the growth of a true goodness of the heart in the attempt to promote a goodness which is merely on the surface. This, however, is not to be understood as meaning that the punishment of crime serves no moral purpose. It does serve such a purpose, and has its value in doing so, but only in the sense that the protection of rights, and the association of terror with their violation, is the condition antecedent of any general advance in moral wellbeing.

197. The punishment of crime, then, neither is, nor can, nor should be adjusted to the degree of moral depravity, properly so called, which is implied in the crime. But it does not therefore follow that it does not represent the disapproval which the community feels for the crime. On the whole, making allowance for the fact that law and judicial custom vary more slowly than popular feeling, it does represent such disapproval. And the disapproval may fitly be called moral, so far as that merely means that it is a disapproval relating to voluntarily action. But it is disapproval founded on a sense of what is necessary for the protection of rights, not on a judgement of moral good and evil of that kind which we call conscience when it is applied to our own actions, and which is founded on an ideal of moral goodness with which we compare our inward conduct ("inward," as representing motives and character). It is founded essentially on the outward aspect of a man's conduct, on the view of it as related to the security and freedom in action and acquisition of other members of society. It is true that this distinction between the outward and inward aspects of conduct is not present to the popular mind. It has not been recognised by those who have been the agents in establishing

the existing law of crimes in civilised nations. As the state came to control the individual or family in revenging hurts, and to substitute its penalties for private vengeance, rules of punishment came to be enacted expressive of general disapproval, without any clear consciousness of what was the ground of the disapproval. But in fact it was by what have been just described as the outward consequences of conduct that a general disapproval of it was ordinarily excited. Its morality in the stricter or inward sense was not matter of general social consideration. Thus in the main it has been on the ground of its interference with the general security and freedom in action and acquisition, and in proportion to the apprehension excited by it in this respect, that conduct has been punished by the state. Thus the actual practice of criminal law has on the whole corresponded to its true principle. So far as this principle has been departed from, it has not been because the moral badness of conduct, in the true or inward sense, has been taken account of in its treatment as a crime for this has not been generally contemplated at all, but because "religious" considerations have interfered. Conduct which did not call for punishment by the state as interfering with any true rights (rights that should be rights) has been punished as "irreligious." This, however, did not mean that it was punished on the ground of moral badness, properly so called. It meant that its consequences were feared either as likely to weaken the belief in some divine authority on which the established system of rights was supposed to rest, or as likely to bring evil on the community through provoking the wrath of some unseen power.

198. This account of the considerations which have regulated the punishment of crimes explains the severity with which "criminal negligence," is in some cases punished, and that severity is justified by the account given of the true principle of criminal law, the principle, viz., that crime should be punished according to the importance of the right which it violates and to the degree of terror which in a well-organised society needs to be associated with the crime in order to the protection of the right. It cannot be held that the carelessness of an engine-driver who overlooks a signal and causes a fatal accident implies more moral depravity than is implied in such negligence as all of us are constantly guilty of. Considered with reference to the state of mind of the agent, it is on a level with multitudes of actions and omissions which are not punished at all. Yet the engine-driver would be found guilty of man-slaughter and sentenced to penal servitude. The justification is not to be found in distinctions between different kinds of negligence on the part of dif-

ferent agents but in the effect of the negligence in different cases upon the rights of others. In the case supposed, the most important of all rights, the right to life, on the part of railway passengers depends for its maintenance on the vigilance of the drivers. Any preventible failure in such vigilance requires to have sufficient terror associated with it in the mind of other engine-drivers to prevent the recurrence of a like failure in vigilance. Such punishment is just, however generally virtuous the victim of it, because necessary to the protection of rights of which the protection is necessary to social well-being; and the victim of it, in proportion to his sense of justice, which means his habit of practically recognising true rights, will recognise it as just.

199. On this principle crimes committed in drunkenness must be dealt with. Not only is all depravity of motive specially inapplicable to them, since the motives actuating a drunken man often seem to have little connection with his habitual character; it is not always the case that a crime committed in drunkenness is even intentional. When a man in a drunken rage kills another, he no doubt intends to kill him, or at any rate to do him "grievous bodily harm," and perhaps the association of great penal terror with such an offence may tend to restrain men from committing it even when drunk; but when a drunken mother lies on her child and smothers it, the hurt is not intentional but accidental. The drunkenness, however, is not accidental, but preventible by the influence of adequate motives. It is therefore proper to treat such a violation of right, though committed unknowingly, as a crime, and to associate terror with it in the popular imagination, in order to the protection of rights by making people more careful about getting drunk, about allowing or promoting drunkenness, and about looking after drunken people. It is unreasonable, however, to do this and at the same time to associate so little terror, as in practice we do, with the promotion of dangerous drunkenness. The case of a crime committed by a drunkard is plainly distinguishable from that of a crime committed by a lunatic, for the association of penal terror with the latter would tend neither to prevent a lunatic from committing a crime nor people from becoming lunatics.

200. The principle above stated, as that according to which punishment by the state should be inflicted and regulated, also justifies a distinction between crimes and civil injuries, i.e., between breaches of right for which the state inflicts punishment without redress to the person injured, and those for which it procures or seeks to procure redress to the person injured without punishment of the person causing the injury. We

are not here concerned with the history of this distinction (for which see Maine, *Ancient Law*, Ch. X, and W. E. Hearn, *The Aryan Household,* Ch. XIX), nor with the question whether many breaches of right now among us treated as civil injuries ought not to be treated as crimes, but with the justification that exists for treating certain kinds of breach of right as cases in which the state should interfere to procure redress for the person injured, but not in the way of inflicting punishment on the injurer until he wilfully resists the order to make redress. The principle of the distinction as ordinarily laid down, viz. that civil injuries "are violations of^{70} rights, when considered in reference to the injury sustained by the individual," while crimes are "violations of rights, when considered in reference to their evil tendency as regards the community at large," (Stephen, Book V, Ch. I), is misleading; for if the well-being of the community did not suffer in the hurt done to the individual, that hurt would not be a violation of a right in the true sense at all, nor would the community have any ground for insisting that the hurt shall be redressed, and for determining the mode in which it shall be redressed. A violation of right cannot in truth be considered merely in relation to injury sustained by an individual, for thus considered it would not be a violation of right. It may be said that the state is only concerned in procuring redress for civil injuries because if it left an individual to procure redress in his own way, there would be no public peace. But there are other and easier ways of preventing fighting than by procuring redress of wrong. We prevent our dogs from fighting, not by redressing wrongs which they sustain from each other (of wrongs as of rights they are in the proper sense incapable), but by beating them or tying them up. The community would not keep the peace by procuring redress for hurt or damage sustained by individuals, unless it conceived itself as having interest in the security of individuals from hurt and damage, unless it considered the hurt done to individuals as done to itself. The true justification for treating some breaches of right as cases merely for redress, others as cases for punishment, is that, in order to the general protection of rights, with some it is necessary to associate a certain terror, with others it is not.

201. What then is the general ground of distinction between those with which terror does, and those with which it does not, need to be associated? Clearly it is purposeless to seek to associate terror with breaches of right in the case where the breaker does not know that he is violating a right, and is not responsible for not knowing it. No association of terror with such a breach of right can prevent men from similar

breaches under like conditions. In any case, therefore, in which it is, to begin with, open to dispute whether a breach of right has been committed at all, e.g., when it is a question whether a contract has been really broken owing to some doubt as to the interpretation of the contract or its application to a particular set of circumstances, or whether a commodity of which someone is in possession properly belongs to another—in such a case, though the judge finally decides that there has been a breach of right, there is no ground for treating it as a crime or punishing it. If in the course of judicial inquiry it turns out that there has been fraud by one or other of the parties to the litigation, a criminal prosecution, having punishment, not redress, for its object, should properly supervene upon the civil suit, unless the consequences of the civil suit are incidentally such as to amount to a sufficient punishment of the fraudulent party. Again, it is purposeless to associate terror with a breach of obligation which the person committing it knows to be so, but of an obligation which he has no means of fulfilling, e.g., non-payment of an acknowledged debt by a man who, through no fault of his own, is without means of paying it. It is only in cases of one or other of the above kinds—cases in which the breach of right, supposing it to have been committed, has presumably arisen either from inability to prevent it or from ignorance of the existence of the right—that it can be held as an absolute rule to be no business of the state to interfere penally but only in the way of restoring, so far as possible, the broken right.

202. But there are many cases of breach of right which can neither be definitely reduced to one of the above kinds nor distinguished from them by any broad demarcation; cases in which the breaker of a right has been ignorant of it because he has not cared to know, or in which his inability to fulfil it is the result of negligence or extravagance. Whether these should be treated penally or no will depend partly on the seriousness of the wrong done through avoidable ignorance or negligence, partly on the sufficiency of the deterrent effect incidentally involved in the civil remedy. In the case e.g., of inability to pay a debt through extravagance or recklessness, it may be unnecessary and inadvisable to treat the breach of right penally, in consideration that it is indirectly punished by poverty and loss of reputation incidental to bankruptcy, and that creditors should not look to the state to protect them from the consequences of lending on bad security. The negligence of a trustee, again, may be indirectly punished by his being obliged to make good the property lost through his neglect to the utmost of his means. This may serve as a sufficiently deter-

rent example without the negligence being proceeded against criminally. Again, damage done to property, by negligence is in England dealt with civilly, not criminally; and it may be held that in this case the liability to civil action is a sufficient deterrent. On the other hand, negligence which, as negligence, is not really distinguishable from the above, is rightly treated criminally when its consequences are more serious; e.g., that of the railway-servant whose negligence results in a fatal accident, that of the bank-director who allows a misleading statement of accounts to be published, fraudulently perhaps in the eye of the law, but in fact negligently. As a matter of principle, no doubt, if intentional violation of the right of property is treated as penal equally with the violation of the right of life, the negligent violation should be treated as penal in the one case as much as in the other. But as the consequences of an action for damages may be virtually though not ostensibly penal to the person proceeded against, it may be convenient to leave those negligences which do not, like the negligence of a railway-servant, affect the most important rights, or do not affect rights on a very large scale as does that of a bank-director, to be dealt with by the civil process.

203. The actual distinction between crimes and civil injuries in English law is no doubt largely accidental. As the historians of law point out, the civil process, having compensation, not punishment, for its object, is the form which the interference of the community for the maintenance of rights originally takes. The community restraining private vengeance, helps the injured person to redress, and regulates the way in which redress shall be obtained. This procedure no doubt implies the conviction that the community is concerned in the injury done to an individual, but it is only by degrees that this conviction becomes explicit, and that the community comes to treat all preventible breaches of right as offences against itself or its sovereign representative, i.e., as crimes or penal; in the language of English law, as "breaches of the king's peace." Those offences are first so treated which happen to excite most public alarm— most fear for general safety (hence, among others, anything thought sacrilegious). In a country like England, where no code has been drawn up on general principles, the class of injuries that are treated penally is gradually enlarged as public alarm happens to be excited in particular directions, but it is largely a matter of accident how the classification of crimes on one side and civil injuries on the other happens to stand at any particular time.[71]

204. According to the view here taken, then, there is no direct reference in punishment by the state, either retrospective or prospective, to moral good or evil. The state in its judicial action does not look to the moral guilt of the criminal whom it punishes, or to the promotion of moral good by means of his punishment in him or others. It looks not to virtue and vice but to rights and wrongs. It looks back to the wrong done in the crime which it punishes; not, however, in order to avenge it but in order to the consideration of the sort of terror which needs to be associated with such wrong-doing in order to the future maintenance of rights. If the character of the criminal comes into account at all, it can only be properly as an incident of this consideration. Thus punishment of crime is preventive in its object; not, however, preventive of any or every evil or by any and every means, but (according to its idea or as it should be) *justly* preventive of *injustice*; preventive of interference with those powers of action and acquisition which it is for the general well-being that individuals should possess, and according to laws which allow those powers equally to all men. But in order effectually to attain its preventive object and to attain it justly, it should be reformatory. When the reformatory office of punishment is insisted on, the reference may be, and from the judicial point of view must be, not to the moral good of the criminal as an ultimate end, but to his recovery from criminal habits as a means to that which is the proper and direct object of state-punishment, viz., the general protection of rights. The reformatory function of punishment is from this point of view an incident of its preventive function, as regulated by consideration of what is just to the criminal as well as to others. For the fulfilment of this latter function, the great thing, as we have seen, is by the punishment of an actual criminal to deter other possible criminals, but for the same purpose, unless the actual criminal is to be put out of the way or locked up for life, it must be desirable to reform him so that he may not be dangerous in future. Now when it is asked why he should not be put out of the way it must not be forgotten that among the rights which the state has to maintain are included rights of the criminal himself. These indeed are for the time suspended by his action in violation of rights, but founded as they are on the capacity for contributing to social good, they could only be held to be finally forfeited on the ground that this capacity was absolutely extinct.

205. This consideration limits the kind of punishment which the state may justly inflict. It ought not in punishing unnecessarily to sacrifice to the maintenance of rights in general what may be called the reversionary

rights of the criminal, rights which, if properly treated, he might ultimately become capable of exercising for the general good. Punishment
therefore either by death or by perpetual imprisonment is justifiable only
on one of two grounds; either that association of the extremest terror
with certain actions is under certain conditions necessary to preserve the
possibility of a social life based on observance of rights, or that the crime
punished affords a presumption of a permanent incapacity for rights on
the part of the criminal. The first justification may be pleaded for the
executions of men concerned in treasonable outbreaks, or guilty of certain breaches of discipline in war (on the supposition that the war is
necessary for the safety of the state and that such punishments are a necessary incident of war). Whether the capital punishment is really just in
such cases must depend, not only on its necessity as an incident in defence of a certain state, but on the question whether that state itself is
fulfilling its function as a sustainer of true rights. For the penalty of death
for murder both justifications may be urged. It cannot be defended on
any other ground, but it may be doubted whether the presumption of
permanent incapacity for rights is one which in our ignorance we can
ever be entitled to make. As to the other plea, the question is whether,
with a proper police system and sufficient certainty of detection and conviction, the association of this extremest terror with the murderer is necessary to the security of life. Where the death-penalty, however, is unjustifiable, so must be that of really permanent imprisonment; one as much
as the other is an absolute deprivation of free social life, and of the possibilities of moral development which that life affords. The only justification for a sentence of permanent imprisonment in a case where there
would be none for capital punishment would be that, though inflicted as
permanent, the imprisonment might be brought to an end in the event of
any sufficient proof appearing of the criminal's amendment. But such
proof could only be afforded if the imprisonment were so modified as to
allow the prisoner a certain amount of liberty.

206. If punishment then is to be just, in the sense that in its infliction
due account is taken of all rights, including the suspended rights of the
criminal himself, it must be, so far as public safety allows, reformatory.
It must tend to qualify the criminal for the resumption of rights. As reformatory, however, punishment has for its direct object the qualification for the exercise of rights, and is only concerned with true moralisation of the criminal indirectly so far as it may result from the exercise of
rights. But even where it cannot be reformatory in this sense, and over

and above its reformatory function in cases where it has one, it has a moral end. Just because punishment by the state has for its direct object the maintenance of rights, it has, like every other function of the state, indirectly a moral object, because true rights according to our definition, are powers which it is for the general well-being that the individual (or association) should possess, and that well-being is essentially a moral well-being. Ultimately, therefore, the just punishment of crime is for the moral good of the community. It is also for the moral good of the criminal himself, unless—and it is a supposition which we ought not to make– –he is beyond the reach of moral influences. Though not inflicted for that purpose, and though it would not the less have to be inflicted if no moral effect on the criminal could be discerned, it is morally the best thing that can happen to him. It is so, even if a true social necessity requires that he be punished with death. The fact that society is obliged so to deal with him affords the best chance of bringing home to him the anti-social nature of his act. It is true that the last utterances of murderers generally convey the impression that they consider themselves interesting persons, quite sure of going to heaven; but these are probably conventional. At any rate if the solemn infliction of punishment on behalf of human society, and without any sign of vindictiveness, will not breed the shame, which is the moral new birth, presumably nothing else within human reach will.

Chapter 12
The Right of the State to Promote Morality

207. The right of the individual man, as such, to free life on its negativeside is constantly gaining more general recognition. It is the basis of the growing scrupulosity in regard to punishments which are not reformatory, which put rights finally out of the reach of a criminal instead of qualifying him for their renewed exercise. But the only rational foundation for the ascription of this right is ascription of capacity for free contribution to social good. Is it then reasonable for us as a community to treat this capacity in the man whose crime has given proof of its having been overcome by anti-social tendencies, as yet giving him a title to a further chance of its development; on the other hand, to act as if it conferred no title on its possessors, before a crime has been committed, to be placed under conditions in which its realisation would be possible? Are not all modern states so acting allowing their ostensible members to grow up under conditions which render the development of social capacity practically impossible? Was it no more reasonable, as in the ancient states, to deny the right to life in the human subject as such, than to admit it under conditions which prevent the realisation of the capacity that forms the ground of its admission? This brings us to the fourth of the questions that arose[72] out of the assertion of the individual's right to free life. What is the nature and extent of the individual's claim to be enabled positively to realise that capacity for freely contributing to social good which is the foundation of his right to free life?

208. In dealing with this question, it is important to bear in mind that the capacity we are considering is essentially a free or (what is the same) a moral capacity. It is a capacity, not for action determined by relation to a certain end, but for action determined by a conception of the end to which it is relative. Only thus is it a foundation of rights. The action of an animal or plant may be made contributory to social good, but it is not therefore a foundation of rights on the part of an animal or plant, because they are not affected by the conception of the good to which they contribute. A right is a power of acting for his own ends for—what he conceives to be his good—secured to an individual by the community, on the supposition that its exercise contributes to the good of the commu-

nity. But the exercise of such a power cannot be so contributory unless the individual, in acting for his own ends, is at least affected by the conception of a good as common to himself with others. The condition of making the animal contributory to human good is that we do not leave him free to determine the exercise of his powers; that we determine them for him; that we use him merely as an instrument; and this means that we do not, because we cannot, endow him with rights. We cannot endow him with rights because there is no conception of a good common to him with us which we can treat as a motive to him to do to us as he would have us do to him. It is not indeed necessary to a capacity for rights, as it is to true moral goodness, that interest in a good conceived as common to himself with others should be a man's dominant motive. It is enough if that which he presents to himself from time to time as his good, and which accordingly determines his action, is so far affected by consideration of the position in which he stands to others—of the way in which this or that possible action of his would affect them in return—as to result habitually without force or fear of force, in action not incompatible with conditions necessary to the pursuit of a common good on the part of others. In other words, it is the presumption that a man in his general course of conduct will of his own motion have respect to the common good, which entitles him to rights at the hands of the community. The question of the moral value of the motive which may induce this respect—whether an unselfish interest in common good or the wish for personal pleasure and fear of personal pain—does not come into the account at all. An agent, indeed, who could only be induced by fear of death or bodily harm to behave conformably to the requirements of the community would not be a subject of rights, because this influence could never be brought to bear on him so constantly, if he were free to regulate his own life, as to secure the public safety. But a man's desire for pleasure to himself and aversion from pain to himself, though dissociated from any desire for a higher object for any object that is desired because good for others may constitute a capacity for rights, if his imagination of pleasure and pain is so far affected by sympathy with the feeling of others about him as to make him, independently of force or fear of punishment, observant of established rights. In such a case the fear of punishment may be needed to neutralise anti-social impulses under circumstances of special temptation, but by itself it could never be a sufficiently uniform motive to qualify a man, in the absence of more spontaneously social feelings, for the life of a free citizen. The qualification for such a life is a spontaneous habit of acting with reference to a common good, whether that habit be founded on an imagination of pleasures and pains or on a conception of what ought to be. In either case the habit implies at least an understanding that there is such a thing as a common good, and a regulation of egoistic hopes and fears, if not an inducing of more "disinterested" motives, in consequence of that understanding.

209. The capacity for rights, then, being a capacity for spontaneous action regulated by a conception of a common good, either so regulated through an interest which flows directly from that conception or through hopes and fears which are affected by it through more complex channels of habit and association is a capacity which cannot be generated—which on the contrary is neutralised—by any influences that interfere with the spontaneous action of social interests. Now any direct enforcement of the outward conduct, which ought to flow from social interests, by means of threatened penalties—and a law requiring such conduct necessarily implies penalties for disobedience to it—does interfere with the spontaneous action of those interests, and consequently checks the growth of the capacity which is the condition of the beneficial exercise of rights. For this reason the effectual action of the state, i.e., the community as acting through law, for the promotion of habits of true citizenship, seems necessarily to be confined to the removal of obstacles. Under this head, however, there may and should be included much that most states have hitherto neglected, and much that at first sight may have the appearance of an enforcement of moral duties, e.g., the requirement that parents have their children taught the elementary arts. To educate one's children is no doubt a moral duty, and it is not one of those duties, like that of paving debts, of which the neglect directly interferes with the rights of someone else. It might seem, therefore, to be a duty with which positive law should have nothing to do, any more than with the duty of striving after a noble life. On the other hand, the neglect of it does tend to prevent the growth of the capacity for beneficially exercising rights on the part of those whose education is neglected, and it is on this account not as a purely moral duty on the part of a parent, but as the prevention of a hindrance to the capacity for rights on the part of children that education should be enforced by the state. It may be objected, indeed, that in enforcing it we are departing in regard to the parents from the principle above laid down; that we are interfering with the spontaneous action of social interests, though we are doing so with a view to promoting this spontaneous action in another generation. But the answer to this objection is, that a law of

compulsory education, if the preferences, ecclesiastical or otherwise, of those parents who show any practical sense of their responsibility are duly respected, is from the beginning only felt as compulsion by those in whom, so far as this social function is concerned, there is no spontaneity to be interfered with; and that in the second generation, though the law with its penal sanctions still continues, it is not felt as a law, as an enforcement of action by penalties, at all.

210. On the same principle the freedom of contract ought probably to be more restricted in certain directions than is at present the case. The freedom to do as they like on the part of one set of men may involve the ultimate disqualification of many others, or of a succeeding generation, for the exercise of rights. This applies most obviously to such kinds of contract or traffic as affect the health and housing of the people, the growth of population relatively to the means of subsistence, and the accumulation or distribution of landed property. In the hurry of removing those restraints on free dealing between man and man, which have arisen partly perhaps from some confused idea of maintaining morality but much more from the power of class-interests, we have been apt to take too narrow a view of the range of persons—not one generation merely but succeeding generations—whose freedom ought to be taken into account, and of the conditions necessary to their freedom ("freedom" here meaning their qualification for the exercise of rights). Hence the massing of population without regard to conditions of health; unrestrained traffic in deleterious commodities; unlimited upgrowth of the class of hired labourers in particular industries which circumstances have suddenly stimulated, without any provision against the dangers of an impoverished proletariate in following generations. Meanwhile, under pretence of allowing freedom of bequest and settlement, a system has grown up which prevents the landlords of each generation from being free either in the government of their families or in the disposal of their land, and aggravates the tendency to crowd into towns, as well as the difficulties of providing healthy house-room, by keeping land in a few hands. It would be out of place here to consider in detail the remedies for these evils, or to discuss the question how far it is well to trust to the initiative of the state or individuals in dealing with them. It is enough to point out the directions in which the state may remove obstacles to the realisation of the capacity for beneficial exercise of rights without defeating its own object by vitiating the spontaneous character of that capacity.

Chapter 13
The Right of the State in Regard to Property

211. We have now considered the ground of the right to free life, and what is the justification, if any, for the apparent disregard of that right (a) in war, (b) in the infliction of punishment. We have also dealt with the question of the general office of the state in regard to the development of that capacity in individuals which is the foundation of the right, pointing out on the one hand the necessary limitation of its office in this respect, on the other hand the directions in which it may remove obstacles to that development. We have next to consider the rationale of the rights of property.

In discussions on the "origin of property" two questions are apt to be mixed up which, though connected, ought to be kept distinct. One is the question how men have come to appropriate; the other the question how the idea of right has come to be associated with their appropriations. As the term "property" not only implies a permanent possession of something, or a possession which can only be given up with the good will of the possessor, but also a possession recognised as a right, an inquiry into the origin of property must involve both these questions, but it is not the less important that the distinction between them should be observed. Each of them again has both its analytical and its historical side. In regard to the first question it is important to learn all that can be learnt as to the kind of things that were first, and afterwards at successive periods, appropriated; as to the mode in which, and the sort of persons or societies by whom, they were appropriated. This is an historical inquiry. But it cannot take the place of a metaphysical or psychological analysis of the conditions on the part of the appropriating subject implied in the fact that he does such a thing as appropriate. So too, in regard to the second question, it is important to investigate historically the forms in which the right of men in their appropriations has been recognised; the parties, whether individuals or societies, to whom the right has been allowed; and the sort of objects, capable of appropriation, to which it has been considered to extend. But neither can these inquiries help us to understand, in the absence of a metaphysical or moral analysis, either what is implied in the ascription of a right to certain appropriations, or why there should be a right to them.

212. We have then two questions, as above stated, each requiring two different methods of treatment. But neither have the questions themselves, nor the different methods of dealing with them, been duly distinguished.

It is owing to confusion between them that the right of property in things has been supposed to originate in the first occupancy of them. This supposition, in truth, merely disguises the identical proposition that in order to property there must to begin with have been some appropriation. The truism that there could be no property in anything which had not been at some time and in some manner appropriated tells us nothing as to how or why property in it, as a right, came to be recognised, or why that right should be recognised. But owing to the confusion between the origin of appropriation and the origin of property as a right, an identical proposition as to the beginning of appropriation seemed to be an instructive statement as to the basis of the rights of property. Of late, in a revulsion from theories founded on identical propositions, "historical" inquiries into the "origin of property" have come into vogue. The right method of dealing with the question has been taken to lie in an investigation of the earliest forms in which property has existed. But such investigation, however valuable in itself, leaves untouched the questions, (1) what it is in the nature of men that makes it possible for them, and moves them, to appropriate; (2) why it is that they conceive of themselves and each other as having a right in their appropriations; (3) on what ground is this conception treated as of moral authority—as one that should be acted on.

213. (1) Appropriation is an expression of will; of the individual's effort to give reality to a conception of his own good; of his consciousness of a possible self-satisfaction as an object to be attained. It is different from mere provision to supply a future want. Such provision appears to be made by certain animals, e.g. ants. It can scarcely be made under the influence of the imagination of pain incidental to future want derived from previous experience, for the ant lays up for the winter though it has not previously lived through the winter. It may be suggested that it does so from inherited habit, but that this habit has originally arisen from an experience of pain on the part of ants in the past. Whether this is the true account of the matter we have not, I think—perhaps from the nature of the case, cannot have—the means of deciding. We conceal our ignorance by saying that the ant acts instinctively, which is in effect a merely negative statement, that the ant is not moved to make provision for win-

ter either by imagination of the pain which will be felt in winter if it does not, or by knowledge of the fact (conception of the fact) that such pain will be felt. In fact, we know nothing of the action of the ant from the inside, or as an expression of consciousness. If we are not entitled to deny dogmatically that it expresses consciousness at all, neither are we entitled to say that it does express consciousness, still less what consciousness it expresses. On the other hand we are able to interpret the acts of ourselves, and of those with whom we can communicate by means of signs to which we and they attach the same meaning, as expressions of consciousness of a certain kind, and thus by reflective analysis to assure ourselves that acts of appropriation in particular express a will of the kind stated; that they are not merely a passing employment of such materials as can be laid hands on to satisfy this or that want, present or future, felt or imagined, but reflect the consciousness of a subject which distinguishes itself from its wants; which presents itself to itself as still there and demanding satisfaction when this or that want, or any number of wants, have been satisfied; which thus not merely uses a thing to fill a want, and in so doing at once destroys the thing and for the time removes the want, but says to itself, "this shall be mine to do as I like with, to satisfy my wants and express my emotions as they arise."

214. One condition of the existence of property, then, is appropriation, and that implies the conception of himself on the part of the appropriator as a permanent subject for whose use, as instruments of satisfaction and expression, he takes and fashions certain external things certain things external to his bodily members. These things, so taken and fashioned, cease to be external as they were before. They become a sort of extension of the man's organs, the constant apparatus through which he gives reality to his ideas and wishes. But another condition must be fulfilled in order to constitute property, even of the most simple and primitive sort. This is the recognition by others of a man's appropriations as something which they will treat as his, not theirs, and the guarantee to him of his appropriations by means of that recognition. What then is the ground of the recognition? The writers of the seventeenth and eighteenth centuries, who discussed the basis of the rights of property, took it for granted, and in so doing begged the question. Grotius makes the right of property rest on contract, but clearly until there is a recognised "meum" [mine] and "tuum" [yours] there can be no contract. Contract presupposes property. The property in a particular thing may be derived from a contract through which it has been obtained in exchange for another thing

or for some service rendered, but that implies that it was previously the property of another, and that the person obtaining it had a property in something else if only in the labour of his hands, which he could exchange for it.[73] Hobbes is so far more logical that he does not derive property from contract, but treats property and "the validity of covenants," as coordinately dependent on the existence of a sovereign power of compulsion.[74] But his account of this, as of all other forms of right, is open to the objection (before dwelt on) that if the sovereign power is merely a strongest force it cannot be a source of rights; and that if it is other than this, if it is a representative and maintainer of rights, its existence presupposes rights, which remain to be accounted for. As previously shown, Hobbes, while professing to make all rights dependent on the sovereign power, presupposes rights in his account of the institution of this power. The validity of contracts "begins not but with its institution," yet its own right is derived from an irrevocable contract of all with all in which each devolves his "persona" the body of his rights, upon it. Without pressing his particular forms of expression unfairly against him, it is clear that he could not really succeed in thinking of rights as derived simply from supreme force; that he could not associate the idea of absolute right with the sovereign without supposing prior rights which it was made the business of the sovereign to enforce, and in particular such a recognised distinction between "meum" and "tuum" as is necessary to a covenant. Nor when we have dropped Hobbes's notion of government or law-making power, as having originated in a covenant of all with all, shall we succeed any better in deriving rights of property, any more than other rights, from law or a sovereign which makes law, unless we regard the law or sovereign as the organ or sustainer of a general social recognition of certain powers, as powers which should be exercised.

215. Locke[75] treats property—fairly enough so long as only its simplest forms are in question—as derived from labour. By the same law of nature and reason by which a man has "a property in his own person," "the labour of his body, and the work of his hand are properly his" too. Now that the right to free life, which we have already dwelt on, carries with it a certain right to property to a certain permanent apparatus beyond the bodily organs for the maintenance and expression of that life, is quite true. But apart from the difficulty of tracing some kinds of property in which men are in fact held to have a right, to the labour of anyone even of someone from whom it has been derived by inheritance or bequest (a difficulty to be considered presently), to say that it is a "law of nature and

reason" that a man should have a property in the work of his hands is no more than saying that that on which a man has impressed his labour is recognised by others as something which should be his, just as he himself is recognised by them as one that should be his own master. The ground of the recognition is the same in both cases and it is Locke's merit to have pointed this out, but what the ground is he does not consider, shelving the question by appealing to a law of nature or reason.

216. The ground of the right to free life, the reason why a man is secured in the free exercise of his powers through recognition of that exercise by others as something that should be, lay, as we saw, in the conception on the part of everyone who concedes the right to others and to whom it is conceded, of an identity of good for himself and others. It is only as within a society as a relation between its members, though the society be that of all men, that there can be such a thing as a right; and the right to free life rests on the common will of the society, in the sense that each member of the society within which the right subsists in seeking to satisfy himself contributes to satisfy the others, and that each is aware that the other does so; whence there results a common interest in the free play of the powers of all. And just as the recognised interest of a society constitutes for each member of it the right to free life, just as it makes each conceive of such life on the part of himself and his neighbour as what should be, and thus forms the basis of a restraining custom which secures it for each so it constitutes the right to the instruments of such life, making each regard the possession of them by the other as for the common good, and thus through the medium first of custom, then of law, securing them to each.

217. Thus the doctrine that the foundation of the right of property lies in the will that property is "realised will" is true enough if we attach a certain meaning to "will;" if we understand by it, not the momentary spring of any and every spontaneous action, but a constant principle, operative in all men qualified for any form of society, however frequently overborne by passing impulses, in virtue of which each seeks to give reality to the conception of a well-being which he necessarily regards as common to himself with others. A will of this kind at once explains the effort to appropriate, and the restraint placed on each in his appropriations by a customary recognition of the interest which each has in the success of the like effort on the part of the other members of a society with which he shares a common well-being. This customary recognition, founded on a moral or rational will, requires indeed to be represented by

some adequate force before it can result in a real maintenance of rights of property. The wild beast in man will not otherwise yield obedience to the rational will. And from the operation of this compulsive force, very imperfectly controlled by the moral tendencies which need its co-operation—in other words from the historical incidents of conquest and government—there result many characteristics of the institution of property, as it actually exists, which cannot be derived from the spiritual principle which we have assigned as its foundation. Still, without that principle it could not have come into existence, nor would it have any moral justification at all.

218. It accords with the account given of this principle that the right of property, like every other form of right, should first appear within societies founded on kinship, these being naturally the societies within which the restraining conception of a common wellbeing is first operative. We are apt indeed to think of the state of things in which the members of a family or clan hold land and stock in common, as the antithesis of one in which rights of property exist. In truth it is the earliest stage of their existence, because the most primitive form of society in which the fruit of his labour is secured to the individual by the society under the influence of the conception of a common well-being. The characteristic of primitive communities is not the absence of distinction between "meum" and "tuum," without which no society of intelligent as opposed to instinctive agents would be possible at all, but the common possession of certain materials, in particular land, on which labour may be expended. It is the same common interest which prevents separate appropriation of these materials and which secures the individual in the enjoyment and use of that which his labour can extract from them.

219. From the moral point of view, however, the clan-system is defective because under it the restraint imposed upon the individual by his membership of a society is not, and has not the opportunity of becoming, a self-imposed restraint a free obedience to which, though the alternative course is left open to him, the individual submits, because he conceives it as his true good. The area within which he can shape his own circumstances is not sufficient to allow of the opposite possibilities of right and wrong being presented to him, and thus of his learning to love right for its own sake. And the other side of this moral tutelage of the individual, this withholding from him of the opportunity of being freely determined by recognition of his moral relations, is the confinement of those relations themselves, which under the clan-system have no actual existence

except as between members of the same clan. A necessary condition at once of the growth of a free morality, i.e., a certain behaviour of men determined by an understanding of moral relations and by the value which they set on them as understood, and of the conception of those relations as relations between all men, is that free play should be given to every man's powers of appropriation. Moral freedom is not the same thing as a control over the outward circumstances and appliances of life. It is the end to which such control is a generally necessary means and which gives it its value. In order to obtain this control men must cease to be limited in their activities by the customs of the clan. The range of their appropriations must be extended; they must include more of the permanent material on which labour may be expended, and not merely the passing products of labour spent on unappropriated material; and they must be at once secured and controlled in it by the good-will, by the sense of common interest, of a wider society, of a society to which any and every one may belong who will observe its conditions, and not merely those of a particular parentage; in other words by the law, written or unwritten, of a free state.

220. It is too long a business here to attempt an account of the process by which the organisation of rights in the state has superseded that of the clan, and at the same time the restriction of the powers of appropriation implied in the latter has been removed. It is important to observe, however, that this process has by no means contributed unmixedly to the end to which, from the moral point of view, it should have contributed. That end is at once the emancipation of the individual from all restrictions upon, and his provision with means for, the free moral life. But the actual result of the development of rights of property in Europe, as part of its general political development, has so far been a state of things in which all indeed *may* have property, but great numbers in fact cannot have it in that sense in which alone it is of value, viz. as a permanent apparatus for carrying out a plan of life, for expressing ideas of what is beautiful, or giving effect to benevolent wishes. In the eye of the law they have rights of appropriation, but in fact they have not the chance of providing means for a free moral life, of developing and giving reality or expression to a good will, an interest in social well-being. A man who possesses nothing but his powers of labour and who has to sell these to a capitalist for bare daily maintenance, might as well, in respect of the ethical purposes which the possession of property should serve, be denied rights of property altogether. Is the existence of so many men in this position, and the ap-

parent liability of many more to be brought to it by a general fall of wages, if increase of population goes along with decrease in the productiveness of the earth, a necessary result of the emancipation of the individual and the free play given to powers of appropriation? Or is it an evil incident, which may yet be remedied, of that historical process by which the development of the rights of property has been brought about, but in which the agents have for the most part had no moral objects in view at all?

221. Let us first be clear about the points in which the conditions of property, as it actually exists, are at variance with property according to its idea or as it should be. The rationale of property as we have seen, is that everyone should be secured by society in the power of getting and keeping the means of realising a will, which in possibility is a will directed to social good. Whether anyone's will is actually and positively so directed, does not affect his claim to the power. This power should be secured to the individual irrespectively of the use which he actually makes of it, so long as he does not use it in a way that interferes with the exercise of like power by another, on the ground that its uncontrolled exercise is the condition of attainment by man of that free morality which is his highest good. It is not then a valid objection to the manner in which property is possessed among us, that its holders constantly use it in a way demoralising to themselves and others, any more than such misuse of any other liberties is an objection to securing men in their possession. Only then is property held in a way inconsistent with its idea, and which should, if possible, be got rid of, when the possession of property by one man interferes with the possession of property by another when one set of men are secured in the power of getting and keeping the means of realising their will, in such a way that others are practically denied the power. In that case it may truly be said that "property is theft." The rationale of property, in short, requires that everyone who will conform to the positive condition of possessing it, viz. labour, and the negative condition, viz. respect for it as possessed by others, should, so far as social arrangements can make him so, be a possessor of property himself, and of such property as will at least enable him to develop a sense of responsibility, as distinct from mere property in the immediate necessaries of life.

222. But then the question arises, whether the rationale of property, as thus stated, is not inconsistent with the unchecked freedom of appropriation, or freedom of appropriation checked only by the requirement that

the thing appropriated shall not have previously been appropriated by another. Is the requirement that every honest man should be a proprietor to the extent stated, compatible with any great inequalities of possession? In order to give effect to it, must we not remove those two great sources of the inequality of fortunes, (1) freedom of bequest, and the other arrangements by which the profits of the labour of several generations are accumulated on persons who do not labour at all; (2) freedom of trade, of buying in the cheapest market and selling in the dearest, by which accumulated profits of labour become suddenly multiplied in the hands of a particular proprietor? Now clearly, if an inequality of fortunes, of the kind which naturally arises from the admission of these two forms of freedom, necessarily results in the existence of a proletariate, practically excluded from such ownership as is needed to moralise a man, there would be a contradiction between our theory of the right of property and the actual consequence of admitting the right according to the theory; for the theory logically necessitates freedom both in trading and in the disposition of his property by the owner, so long as he does not interfere with the like freedom on the part of others; and in other ways as well its realisation implies inequality.

223. Once admit as the idea of property that nature should be progressively adapted to the service of man by a process in which each, while working freely or for himself, i.e., as determined by a conception of his own good, at the same time contributes to the social good, and it will follow that property must be unequal. If we leave a man free to realise the conception of a possible well-being, it is impossible to limit the effect upon him of his desire to provide for his future well-being, as including that of the persons in whom he is interested, or the success with which at the prompting of that desire he turns resources of nature to account. Considered as representing the conquest of nature by the effort of free and variously gifted individuals, property must be unequal; and no less must it be so if considered as a means by which individuals fulfil social functions. As we may learn from Aristotle, those functions are various and the means required for their fulfilment are various. The artist and man of letters require different equipment and apparatus from the tiller of land and the smith. Either then the various apparatus needed for various functions must be provided for individuals by society, which would imply a complete regulation of life, incompatible with that highest object of human attainment, a free morality; or we must trust for its

provision to individual effort, which will imply inequality between the property of different persons.

224. The admission of freedom of trade follows from the same principle. It is a condition of the more complete adaptation of nature to the service of man by the free effort of individuals. "To buy in the cheapest and sell in the dearest market" is a phrase which may no doubt be used to cover objectionable transactions, in which advantage is taken of the position of sellers who from circumstances are not properly free to make a bargain. It is so employed when the cheapness of buying arises from the presence of labourers who have no alternative but to work for "starvation wages." But in itself it merely describes transactions in which commodities are bought where they are of least use and sold where they are of most use. The trader who profits by the transaction is profiting by what is at the same time a contribution to social well-being.

In regard to the freedom which a man should be allowed in disposing of his property by will or gift, the question is not so simple. The same principle which forbids us to limit the degree to which a man may provide for his future, forbids us to limit the degree to which he may provide for his children, these being included in his forecast of his future. It follows that the amount which children may inherit may not rightly be limited; and in this way inequalities of property, and accumulations of it to which possessors have contributed nothing by their own labour, must arise. Of course the possessor of an estate, who has contributed nothing by his own labour to its acquisition, may yet by his labour contribute largely to the social good, and a well-organised state will in various ways elicit such labour from possessors of inherited wealth. Nor will it trust merely to encouraging the voluntary fulfilment of social functions, but will by taxation make sure of some positive return for the security which it gives to inherited wealth. But while the mere permission of inheritance, which seems implied in the permission to a man to provide unlimitedly for his future, will lead to accumulations of wealth, on the other hand, if the inheritance is to be equal among all children, and, failing children, is to pass to the next of kin, the accumulation will be checked. It is not therefore the right of inheritance, but the right of bequest, that is most likely to lead to accumulation of wealth, and that has most seriously been questioned by those who hold that universal ownership is a condition of moral well-being. Is a proprietor to be allowed to dispose of his property as he likes among his children (or, if he has none, among others), making one very rich as compared with the others, or is he to be checked by a law requiring approximately equal inheritance?

225. As to this, consider that on the same principle on which we hold that a man should be allowed to accumulate as he best can for his children, he should have discretion in distributing among his children. He should be allowed to accumulate, because in so doing he at once expresses and develops the sense of family responsibility which naturally breeds a recognition of duties in many other directions. But if the sense of family responsibility is to have free play, the man must have due control over his family, and this he can scarcely have if all his children as a matter of necessity inherit equally, however undutiful or idle or extravagant they may be. For this reason the true theory of property would seem to favour freedom of bequest, at any rate in regard to wealth generally. There may be special reasons, to be considered presently, for limiting it in regard to land. But as a general rule, the father of a family, if left to himself and not biased by any special institutions of his country, is most likely to make that distribution among his children which is most for the public good. If family pride moves him to endow one son more largely than the rest, in order to maintain the honour of his name, family affection will keep this tendency within limits in the interest of the other children, unless the institutions of his country favour the one tendency as against the other. And this they will do if they maintain great dignities, e.g. peerages, of which the possession of large hereditary wealth is virtually the condition, and if they make it easy, when the other sons have been impoverished for the sake of endowing the eldest, to maintain the former at the public expense by means of appointments in the church or state.

It must be borne in mind, further, that the freedom of bequest which is to be justified on the above principles must not be one which limits that freedom in a subsequent generation. It must therefore be distinguished from the power of settlement allowed by English law and constantly exercised in dealing with landed estate; for this power, as exercised by the landowning head of a family in one generation, prevents the succeeding head of the family from being free to make what disposition he thinks best among his children and ties up the succession to the estate to his eldest son. The practice of settlement in England, in short, as applied to landed estate, cancels the freedom of bequest in the case of most landowners and neutralises all the dispersive tendency of family affection, while it maintains in full force all the accumulative tendency of family pride. This, however, is no essential incident of a system in which the rights of individual ownership are fully developed, but just the contrary.

226. The question then remains, whether the full development of those rights, as including that of unlimited accumulation of wealth by the individual and of complete freedom of bequest on his part, necessarily carries with it the existence of a proletariate, nominal owners of their powers of labour, but in fact obliged to sell these on such terms that they are in fact owners of nothing beyond what is necessary from day to day for the support of life, and may at any time lose even that, so that, as regards the moral functions of property, they may be held to be not proprietors at all; or whether the existence of such a class is due to causes only accidentally connected with the development of rights of individual property.

We must bear in mind (1) that the increased wealth of one man does not naturally mean the diminished wealth of another. We must not think of wealth as a given stock of commodities of which a larger share cannot fall to one without taking from the share that falls to another. The wealth of the world is constantly increasing in proportion as the constant production of new wealth by labour exceeds the constant consumption of what is already produced. There is no natural limit to its increase except such as arises from the fact that the supply of the food necessary to sustain labour becomes more difficult as more comes to be required owing to the increase in the number of labourers, and from the possible ultimate exhaustion of the raw materials of labour in the world. Therefore in the accumulation of wealth, so far as it arises from the saving by anyone of the products of his labour, from his bequest of this capital to another who farther adds to it by saving some of the profit which the capital yields, as employed in the payment for labour or in trade either by the capitalist himself or someone to whom he lends it, and from the continuation of this process through generations, there is nothing which tends to lessen for anyone else the possibilities of ownership. On the contrary, supposing trade and labour to be free, wealth must be constantly distributed throughout the process in the shape of wages to labourers and of profits to those who mediate in the business of exchange.

227. It is true that the accumulation of capital naturally leads to the employment of large masses of hired labourers. But there is nothing in the nature of the case to keep these labourers in the condition of living from hand to mouth, to exclude them from that education of the sense of responsibility which depends on the possibility of permanent ownership.

There is nothing in the fact that their labour is hired in great masses by great capitalists to prevent them from being on a small scale capitalists themselves. In their position they have not indeed the same stimulus to saving, or the same constant opening for the investment of savings, as a man who is *αυτουργός* [self-employed]; but their combination in work gives them every opportunity if they have the needful education and self-discipline, for forming societies for the investment of savings. In fact, as we know, in the well-paid industries of England the better sort of labourers do become capitalists, to the extent often of owning their houses and a good deal of furniture, of having an interest in stores, and of belonging to benefit-societies through which they make provision for the future. It is not then to the accumulation of capital, but to the condition, due to antecedent circumstances unconnected with that accumulation, of the men with whom the capitalist deals and whose labour he buys on the cheapest terms, that we must ascribe the multiplication in recent times of an impoverished and reckless proletariate.

228. It is difficult to summarise the influences to which is due the fact that in all the chief seats of population in Europe the labour market is constantly thronged with men who are too badly reared and fed to be efficient labourers; who for this reason, and from the competition for employment with each other, have to sell their labour very cheap; who have thus seldom the means to save, and whose standard of living and social expectation is so low that, if they have the opportunity of saving, they do not use it, and keep bringing children into the world at a rate which perpetuates the evil. It is certain, however, that these influences have no necessary connection with the maintenance of the right of individual property and consequent unlimited accumulation of capital, though they no doubt are connected with that régime of force and conquest by which existing governments have been established—governments which do not indeed create the rights of individual property, any more than other rights, but which serve to maintain them. It must always be borne in mind that the appropriation of land by individuals has in most countries—probably in all where it approaches completeness—been originally effected, not by the expenditure of labour or the results of labour on the land, but by force. The original landlords have been conquerors.

229. This has affected the condition of the industrial classes in at least two ways: (1) When the application of accumulated capital to any work in the way of mining or manufacture has created a demand for labour, the supply has been forthcoming from men whose ancestors, if not them-

selves, were trained in habits of serfdom men whose life has been one of virtually forced labour, relieved by church-charities or the poor law (which in part took the place of these charities) who were thus in no condition to contract freely for the sale of their labour, and had nothing of that sense of family responsibility which might have made them insist on having the chance of saving. Landless countrymen, whose ancestors were serfs, are the parents of the proletariate of great towns. (2) Rights have been allowed to landlords, incompatible with the true principle on which rights of property rest, and tending to interfere with the development of the proprietorial capacity in others. The right to freedom in unlimited acquisition of wealth, by means of labour and by means of the saving and successful application of the results of labour, does not imply the right of anyone to do as he likes with those gifts of nature, without which there would be nothing to spend labour upon. The earth is just as much an original natural material necessary to productive industry as are air, light, and water, but while the latter from the nature of the case cannot be appropriated, the earth can be and has been. The only justification for this appropriation, as for any other, is that it contributes on the whole to social well-being; that the earth as appropriated by individuals under certain conditions becomes more serviceable to society as a whole, including those who are not proprietors of the soil, than if it were held in common. The justification disappears if these conditions are not observed; and from government having been chiefly in the hands of appropriators of the soil, they have not been duly observed. Landlords have been allowed to "do what they would with their own," as if land were merely like so much capital, admitting of indefinite extension. The capital gained by one is not taken from another, but one man cannot acquire more land without others having less; and though a growing reduction in the number of landlords is not necessarily a social evil, if it is compensated by the acquisition of other wealth on the part of those extruded from the soil, it is only not an evil if the landlord is prevented from so using his land as to make it unserviceable to the wants of men (e.g. by turning fertile land into a forest), and from taking liberties with it incompatible with the conditions of general freedom and health; e.g. by clearing out a village and leaving the people to pick up house-room as they can elsewhere a practice common under the old poor-law, when the distinction between close and open villages grew up, or, on the other hand, by building houses in unhealthy places or of unhealthy structure, by stopping up means of communication, or forbidding the erection of dissenting chapels. In fact the restraints which the public interest requires to be placed on the use of land if individual property in it is to be allowed at all, have been pretty much ignored, while on the other hand, that full development of its resources, which individual ownership would naturally favour, has been interfered with by laws or customs which, in securing estates to certain families, have taken away the interest, and tied the hands, of the nominal owner—the tenant for life—in making the most of his property.

230. Thus the whole history of the ownership of land in Europe has been of a kind to lead to the agglomeration of a proletariate, neither holding nor seeking property, wherever a sudden demand has arisen for labour in mines or manufactures. This at any rate was the case down to the epoch of the French Revolution; and this, which brought to other countries deliverance from feudalism, left England, where feudalism had previously passed into unrestrained landlordism, almost untouched. And while those influences of feudalism and landlordism which tend to throw a shiftless population upon the centres of industry have been left unchecked, nothing till quite lately was done to give such a population a chance of bettering itself, when it had been brought together. Their health, housing, and schooling were unprovided for. They were left to be freely victimised by deleterious employments, foul air, and consequent craving for deleterious drinks. When we consider all this, we shall see the unfairness of laying on capitalism or the free development of individual wealth the blame which is really due to the arbitrary and violent manner in which rights over land have been acquired and exercised, and to the failure of the state to fulfil those functions which under a system of unlimited private ownership are necessary to maintain the conditions of a free life.

231. Whether, when those functions have been more fully recognised and executed, and when the needful control has been established in the public interest over the liberties which landlords may take in the use of their land, it would still be advisable to limit the right of bequest in regard to land, and establish a system of something like equal inheritance, is a question which cannot be answered on any absolute principle. It depends on circumstances. Probably the question should be answered differently in a country like France or Ireland, where the most important industries are connected directly with the soil, and in one like England where they are not so. The reasons must be cogent which could justify that interference with the control of the parent over his family, which seems to be implied in the limitation of the power of bequeathing land when the parent's wealth lies solely in land, and which arises, be it re-

membered, in a still more mischievous way from the present English practice of settling estates. But it is important to bear in mind that the question in regard to land stands on a different footing from that in regard to wealth generally, owing to the fact that land is a particular commodity limited in extent, from which alone can be derived the materials necessary to any industry whatever, on which men must find house-room if they are to find it at all, and over which they must pass in communicating with each other, however much water or even air may be used for that purpose. These are indeed not reasons for preventing private property in land or even free bequest of land, but they necessitate a special[76] control over the exercise of rights of property in land, and it remains to be seen whether that control can be sufficiently established in a country where the power of great estates has not first been broken, as in France, by a law of equal inheritance.

232. To the proposal that "unearned increment" in the value of the soil, as distinct from value produced by expenditure of labour and capital, should be appropriated by the state, though fair enough in itself, the great objection is that the relation between earned and unearned increment is so complicated, that a system of appropriating the latter to the state could scarcely be established without lessening the stimulus to the individual to make the most of the land, and thus ultimately lessening its serviceableness to society.

Chapter 14
The Right of the State in Regard to the Family

233. In the consideration of those rights which do not arise out of the existence of the state, but which are antecedent to it (though of course, implying society in some form), and which it is its office to enforce, we now come to family or household rights—also called, though not very distinctively, rights in private relations—of which the most important are the reciprocal rights of husband and wife, parent and child. The distinctive thing about these is that they are not merely rights of one person as against all or some other persons over some thing, or to the performance of or abstention from some action; they are rights of one person as against all other persons to require or prevent a certain behaviour on the part of another. Right to free life is a right on the part of any and every person to claim from all other persons that course of action or forbearance which is necessary to his free life. It is a right against all the world, but not a right over any particular thing or person. A right of property, on the other hand, is a right against all the world, and also over a particular thing; a right to claim from any and every one certain actions and forbearances in respect of a particular thing (hence called "jus in rem"). A right arising from contract, unlike the right of property or the right of free life, is not a right as against all the world, but a right as against a particular person or persons contracted with to claim a certain performance or forbearance. It may or may not be a right over a particular thing, but as it is not necessarily so, while it is a right against a particular person or persons in distinction from all the world, it is called "jus in personam" as distinct from "in rem." The right of husband over wife and that of parent over children (or *vice versa*) differs from the right arising out of contract, inasmuch as it is not merely a right against the particular person contracted with, but a right against all the world. In this respect it corresponds to the right of property; but differs again from this, since it is not a right over a thing but over a person. It is a right to claim certain acts or forbearances from all other persons in respect of a particular person: or (more precisely) to claim a certain behaviour from a certain person, and

at the same time to exclude all others from claiming it. Just because this kind of right is a right over a person, it is always reciprocal as between the person exercising it and the person over whom it is exercised. All rights are reciprocal as between the person exercising them and the person against whom they are exercised. My claim to the right of free life implies a like claim upon me on the part of those from whom I claim acts and forbearances necessary to my free life. My claim upon others in respect of the right of property, or upon a particular person in respect of an action which he has contracted to perform, implies the recognition of a corresponding claim upon me on the part of all persons or the particular party to the contract. But the right of a husband in regard to his wife not merely implies that all those as against whom he claims the right have a like claim against him, but that the wife over whom he asserts the right has a right, though not a precisely like right, over him. The same applies to the right of a father over a son, and of a master over a servant.

234. A German would express the peculiarity of the rights now under consideration by saying that, not only are persons the subjects of them, but persons are the objects of them. By the "subject" of rights he would mean the person exercising them or to whom they belong; by "object" that in respect of which the rights are exercised. The piece of land or goods which I own is the "object" of the right of property, the particular action which one person contracts to perform for another is the "object" of a right of contract; and in like manner the person from whom I have a right to claim certain behaviour, which excludes any right on the part of anyone else to claim such behaviour from him or her, is the "object" of the right. But English writers commonly call that the subject of a right which the Germans would call the object. By the subject of a right of property they would not mean the person to whom the right belongs, but the thing over which, or in respect of which, the right exists. And in like manner, when a right is exercised over, or in respect of a person, such as a wife or a child, they would call that person, and not the person exercising the right, the subject of it. By the object of a right, on the other hand, they mean the action or forbearance which someone has a right to claim. The object of a right arising out of contract would be the action which the person contracting agrees to perform. The object of a connubial right would not be, as according to German usage, the person in regard to, or over, whom the right is exercised—that person would be the subject of the right—but either the behaviour which the person possessing the right is entitled to claim from that person, or the forbearances in respect to

that person, which he is entitled to claim from others (Austin, I. 378 and II. 736). Either usage is justifiable in itself. The only matter of importance is not to confuse them. There is a convenience in expressing the peculiarity of family rights by saying, according to the sense of the terms adopted by German writers, that not only are persons subjects of them but persons are objects of them. It is in this sense that I shall use these terms, if at all.

235. So much for the peculiarity of family rights, as distinct from other rights. The distinction is not merely a formal one. From the fact that these rights have persons for their objects, there follow important results, as will appear, in regard to the true nature of the right, to the manner in which it should be exercised. The analytical, as distinct from the historical, questions which have to be raised with reference to family rights correspond to those raised with reference to rights of property. As we asked what in the nature of man made appropriation possible for him, so now we ask (1) what it is in the nature of man that makes him capable of family life. As we asked next how appropriations came to be so sanctioned by social recognition as to give rise to rights of property, so now we have to ask (2) how certain powers exercised by a man, certain exemptions which he enjoys from the interference of others, in his family life, come to be recognised as rights. And as we inquired further how far the actual institutions of property correspond with the idea of property as a right which for social good should be exercised, so now we have to inquire (3) into the proper adjustment of family rights, as determined by their idea; in what form these rights should be maintained; bearing in mind (a) that, like all rights, their value depends on their being conditions of which the general observance is necessary to a free morality, and (b) their distinctive character as rights of which, in the sense explained, persons are the objects.

236. (1) We saw that appropriation of that kind which, when secured by a social power, becomes property, supposes an effort on the part of the individual to give reality to a conception of his own good, as a whole or as something permanent, in distinction from the mere effort to satisfy a want as it arises. The formation of family life supposes that in the conception of his own good to which a man seeks to give reality there is included a conception of the well-being of others, connected with him by sexual relations or by relations which arise out of these. He must conceive of the well-being of these others as a permanent object bound up with his own, and the interest in it as thus conceived must be a motive to

him over and above any succession of passing desires to obtain pleasure from, or give pleasure to, the others; otherwise there would be nothing to lead to the establishment of a household, in which the wants of the wife or wives are permanently provided for, in the management of which a more or less definite share is given to them (more definite, indeed, as approach is made to a monogamistic system, but not wholly absent anywhere where the wife is distinguished from the female), and upon which the children have a recognised claim for shelter and sustenance.

237. No doubt family life as we know it is an institution of gradual growth. It may be found in forms where it is easy to ignore the distinction between it and the life of beasts. It is possible that the human beings with whom it first began—beings "human" because capable of it—may have been "descended" from animals not capable of it, they may have been connected with such animals by certain processes of generation. But this makes no difference in the nature of the capacity itself, which is determined not by a past history but by its results, its functions, that of which it is a capacity. As the foundation of any family life, in the form in which we know it, implies that upon the mere sexual impulse there has supervened on the part of the man a permanent interest in a woman as a person with whom his own well-being is united, and a consequent interest in the children born of her, so in regard to every less perfect form out of which we can be entitled to say that the family life, as we know it, has developed, we must be also entitled to say that it expresses some interest which is in principle identical with that described, however incompletely it has emerged from lower influences.

238. (2) Such an interest being the basis of family relations, it is quite intelligible that everyone actuated by the interest should recognise, and be recognised by, everyone else to whom he ascribes an interest like his own, as entitled to behave towards the objects of the interest—towards his wife and children—in a manner from which everyone else is excluded; that there should thus come to be rights in family relations to a certain privacy in dealing with them; to deal with them as his alone and not another's; claims, ratified by the general sense of their admission being for the common good, to exercise certain powers and demand certain forbearances from others, in regard to wife and children. It is only indeed at an advanced stage of reflection that men learn to ascribe to other men, simply as men, the interests which they experience themselves; and hence it is at first only within narrow societies that men secure to each other the due privileges and privacies of family life. In others of the same

kin or tribe they can habitually imagine an interest like that of which each feels his own family life to be the expression, and hence in them they spontaneously respect family rights; but they cannot thus practically think themselves into the position of a stranger, and hence towards him they do not observe the same restraints. They do not regard the women of another nation as sacred to the husbands and families of that nation. But that power of making another's good one's own, which in the more intense and individualised form is the basis of family relations, must always at the same time exist in that more diffused form in which it serves as the basis of a society held together by the recognition of a common good. Wherever, therefore, the family relations exist, there is sure to exist also a wider society which by its authority gives to the powers exercised in those relations the character of rights. By what process the relations of husband and wife and the institution of the house-hold may have come to be formed among descendants of a single pair, it is impossible to conceive or to discover, but in fact we find no trace in primitive history of households except as constituents of a clan recognising a common origin; and it is by the customs of the clan, founded in the conception of a common good, that those forbearances on the part of members of one household in dealing with another, which are necessary to the privacy of the several households, are secured.

239. The history of the development of family life is the history of the process (a) by which family rights have come to be regarded as independent of the special custom of a clan and the special laws of a state, as rights which all men and women, as such, are entitled to. This, however, characterises the history of all rights alike. It is a history farther (b) of the process by which the true nature of these rights has come to be recognised, as rights over persons; rights of which persons are the objects, and which therefore imply reciprocal claims on the part of those over whom they are exercised and of those who exercise them. The establishment of monogamy, the abolition of "patria potestas" [paternal authority] in its various forms, the, emancipation of women' (in the proper sense of the phrase), are involved in these two processes. The principles (1) that all men and all women are entitled to marry and form households, (2) that within the household the claims of the husband and wife are throughout reciprocal, cannot be realised without carrying with them not merely monogamy, but the removal of those faulty relations between men and women which survive in countries where monogamy is established by law.

240. Under a system of polygamy, just so far as it is carried out, there must be men who are debarred from marrying. It can only exist, indeed, alongside of a slavery, which excludes masses of men from the right of forming a family. Nor does the wife, under a polygamous system, though she ostensibly marries, form a household, or become the co-ordinate head of a family, at all. The husband alone is head of the family and has authority over the children. The wife, indeed, who for the time is the favourite, may practically share the authority, but even she has no equal and assured position. The "consortium omnis vitae" [sharing of an entire life], the "individua vitae consuetude" [indivisible common life], which according to the definition in the Digest is an essential element in marriage, is not hers.[77]

And further as the polygamous husband requires a self-restraint from his wife which he does not put on himself, he is treating here unequally. He demands a continence from her which, unless she is kept in the confinement of slavery, can only rest on the attachment of a person to a person and on a personal sense of duty and at the same time is practically ignoring the demand, which this personal attachment on her part necessarily carries with it, that he should keep himself for her as she keeps herself for him. The recognition of children as having claims upon their parents reciprocal to those of the parents over them, equally involves the condemnation of polygamy. For these claims can only be duly satisfied the responsibilities of father and mother towards the children (potentially persons) whom they have brought into the world can only be fulfilled if father and mother jointly take part in the education of the children; if the children learn to love and obey father and mother as one authority. But if there is no permanent "consortium vitae" [sharing of life] of one husband with one wife, this joint authority over the children becomes impossible. The child, when its physical dependence on the mother is over, ceases to stand in any special relation to her. She has no recognised duties to him, or he to her. These lie between him and his father only, and just because the father's interests are divided between the children of many wives, and because these render their filial offices to the father separately not to father and mother jointly, the true domestic training is lost.

241. Monogamy, however, may be established, and an advance so far made towards the establishment of a due reciprocity between husband and wife, as well as towards a fulfilment of the responsibilities incurred in bringing children into the world, while yet the true claims of men in

respect of women, and of women in respect of men, and of children upon their parents, are far from being generally realised. Wherever slavery exists alongside of monogamy on the one side, people of the slave class are prevented from forming family ties, and on the other those who are privileged to marry, though they are confined to one wife, are constantly tempted to be false to the true monogamistic idea by the opportunity of using women as chattels to minister to their pleasures. The wife is thus no more than an institution, invested with certain dignities and privileges, for the continuation of the family; a continuation, which under pagan religions is considered necessary for the maintenance of certain ceremonies, and to which among ourselves an importance is attached wholly unconnected with the personal affection of the man for the wife.[78] When slavery is abolished, and the title of all men and women equally to form families is established by law, the conception of the position of the wife necessarily rises. The ἑταίρα [courtesan] and παλλακή [concubine] cease at any rate to be recognised accompaniments of married life, and the claim of the wife upon the husband's fidelity, as reciprocal to his claim upon hers, becomes established by law.

242. Thus that marriage should only be lawful with one wife, that it should be for life, that it should be terminable by the infidelity of either husband or wife, are rules of right; not of morality, as such, but of right. Without such rules the rights of the married persons are not maintained. Those outward conditions of family life would not be secured to them, which are necessary on the whole for the development of a free morality. Polygamy is a violation of the rights (1) of those who through it are indirectly excluded from regular marriage, and thus from the moral education which results from this; (2) of the wife, who is morally lowered by exclusion from her proper position in the household and by being used, more or less, as the mere instrument of the husband's pleasure; (3) of the children, who lose the chance of that full moral training which depends on the connected action of father and mother. The terminability of marriage at the pleasure of one of the parties to it (of its terminability at the desire of both we will speak presently) is a violation of the rights at any rate of the unconsenting party, on the grounds (a) that liability to it tends to prevent marriage from becoming that "individua vitae consuetude" which gives it its moral value, and (b) that, when the marriage is dissolved, the woman, just in proportion to her capacity for self-devotion and the degree to which she has devoted herself to her original husband, is debarred from forming that "individua vitae consuetude" again, and

thus crippled in her moral possibilities. It is a violation of the rights of children for the same reason for which polygamy is so.

On the other hand, that the wife should be bound indissolubly by the marriage-tie to an unfaithful husband (or *vice versa*), is a violation of the right of wife (or husband, as the case may be), because on the one hand the restraint which makes her liable to be used physically as the instrument of the husband's pleasures, when there is no longer reciprocal devotion between them, is a restraint which (except in peculiar cases) renders moral elevation impossible; and on the other, she is prevented from forming such a true marriage as would be, according to ordinary rules, the condition of the realisation of her moral capacities. Though the husband's right to divorce from an unfaithful wife has been much more thoroughly recognised than the wife's to divorce from an unfaithful husband, he would be in fact less seriously wronged by the inability to obtain a divorce, for it is only the second of the grounds just stated that fully applies to him. The rights of the children do not seem so plainly concerned in the dissolution of a marriage to which husband or wife has been unfaithful. In some cases the best chance for them might seem to lie in the infidelities being condoned and an outward family peace re-established. But that their rights are violated by the infidelity itself is plain. In the most definite way it detracts from their possibilities of goodness. Without any consent on their part, quite independently of any action of their own will, they are placed by it in a position which tends—though special grace may counteract it—to put the higher kinds of goodness beyond their reach.

243. These considerations suggest some further questions which may be discussed under the following heads. (1) If infidelity in marriage is a violation of rights in the manner stated, and if (as it must be) it is a wilful and knowing violation, why is it not treated as a crime, and, like other such violations of rights, punished by the state in order to the better maintenance of rights? (2) Should any other reason but the infidelity of husband or wife be allowed for the legal dissolution of the marriage tie? (3) How are the rights connected with marriage related to the morality of marriage?

(1) There is good reason why the state should not take upon itself to institute charges of adultery, but leave them to be instituted by the individuals whose rights the adultery violates. The reasons ordinarily alleged would be (a) the analogy of ordinary breaches of contract, against which the state leaves it to the individual injured to set the law in motion; (b)

the practical impossibility of preventing adultery through the action of the functionaries of the state. The analogy however, from ordinary breaches of contract does not really hold. In the first place, though marriage involves contract, though without contract there can be no marriage, yet marriage at once gives rise to right and obligations of a kind which cannot arise out of contract—in particular to obligations towards the children born of the marriage. These children, at any rate, are in no condition to seek redress—even if from the nature of the case redress could be had—for the injuries inflicted on them by a parent's adultery as a person injured by a breach of contract can seek redress for it. Again, though the state leaves it to the individual injured by a breach of contract to institute proceedings for redress, if the breach involves fraud, it—at any rate in certain cases treats the fraud as a crime and punishes. Now in every breach of the marriage-contract by adultery there is that which answers to fraud in the case of ordinary breach of contract. The marriage-contract is broken knowingly and intentionally. If there were no reason to the contrary, then, it would seem that the state, though it might leave to the injured individuals the institution of proceedings against adultery should yet treat adultery as a crime and seek to prevent it by punishment in the interest of those whose virtual rights are violated by it, though not in the way of breach of contract. But there are reasons to the contrary—reasons that arise out of the moral purposes served by the marriage-tie—which make it desirable both that it should be at the discretion of the directly injured party whether a case of adultery should be judicially dealt with at all, and that in no case should penal terror be associated with such a violation of the marriage-bond. Under ordinary conditions, it is a public injury that a violation of his rights should be condoned by the person suffering it. If the injured individual were likely to fail in the institution of proceedings for his own redress or defence, the public interest would require that the matter should be taken out of his hands. But if an injured wife or husband is willing to condone a breach of his or her rights through adultery, it is generally best that it should be condoned. That married life should be continued in spite of anything like dissoluteness on the part of husband or wife, is no doubt undesirable. The moral purposes which married life should serve cannot be served, either for the married persons themselves or for the children, under such conditions. On the other hand, the condonation of a single offence would generally be better for all concerned than an application for divorce. The line cannot be drawn at which, with a view to the higher ends which marriage should serve, divorce becomes desirable. It is therefore best that the state, while uniformly allowing the right of divorce where the marriage-bond has been broken by adultery, since otherwise the right of everyone to form a true marriage (a marriage which shall be the basis of family life) is neutralised, and taking care that procedure for divorce be cheap and easy, should leave the enforcement of the right to the discretion of individuals.

244. On similar grounds, it is undesirable that adultery as such should be treated as a crime that penal terror should be associated with it. Though rights, in the strict sense, undoubtedly arise out of marriage, though marriage has thus its strictly legal aspect, it is undesirable that this legal aspect should become prominent. It may suffer in respect of its higher moral purposes, if the element of force appears too strongly in the maintenance of the rights to which it gives rise. If a husband who would otherwise be false to the marriage bond is kept outwardly faithful to it by fear of the punishment which might attend its breach, the right of the wife and children is indeed so far protected, but is anything gained for those moral ends, for the sake of which the maintenance of these rights is alone of value? The man in whom disloyal passion is neutralised by fear of punishment will contribute little in his family life to the moral development of himself, his wife, or his children. If he cannot be kept true by family affection and sympathy with the social disapprobation attaching to matrimonial infidelity (and unless it is a matter of social disapprobation no penalties will be effectually enforced against it) he will not be kept true in a way that is of any value to those concerned by fear of penalties. In other words, the rights that arise out of marriage are not of a kind which can in their essence be protected by associating penal terror with their violation, as the rights of life and property can be. They are not rights to claim mere forbearances or to claim the performance of certain outward actions, by which a right is satisfied irrespectively of the disposition with which the act is done. They are claims which cannot be met without a certain disposition on the part of the person upon whom the claim rests, and that disposition cannot be enforced. The attempt to enforce the outward behaviour in order to satisfy the claim, which is a claim not to the outward behaviour merely but to this in connection with a certain disposition, defeats its own end.

245. For the protection, therefore, of the rights of married persons and their children against infidelity it does not appear that the law can do more than secure facilities of divorce in the case of adultery. This indeed

is not in itself a protection against the wrong involved in adultery, but rather a deliverance from the further wrong to the injured husband or wife and to the children that would be involved in the continuance of any legal claim over them on the part of the injurer. But indirectly it helps to prevent the wrong being done by bringing social disapprobation to bear on cases of infidelity, and thus helping to keep married persons faithful through sympathy with the disapprobation of which they feel that they would be the objects when they imagine themselves unfaithful. The only other effectual way in which the state can guard against the injuries in question is by requiring great precaution and solemnity in the contraction of marriages. This it can do by insisting on the consent of parents to the marriage of all minors, exacting a long notice (perhaps even a preliminary notice of betrothal), and, while not preventing civil marriage by encouraging the celebration of marriage in the presence of religious congregations and with religious rites.

246. Question (2) is one that does not admit of being answered on any absolute principle. We must bear in mind that all rights—in idea or as they should be—are relative to moral ends. The ground for securing to individuals in respect of the marriage-tie certain powers as rights, is that in a general way they are necessary to the possibility of a morally good life, either directly to the persons exercising them or to their Children. The more completely marriage is a "consortium omnis vitae" in the sense of a unity in all interests and for the whole of a lifetime, the more likely are the external conditions of a moral life to be fulfilled in regard both to married persons and their children. Therefore the general rule of the state in dealing with marriage should be to secure such powers as are favourable and withhold such as are not favourable to the "consortium omnis vitae." But in the application of the principle great difficulties arise. Lunacy may clearly render the "consortium omnis vitae" finally impossible; but what kind and degree of lunacy? If the lunatic may possibly recover, though there is undoubtedly reason for the separation from husband or wife during lunacy, should permanent divorce be allowed? If it is allowed, and the lunatic recovers, a wrong will have been done both to him and to the children previously born of the marriage. On the other hand, to reserve the connubial rights of a lunatic of whose recovery there is hope, and to restore them when he recovers, may involve the wrong of bringing further children into the world with the taint of lunacy upon them. Is cruelty to be a ground of divorce, and if so, what amount? There is a degree of persistent cruelty which renders "consortium omnis vitae"

impossible, but unless it is certain that cruelty has reached the point at which a restoration of any sort of family life becomes impossible, a greater wrong both to wife and children may be involved in allowing divorce than in refusing it. A husband impatient for the time of the restraint of marriage may be tempted to passing cruelty as a means of ridding himself of it, while if no such escape were open to him he might get the better of the temporary disturbing passion and settle down into a decent husband. The same consideration applies still more strongly to allowing incompatibility of temper as a ground of divorce. It would be hard to deny that it might be of a degree and kind in which it so destroyed the possibility of "consortium omnis vitae," that, with a view to the interests of the children, who ought in such a case to be chiefly considered, divorce implied less wrong than the maintenance of the marriage-tie. But on the other hand, to hold out the possibility of divorce on the ground of incompatibility is just the way to generate that incompatibility. On the whole, the only conclusion seems to be that this last ground should not be allowed, and that in deciding on other grounds large discretion should be allowed to a well-constituted court.

Chapter 15
Rights and Virtues

247. We have now considered in a perfunctory way those rights which are antecedent to the state, which are not derived from it but may exist where a state is not, and which it is the office of the state to maintain. We have inquired what it is in the nature of man that renders him capable of these rights, what are the moral ends to which the rights are relative, and in what form the rights should be realised in order to the attainment of these ends. In order to make the inquiry into rights complete, we ought to go on to examine in the same way the rights which arise out of the establishment of a state the rights connected with the several functions of government; how these functions come to be necessary, and how they may best be fulfilled with a view to those moral ends to which the functions of the state are ultimately relative. According to my project, I should then have proceeded to consider the social virtues, and the "moral sentiments" which underlie our particular judgements as to what is good and evil in conduct. All virtues are really social; or, more properly, the distinction between social and self-regarding virtues is a false one. Every virtue is self-regarding in the sense that it is a disposition, or habit of will, directed to an end which the man presents to himself as his good; every virtue is social in the sense that unless the good to which the will is directed is one in which the well-being of society in some form or other is involved, the will is not virtuous at all.

248. The virtues are dispositions to exercise positively, in some way contributory to social good, those powers which, because admitting of being so exercised, society should secure to him, which a man has a right to possess, which constitute his rights. It is therefore convenient to arrange the virtues according to the division of rights. E.g., in regard to the right of all men to free life, the obligations, strictly so called, correlative to that right having been considered (obligations which are all of a negative nature, obligations to forbear from meddling with one's neighbour), we should proceed to consider the activities by which a society of men really free is established, or by which some approach is made to its establishment; ("really free," in the sense of being enabled to make the most of their capabilities). These activities will take different forms un-

der different social conditions, but in rough outline they are those by which men in mutual helpfulness conquer and adapt nature, and overcome the influences which would make them victims of chance and accident, of brute force and animal passion. The virtuous disposition displayed in these activities may have various names applied to it according to the particular direction in which it is exerted "industry," "courage," "public spirit." A particular aspect of it was brought into relief among the Greeks under the name of $\alpha\nu\delta\rho\varepsilon\iota\alpha$ [manliness]. The Greek philosophers already gave an extension to the meaning of this term beyond that which belonged to it in popular usage, and we might be tempted further to extend it so as to cover all the forms in which the habit of will necessary to the maintenance and furtherance of free society shows itself. The name, however, does not much matter. It is enough that there are specific modes of human activity which contribute directly to maintain a shelter for man's worthier energies against disturbance by natural forces and by the consequences of human fear and lust. The state of mind which appears in them may properly be treated as a special kind of virtue. It is true that the principle and the end of all virtues is the same. They are all determined by relation to social well-being as their final cause, and they all rest on an interest which dominates the virtuous agent in some form or other of that well-being; but as that interest may take different directions in different persons, as it cannot be equally developed at once in everyone it may be said roughly that a man has one kind of virtue and not others.

249. As the kind of moral duties (in distinction from those obligations which are correlative to rights) which relate to the maintenance of free society and the disposition to fulfil those duties should form a special object of inquiry, so another special kind would be those which have to do with the management of property, with the acquisition and expenditure of wealth. To respect the rights of property in others, to fulfil the obligations correlative to those rights, is one thing; to make a good use of property, to be justly generous and generously just in giving and receiving, is another; and that may properly be treated as a special kind of virtue which appears in the duly blended prudence, equity and generosity of the ideal man of business. Another special kind will be that which appears in family relations; where indeed that merely negative observance of rights which in other relations can be distinguished from the positive fulfilment of moral duties, becomes unmeaning. As we have seen, there are certain aggravations and perpetuations of wrong from

which husband or wife or children can be protected by law, but the fulfilment of the claims which arise out of the marriage-tie requires a virtuous
will in the active and positive sense—a will governed by unselfish interests—on the part of those concerned.

250. What is called "moral sentiment" is merely a weaker form of that
interest in social well-being which, when wrought into a man's habits
and strong enough to determine action, we call virtue. So far as this interest is brought into play on the mere survey of action, and serves merely
to determine our approbation or disapprobation, it is called moral sentiment. The forms of moral sentiment accordingly should be classified on
some[79] principle as forms of virtue, i.e., with relation to the social functions to which they correspond.

251. For the convenience of analysis, we may treat the obligations
correlative to rights, obligations which it is the proper office of law to
enforce, apart from moral duties and from the virtues which are tendencies to fulfil those duties. I am properly *obliged* to those actions and
forbearances which are necessary[80] to the general freedom necessary if
each is not to interfere with the realisation of another's will. My *duty* is
to be interested positively in my neighbour's well-being. And it is important to understand that while the enforcement of obligations is possible,
that of moral duties is impossible. But the establishment of obligations
by law or authoritative custom, and the gradual recognition of moral
duties, have not been separate processes. They have gone on together in
the history of man. The growth of the institutions by which more complete equality of rights is gradually secured to a wider range of persons,
and of those interests in various forms of social well-being by which the
will is moralised, have been related to each other as the outer and inner
side of the same spiritual development; though at a certain stage of reflection it comes to be discovered that the agency of force, by which the
rights are maintained, is ineffectual for eliciting the moral interests. The
result of the twofold process has been the creation of the actual content
of morality; the articulation of the indefinite consciousness that there is
something that should be—a true well-being to be aimed at other than
any pleasure or succession of pleasures—into the sentiments and interests which form an "enlightened conscience." It is thus that when the
highest stage of reflective morality is reached and upon interests in this
or that mode of social good there supervenes an interest in an ideal of
goodness, that ideal has already a definite filling; and the man who pursues Duty for Duty's sake, who does good for the sake of being good or

in order to realise an idea of perfection, is at no loss to say what in particular his duty is, or by what particular methods the perfection of character is to be approached.

Notes

¹ KE places "moral progress of mankind" in quotation marks.
² KE's wording differs considerably here.
³ KE has "or" instead of "and" here.
⁴ There are two definitions of "Recht" or "jus naturae" quoted by Ulrici (*Naturrecht*, p. 219), which embody the truths conveyed in these statements. (1) Krause defines "Recht" as "das organische Ganze der aüsseren Bedingungen des Vernunftlebens," "the organic whole of the outward conditions necessary to the rational life." (2) Henrici says that "Recht" is "was der Idee der Unverletzbarkeit der materiellen wesentlichen Bedingungen des moralischen Menschenthums, d. h. der menschlichen Persönlichkeit nach ihrer Existenz und ihrer Vervollkommnung, oder der unveraüsserlichen Menschengüter im aüsserlichen Verkehr entspricht": i.e. "Right is what" (or, "that is properly matter of legal obligation which") "in the outward intercourse of men corresponds to the idea of the inviolability of the essential material conditions of a moral humanity, i.e. of the human personality in respect of its existence and its perfection;" or, more simply, "Right is that which is really necessary to the maintenance of the material conditions essential to the existence and perfection of human personality." Cf. Trendelenburg, Naturrecht, §46. "Das Recht ist im sittlichen Ganzen der Inbegriff derjenigen allgemeinen Bestimmungen des Handelns, durch welche es geschieht dass das sittliche Ganze und seine Gliederung sich erhalten und weiter bilden kann." Afterwards he emphasises the words "des Handelns," and adds: "Zwar kann das Handeln nicht ohne den Willen gedacht werden der zum Grunde liegt: aber die Rechtbestimmungen sind nicht Bestimmungen des Willens als solchen, was dem innern Gebiet, der Ethik der Gesinnung, anheimfallen würde. Der Wille der nicht Handlung wird entzieht sich dem Recht. Wenn das Recht Schuld und Versehen, dolus und culpa, in sein Bereich zieht, so sind sie als innere aber charakteristische Beschaffenheiten des Handelns anzusehen."
⁵ KE adds at this point, "in which case there is no act at all."
⁶ KE has "rights" in place of "relations."
⁷ KE has "free servant" in place of "servant."
⁸ Or Tractatus Politici.

[9] Per *jus* itaque *naturae* intelligo. . . ipsam naturae potentiam. . . Quicquid unusquisque homo ex legibus suae naturae agit, id summo naturae jure agit, tantumque in naturam habet juris, quantum potentia valet.

[10] Homines magis caeca cupiditate quam ratione ducuntur; ac proinde hominum naturalis potentia sive jus non ratione, sed quocumque appetitu quo ad agendum determinantur, quoque se conservare conantur, definiri debet.

[11] Suum esse conservare.

[12] Quatenus homines ira, invidia aut aliquo odii affectu conflictantur, eatenus diverse trahuntur et invicem contrarii sunt, et propterea eo plus timendi, quo plus possunt, magisque callidi et astuti sunt, quam reliqua animalia; et quia homines ut plurimum his affectibus natura sunt obnoxii, sunt ergo homines ex natura hostes.

[13] Atque adeo concludimus jus naturae vix posse concipi nisi ubi homines jura habent communia, qui simul terras, quas habitare et colere possunt, sibi vindicare, seseque munire, vimque omnem repellere et ex communi omnium sententia vivere possunt. Nam (per art. 13 hujus cap.) quo plures in unum sic conveniunt, eo omnes simul plus juris habent.

[14] Ubi homines jura communia habent omnesque una veluti mente ducuntur, certum est (per art. 13 hujus cap.) eorum unumquemque tanto minus habere juris, quanto reliqui simul ipso potentiores sunt, hoc est, illum revera jus nullum in naturam habere praeter id, quod ipsi commune concedit jus. Ceterum quicquid ex communi consensu ipsi imperatur, teneri exsequi vel (per art. 4 hujus cap.) jure ad id cogi.

[15] Hoc jus, quod multitudinis potentia definitur, imperium apellari solet.

[16] Multitudinis quae una veluti mente ducitur.

[17] Homo ex legibus suae naturae agit suaeque utilitati consulit.

[18] Civitatis jus potentia multitudinis, quae una veluti mente ducitur, determinatur. At haec animorum unio concipi nulla ratione posset, nisi civitas id ipsum maxime indendat, quod sana ratio omnibus hominibus utile esse docet. KE has "And it is a contradiction to say that the state has a right to weaken its own power" following.

[19] Subditi eatenus non sui, sed civitatis juris sint, quatenus ejus potentiam seu minas metuunt, vel quatenus statum civilem amant (per art. 10 praeced. cap.). Ex quo sequitur, quod ea omnia, ad quae agenda nemo praemiis aut minis induci potest, ad jura civitatis non pertineant.

[20] Ad civitatis jus ea minus pertinere, quae plurimi indignantur; "Sicut unusquisque civis sive homo in statu naturali, sic civitas eo minus sui juris est, quo majorem timendi causam habet."

[21] Nam quandoquidem (per art. 2 hujus cap.) jus summae potestatis nihil est praeter ipsum naturae jus, sequitur duo imperia ad invicem sese habere, ut duo homines in statu naturali, excepto hoc, quod civitas sibi cavere potest, ne ab alia opprimatur, quod homo in statu naturali non potest, nimirum qui quotidie somno, saepe morbo aut animi aegritudine, et tandem senectute gravatur, et praeter haec aliis incommodis est obnoxius, a quibus civitas securam se reddere potest.

[22] Duae civitates natura hostes sunt. Homines enim in statu naturali hostes sunt. Qui igitur jus naturae extra civitatem retinent, hostes manent.

[23] Nec dici potest, quod dolo vel pertidia agat, propterea quod fidem solvit, simulatque metus vel spei causa sublata est, quia haec conditio unicuique contrahentium aequalis fuit, ut scilicet quae prima extra metum esse potest, sui juris esset, eoque ex sui animi sententia uteretur, et praeterea quia nemo in futurum contrahit nisi positis praecedentibus circumstantiis.

[24] In statu naturali non dari peccatum, vel sis quis peccat, is sibi, non alteri peccat:...nihil absolute naturae jure prohibetur, nisi quod nemo potest.

[25] Non id omne, quod jure fieri dicimus, optime fieri affirmamus. Aliud namque est agrum jure colere, aliud agrum optime colere; aliud, unquam, est sese jure defendere, conservare, judicium ferre, etc, aliud sese optime defendere, conservare, atque optimum judicium ferre; et consequenter aliud est jure imperare et reipublicae curam habere, aliud optime imperare et rempublicam optime gubernare. Postquam itaque de jure cujuscumque civitatis in genere egimus, tempus est, ut de optimo cujuscumque imperii statu agamus.

[26] Homines enim civiles non nascuntur, sed fiunt. Hominum praeterea naturales affectus ubique iidem sunt.

[27] For the definition of "fortitudo," see *Ethics*, III.59, Schol. "Omnes actiones quae sequuntur ex affectibus qui ad mentem referuntur, quatenus intelligit, ad fortitudinem refero, quam in animositatem et generositatem distinguo. Nam per animositatem intelligo cupiditatem, qua unnusquisque conatur suum esse ex solo rationis dictamine conservare. Per generositatem. . . cupiditatem qua unnusquisque ex solo rationis dictamine conatur reliquos homines juvare et sibi amicitia jungere."

[28] Pax enim non belli privatio, sed virtus est, quae ex animi fortitudine oritur; est namque obsequium constans voluntas id exsequendi, quod ex communi civitatis decreto fieri debet.

[29] Quae maxime ratione, vera mentis virtute et vita, definitur.

[30] Quod multitudo libera instituit, non autem id, quod in multitudinem jure belli acquiritur.

[31] Homini nihil homine utilius.

[32] Homo namque tam in statu naturali quam civili ex legibus suae naturae agit, suaeque utilitati consulit.

[33] Constans voluntas id exsequendi quod ex communi civitatis decreto fieri debet.

[34] Certainly this is so, if we apply to the "libera multitudo" the definition of freedom applied to the "liber homo." "Hominem eatenus *liberum* omnino voco, quatenus ratione ducitur, quia eatenus ex causis, quae per solam eius naturam possunt adaequate intelligi, ad agendum determinatur, tametsi ex iis necessario ad agendum determinetur. Nam libertas agendi necessitatem non tollit, sed ponit."

[35] Jus naturae, quod humani generis proprium est, vix posse concipi, nisi ubi homines jura habent communia, qui simul terras, quas habitare et colere possunt, sibi vindicare, seseque munire, vimque omnem repellere et ex communi omnium sententia vivere possunt.

[36] KE also has "from it" here.

[37] Homines civiles non nascuntur, sed fiunt.

[38] KE has "insensible" here.

[39] Cp. *Eth.* IV. *Appendix*, xxxii. "Ea quae nobis eveniumt contra id, quod nostrae utilitatis ratio postulat, aequo animo feremus, si conscii simus nos functos nostro officio fuisse, et potentiam, quam habemus, non potuisse se eo usque extendere, ut eadem vitare possemus, nosque partem totius naturae esse, cujus ordinem sequimur. Quod si clare et distincte intelligamus, pars illa nostri, quae intelligentia definitur, hoc est, pars melior nostri, in eo plane acquiescet et in ea acquiescentia perseverare conabitur. Nam quatenus intelligimus, nihil appetere nisi id, quod necessarium est, nec absolute nisi in veris acquiescere possumus; adeoque quatenus haec recte intelligimus, eatenus conatus melioris partis nostri cum ordine totius naturae convenit." *Eth.* IV. Preface. . . "Per *bonum*. . . intelligam id, quod certo scimus medium esse, ut ad exemplar humanae naturae, quod nobis proponimus, magis magisque accedamus. . . Deinde homines *perfectiores* aut *imperfectiores* dicemus, quatenus ad hoc idem exemplar magis aut minus accedunt."

[40] Nihil positivum in rebus in se consideratis.

[41] Supremo majistratui in qualibet urbe non plus in subditos juris, quam juxta mensuram potestatis, qua subditum superat, competere statuo.

[42] "The 'jus naturale' is the liberty each man hath to use his own power as he will himself for the preservation of his own nature; that is to say, of his own life; and consequently of doing anything which in his own judgement and reason he shall conceive to be the aptest means thereunto" (Lev., I.14).

[43] KE has "obligatoriness of" here.

[44] KE has "Second Treatise..."

[45] Locke, *Civil Government*, VII. Sec. 87, "Man, being born with a title to perfect freedom, and an uncontrolled enjoyment of all the rights and privileges of the law of nature, equally with any other man or number of men in the world, hath by nature a power not only to preserve his life, liberty, and estate against. . . other men; but to judge of and punish the breaches of that law in others. . . There, and there only, is political society where everyone of the members hath quitted this natural power, resigned it up into the hands of the community in all cases that exclude him not from appealing for protection to the law established by it."

[46] "Laws human of what kind so ever, are available by consent," Hooker, *Ecclesiastical Polity* I.10 (quoted by Locke, *l.c.* Ch. XI. Sec.134). "To be commanded we do consent, when that society, whereof we be a part, hath at any time before consented, without evoking the same after by the like universal agreement," Hooker; *ibid.*

[47] *De jure belli et pacis*, Proleg., Secs. 15 and 16.

[48] KE has "princes and" here.

[49] KE has "supreme legislative and the" here.

[50] KE has "government" in place of "sovereignty."

[51] According to Hobbes, tyranny = "monarchy misliked;" oligarchy = "aristocracy misliked."

[52] "If it happened that the prince had a private will more active than that of the sovereign, and that he made use of the public force placed in his hands as the instrument of this private will, there would result, so to speak, two sovereignties, one "de jure," the other "de facto;" but from that moment the social union would disappear, and the body politic would be dissolved" (III, i). "When the prince ceases to administer the state according to the laws, and usurps the sovereign power. . . then the state in the larger sense is dissolved, and there is formed another within it, composed only of the members of the government. . . the social pact is broken. . . and all the ordinary citizens return as a matter of right to their state of natural liberty, and are merely forced but not obliged to obey" (III, x).

[53] Cf. Maine's statement of Austin's doctrine in *The Early History of Institutions,* pp. 349 and 350 "There is in every independent political community—that is, in every political community not in the habit of obedience to a superior above itself—some single person or some combination of persons which has the power of compelling the other members of the community to do exactly as it pleases. This single person or group—this individual or this collegiate sovereign (to employ Austin's phrase) may be found in every independent political community as certainly as the centre of gravity in a mass of matter. If the community be violently or voluntarily divided into a number of separate fragments, then, as soon as each fragment has settled down (perhaps after an interval of anarchy) into a state of equilibrium, the sovereign will exist, and with proper care will be discoverable in each of the now independent portions. The sovereignty over the North American colonies of Great Britain had its seat in one place before they became the United States, in another place afterwards; but in both cases there was a discoverable sovereign somewhere. This sovereign, this person or combination of persons, universally occurring in all independent political communities, has in all such communities one characteristic, common to all the shapes sovereignty may take, the possession of irresistible force, not necessarily exerted, but capable of being exerted. According to the terminology preferred by Austin, the sovereign, if a single person, is or should be called a monarch; if a small group, the name is an oligarchy; if a group of considerable dimensions, an aristocracy, if very large and numerous, a democracy. Limited monarchy, a phrase perhaps more fashionable in Austin's day than it is now, is abhorred by Austin, and the government of Great Britain he classes with aristocracies. That which all the forms of sovereignty have in common is the power (the power but not necessarily the will) to put compulsion without limit on subjects or fellow-subjects."

[54] [Above, Sec. 80.]

[55] KE has "in any measure" here.

[56] KE has "recognised" in brackets.

[57] KE has "next term" here instead of "next course of lectures."

[58] KE has "ideal realities that force is subordinate" here, instead of in the following sentence.

[59] KE has here: "Next term I hope further to pursue the subject of the functions of the State: to consider the rationale of the rights which it maintains or should maintain, and its further office (if it turns out to have

such an office) in the moralization of man beyond the enforcement of rights. This will lead us on to the consideration of 'social virtues.'"

[60] [Above, Sections 100, 101.]

[61] KE has "in the destruction of the state" here.

[62] Tacitus speaks of it as a peculiarity of the Jews and Germans that they did not allow the killing of younger children (*Hist.*, V, 5; *Germ.* 19). Aristotle (*Pol.* 1335, b, 19) enjoins that μηδεν πεπηρωμένον shall be brought up, but seems to condemn exposure, preferring that the required limit of population should be preserved by destruction of the embryo, on the principle that το όσιον και το μη διωρισμενον τη αισθήσει και τώ ζην έσται. Plato's rule is the same as regards the defective children and the procuring abortion, but he leaves it in the dark whether he meant any healthy children actually born, to be put out of the way (*Rep.* 460 C and 461 C).

[63] Markby, *Elements of Law*, Sec. 226.

[64] [Above, sec. 156].

[65] KE has "more" here.

[66] See above (§156).

[67] "Social right," i.e. right belonging to a society of persons recognising a common good, and belonging through membership of the society to the several persons constituting it. The society to which the right belongs, is in principle or possibility a society of all men as rendered capable of free intercourse with each other by the organisation of the state. Actually, at first it is only this or that family; then some association of families; finally the state, as including all other forms of association, reconciling the rights which arise out of them, and thus the most perfect medium through which the individual can contribute to the good of mankind and mankind to his.

[68] "Happy shall he be that rewardeth thee as thou hast served us."

[69] The conceptions of the just and of justice implied in this statement of the conditions of just punishment may be expressed briefly as follows. "The just" = that complex of social conditions which for each individual is necessary to enable him to realise his capacity of contributing to social good. "Justice" is the habit of mind which leads us to respect those conditions in dealing with others—not to interfere with them so far as they already exist, and to bring them into existence so far as they are not found in existence.

[70] KE has "public or private" here, as in the same phrase which appears later in the sentence.

[71] See Markby, *Element of Law*, Ch. XI, especially note 1, p. 243; and Austin Lecture XXVII. Between crimes and civil injuries the distinction, as it actually exists, is merely one of procedure (as stated by Austin, p. 518). The violation of right in one case is proceeded against by the method of indictment in the other by an "action." The distinction that in one case punishment is the object of the process, in the other redress, is introduced in order to explain the difference of procedure; and to justify this distinction resort is had to the further distinction, that civil injury is considered to affect the individual merely, crime to affect the state. But in fact the action for civil injury may incidentally have a penal result (Austin, p. 521), and if it had not, many violations of right now treated as civil injuries would have to be treated as crimes. As an explanation therefore of the distinction between crimes and injuries as it stands, it is not correct to say that for the former punishment is sought for the latter merely redress. Nor for reasons already given is it true of any civil injury to say that it affects, or should be considered as affecting, injured individuals *merely*. The only distinction of principles is that between violations of right which call for punishment and those which do not; and those only do not call for punishment in some form or other which arise either from uncertainty as to the right violated, or from inability to prevent the violation.

[72] [Above, Sec. 156]

[73] Grotius, *De Jure, etc.* Book II. Ch. II §5. "Simul discimus quomodo res in proprietatem iverint... apcto quodam aut expresso, ut per divisionem, aut tacito, ut per occupationem: simul atque enim communio displicuit, nec instituta est divisio, censeri debet inter omnes convenisse ut, quod quisque occupasset, id proprium haberet." [At the same time we learn how things became subject to private ownership. . . by a kind of agreement, either expressed, as by a decision, or implied, as by occupation. In fact, as soon as community ownership was abandoned, and as yet no division had been made it is supposed that, all agreed, that whatever each one had taken possession of should be his property.] But he supposes a previous process by which things had been appropriated (§4), owing to the necessity of spending labour on them in order to satisfy desire for a more refined kind of living than could be supplied by spontaneous products of the earth. "Hinc discimus quae fuerit causa, ob quam a primaeva communione rerum primo mobilium, deinde et immobilium discessum est: nimirum quod non contenti homines vesci sponte natis, antra habitare. . . vitae genus exquisitius delegissent, industria opus fuit,

quam singuli rebus singulis adhiberent." [The reason was that men were not content to feed on the spontaneous products of the earth, to dwell in caves... but chose a more refined mode of life; this gave rise to industry which some applied to one thing, others to another.] The "communio rerum" [common ownership], thus departed from when labour came to be expended on things, Grotius had previously described (§1) as a state of things in which everyone had a right to whatever he could lay hands on. "Erant omnia communia et indivisa omnibus, veluti unum cunctis patrimonium esset. Hinc factum ut statim quisque hominum ad suos usus arripere posset quod vellet, et quae consumi poterant consumere, ac talis usus universalis juris erat tum vice proprietatis. Nam qudo quisque sic arripuerat, id ei eripere alter nisi per injuriam non poterat." [All things were the undivided possession of all men, as if all possessed a common inheritance. (In consequence), each man could at once take whatever he wished for his own needs, and could consume whatever was capable of being consumed. The enjoyment of this universal right then served the purpose of private ownership; for whatever each had thus taken for his own needs another could not take from him except by an unjust act.] Here then a virtual right of property, though not so called, seems to be supposed in two forms previous to the establishment of what Grotius calls the right of property by contract. There is (1) a right of property in which each can "take to his use and consume" out of the raw material supplied by nature; (2) a further right of each man in that on which he has extended labour. Grotius does not expressly call this a right, but if there is a right, as he says there is, on the part of each man to that which he is able "to take to his use and consume," much more must there be a right to that which he has not only taken but fashioned by his labour. On the nature and rationale of this right Grotius throws no light, but it is clearly presupposed by that right of property which he supposes to be derived from contract, and must be recognised before any such contract could be possible [translations taken from KE].

[74] "There is annexed to the sovereignty the whole power of prescribing the rules whereby every man may know what goods he may enjoy and what actions he may do without being molested by any of his fellow-subjects: and this is what men call propriety. For before constitution of sovereign power, all men had right to all things, which necessarily causeth war; and therefore this propriety, being necessary to peace, and depending on sovereign power, is the act of that power in order to the public peace" (Leviathan, Part II, Ch. XVIII). "The nature of justice consisteth

in keeping a valid covenance, but the validity of covenance begins not but with the constitution of a civil power, sufficient to compel men to keep them, and then it is also that propriety begins." (Ibid. Ch. XV)

[75] *Civil Government*, V. The most important passages are quoted in Fox Bourne's *Life of Locke*, vol. ii, pp. 171 and 172.

[76] KE has "social" in place of "special" here.

[77] "Nuptiae sunt conjunctio maris et feminae, consortium omnis vitae, divini et humani juris communicatio." *Digest*, XXIII. 2,1. "Matrimonium est viri et mulieris conjunctio individuam vitae consuetudinem continens." *Inst.*, I. 9, 2. (Quoted by Trendelenburg, *Naturrecht*, p. 282.)

[78] Her position among the Greeks is well illustrated by a passage from the speech of Demosthenes (?) against Neaera, §122 (quoted by W. E. Hearn, *The Aryan Household*, p. 71), τας μεν γαρ εταίρας ήδονης ένεκ' έχομεν, τας δε παλλακας της καθ' ήμεραν θεραπείας του σώματος, τας δε γυναικας του παιδωποιεισθαι γνησίος και των ενδον φύλακα πιστην έχειν.

[79] KE has "the same" here.

[80] KE has "requisite" here.

Index

adultery 183, 185
Afghans (and Afghanistan) 118, 128
Americans (and America) 35, 36,
    60, 75, 95, 98, 126, 197
appropriation 108, 160-62, 164-66,
    167, 172, 173, 178
Aristotle 17, 25, 26, 48, 168, 198
Austin (and Austinians) 57, 58, 61,
    73, 178, 197, 199
Austrians 63, 89, 93, 121, 131

Bacon 26
Bulgaria 125

Caesar 93, 123
capital (and capitalists) 154, 171,
    172, 175
capital punishment 154
Catholicism 126
Christians (and Christianity) 114,
    115, 123, 124
common good, the 14, 15, 17, 23,
    25, 31, 48, 52, 69-72, 74-77, 82-
    85, 87, 89, 96-98, 102, 108, 109,
    114, 115, 130, 134, 157, 158, 164,
    179, 198
commonwealth, the 20, 22, 30, 40,
    46, 86
crime (and criminals) 7, 134, 136-49,
    151-56, 183-85, 199
Czar, the 64, 95

democracy 42, 50, 51, 60, 197
disinterestedness 9, 10, 48, 79, 80,
    84, 87, 133, 147, 158

disposition 5, 7-9, 168, 170, 185,
    188, 189
divorce 183-86

ecclesiastical (customs, policies,
    etc.) 60, 121, 125, 159
education 25, 158, 171, 181, 182
England (and the English) 4, 15,
    16, 41, 44, 48, 51, 55, 60, 62, 64,
    66, 67, 73, 74, 85, 118, 123, 124,
    127, 128, 131, 152, 170, 172,
    174, 175, 177
English Parliament 44, 51
Ethic (Spinoza) 22
Europe 1, 3, 42, 48, 56, 86, 92, 94,
    98, 123, 130, 166, 172, 174
European wars 121

family, the 24, 29, 62, 64, 82, 89,
    97, 99, 102, 103, 108, 111, 113,
    114, 132, 135, 136, 146, 148,
    165, 170, 173, 174, 176, 178-83,
    185, 187, 189, 198
fear 6-9, 13, 18, 20-22, 30, 59, 83,
    84, 87, 119, 132, 152, 157, 185,
    189
France (and the French) 56, 67, 73,
    92, 93, 99, 121, 127, 128, 130,
    131, 137, 174
fraud 144, 151, 184

Gallic wars 124
Gaul 123
general good, the 87, 108, 154
general will, the 46, 47, 48, 49, 50-
    53, 55, 57, 59, 61-63, 65, 66, 69-
    71, 75, 84
Germany (and Germans) 60, 73, 92,
    121, 123, 124, 127, 128, 131,
    137, 177, 198